T0332808

Authors, Copyright, and Publishing in the Digital Era

Francina Cantatore
Bond University, Australia

Information Science
REFERENCE
An Imprint of IGI Global

Managing Director:	Lindsay Johnston
Production Editor:	Jennifer Yoder
Development Editor:	Austin DeMarco
Acquisitions Editor:	Kayla Wolfe
Typesetter:	Christina Barkanic
Cover Design:	Jason Mull

Published in the United States of America by
Information Science Reference (an imprint of IGI Global)
701 E. Chocolate Avenue
Hershey PA 17033
Tel: 717-533-8845
Fax: 717-533-8661
E-mail: cust@igi-global.com
Web site: http://www.igi-global.com

Library of Congress Cataloging-in-Publication Data

Cantatore, Francina, author.
  Authors, copyright, and publishing in the digital era / by Francina Cantatore.
     pages cm.
  Based on her dissertation (doctoral) -- Bond University, 2011, under title: Negotiating a changing landscape : authors, copyright and the digital revolution.
  Includes bibliographical references and index.
    ISBN 978-1-4666-5214-9 (hardcover) -- ISBN 978-1-4666-5215-6 (ebook) -- ISBN 978-1-4666-5217-0 (print & perpetual access) 1. Copyright--Australia. 2. Copyright--Philosophy. 3. Digital-rights management. I. Title.
  KU1104.C36 2014
  346.9404'82--dc23
                              2013046352

British Cataloguing in Publication Data
A Cataloguing in Publication record for this book is available from the British Library.

All work contributed to this book is new, previously-unpublished material. The views expressed in this book are those of the authors, but not necessarily of the publisher.

Table of Contents

Preface..vi

Acknowledgment..xvi

Chapter 1
Introduction 1
    Background.. 2
    Copyright: An Evolving Concept 4
    Conclusion 7
Chapter 2
History And Development Of Copyright 10
    Introduction.. 10
    The Origins Of Copyright Law.. 11
    Copyright Law In Australia 15
    Global Challenges.. 25
    Conclusion 27
Chapter 3
Theoretical And Philosophical Foundations 33
    Introduction.. 33
    The Public Sphere... 36
    The Public Domain 41
    Utilitarian Approach.. 42
    Natural Right Theory... 44
    Moral Rights Theory... 46
    Public Benefit Theory 49
    Conclusion 52

Chapter 4

Authorship: From Quill To Keyboard And Cyberspace 57

    Authorship And The Law 58

    Critical Theory And The Development Of Authorship................................. 64

    The Keyboard Author 70

    Conclusion 76

Chapter 5

Copyright Support Structures 81

    Introduction.. 81

    International Structures.. 82

    Government Support Structures 83

    Other Support Structures 90

    Conclusion 91

Chapter 6

The Publishing Industry 94

    Introduction.. 95

    Publishing Agreements 96

    Traditional Publishing And The Author/Publisher Relationship 96

    Traditional Publishing Contracts 97

    Digital Considerations 102

    A Changing Industry: Publishing Options For Authors........................... 107

    New Business Models And Copyright Options 118

    Conclusion 124

Chapter 7

Research And Methodology 131

    Introduction: Purpose Of The Research.. 131

    The Research Model 132

    Strategy 134

    Scope Of The Research.. 135

    The Two Stages Of Data Collection 137

    Data Analysis 143

    Conclusion 144

Chapter 8

Research Findings: Authors' Perceptions And The Copyright Framework 147

    Introduction.. 148

    Authors' Perception Of Copyright... 152

    Current Legislative Framework 164

    Supporting Government Structures 174

    Problems Within The Current Framework... 182

    Summary And Conclusion 186

Chapter 9

Research Findings: Authors And Publishing–A Changing Industry 190
    Introduction 190
    Traditional Publishing And Publishing Relationships 191
    Emerging Publishing Models And Business Strategies 200
    Summary And Conclusion 215

Chapter 10

Discussion And Analysis 219
    Introduction 219
    Broad Demographics 220
    Authors' Sources Of Income 220
    Authors And Motivation 222
    Effect Of The Parallel Importing Debate 223
    Authors, Publishers And Publishing Contracts 225
    The Idea Of A 'Heavenly' Library 229
    Digital Copyright Protection 231
    The Google Initiatives: Beyond Copyright 235
    Resale Royalties On Books? 236
    New Business Models 238
    Conclusion 240

Chapter 11

Conclusion And Recommendations 244
    Conclusion 245
    Recommendations 257

List of Abbreviations 263

Compliation of References 264

About the Author 276

Index 277

Preface

Every secret of a writer's soul, every experience of his life, every quality of his mind is written large in his works. - Virginia Woolf

Unprecedented advances in technology have challenged copyright structures globally and are having a disruptive effect on traditional publishing models and the legislative provisions that underpin them. This book focuses on the challenges presented by such a transitional environment from authors' perspectives and considers how the development of a digital publishing arena has impacted authors' copyright expectations. Based on a range of primary sources, including published authors from each Australian State and Territory, publishers and specialist academics, as well as an analysis of legislation, case law, publishing contracts, and relevant literature, the book addresses current copyright structures underpinning Copyright Law in Australia and ventures into new ground in copyright research in written work.

It also considers the global implications of changed copyright models and examines the ways in which authors have responded to the fluid environment of change in practical and progressive ways. Primarily, it has become evident that authors need to equip themselves to deal with the demands of new media technology to ensure that they are adequately rewarded for their creative efforts, and to exert power as a significant stakeholder group in the digital environment. Copyright laws have traditionally adapted to changing technology to meet the needs of copyright users. That was the purpose when the English Crown started to regulate Caxton's revolutionary printing press technology and it remains a focus of copyright legislation today. How authors cope with this transition depends on how they utilise the opportunities that arise as a result of technological change. The findings of the qualitative and quantitative research showed that, whilst publication in the digital sphere poses significant opportunities for book authors, their responses to copyright challenges are varied and inconsistent, depending on their viewpoints.

Recent US Supreme Court decisions such as *Kirtsaeng v. Wiley and Sons, Inc.*—which dealt with the application of the "first sale doctrine" in the cross-border sale of text books on eBay—have significantly affected the enforcement of territorial copyright by authors and publishers. Territorial copyright borders have become blurred, difficult to enforce in view of recent precedent, and are ineffective in preserving authors' copyright and the cultural dimensions of their books. Clearly, new copyright solutions are required, demanding that authors embrace digital technology, improve their knowledge of online publishing, and apply creative publishing models to their advantage.

These issues form the central focus of the book, which has been largely informed by research conducted during the completion of my PhD thesis. A brief summary of the book chapters follows below:

CHAPTER 1: INTRODUCTION

This chapter contains a summary of the issues examined in this research and notes past research conducted in this area. It briefly discusses the evolutionary nature of copyright and provides an overview of the digital considerations forming the backdrop for this book. It concludes that factors such as developments in technology, parallel importing concerns, and changing trends in publishing and marketing are prompting authors to cultivate a greater awareness of issues that affect their livelihood. Google's unauthorised digitalisation of copyrighted work and the resulting legal issues that arose from this action are one such example. These developments imply a movement towards a global awareness of copyright issues – rather than relying on Australian copyright law alone, authors have to consider how their copyright is being impacted on an international scale. This chapter commences the discussion on the way in which authors are navigating their copyright in the expanded literary sphere and how they are dealing with digital technology in their creative work and publishing contracts. On a deeper level, it also introduces the discussion on the author's role in the literary and the greater public sphere and the relationship between the competing groups in the publishing industry.

CHAPTER 2: HISTORY AND DEVELOPMENT OF COPYRIGHT

Chapter 2 deals, first, with the history and development of copyright law internationally and, second, with Australian copyright legislation and legislative objectives. The discussion considers the meaning of copyright and, thereafter, studies the development of the copyright framework in Australia. Recent and current copyright issues, such as the parallel importing debate, are mentioned briefly. Lastly, it reflects on current moral rights provisions in Australian law and concludes with reference to the 2011 Hargreaves Report and possible future implications for Australian copyright law.

In a nutshell, this chapter provides an overview of the development of copyright and copyright legislation, as well as reference to some current challenges in the field of copyright law facing Australian authors. It concludes that copyright law has been evolving to adapt to new technologies and that electronic publishing may require further changes. The UK has recognised the need for transformation pursuant to the Hargreaves Report, and submissions by the Australian Copyright Council Expert Group have subsequently addressed some of the issues covered by the Hargreaves Report. However, a review of the Australian copyright system is imminent in 2012. The *Authors Guild* case is illustrative of the transitional challenges faced by Australian authors in protecting their copyright in the digital domain. However, the proactive involvement of the Australian Society of Authors in this US case is a positive step for Australian authors in the ongoing protection of their digital copyright.

CHAPTER 3: THEORETICAL AND PHILOSOPHICAL FOUNDATIONS

This chapter deals with the theoretical foundation of copyright law and considers the various philosophical theories in this regard. The link between copyright law and the philosophical ideals that underpin its theory and interpretation is noted and considered within the ambits of the public sphere as proposed by Habermas. The discussion also includes an explanation of the public domain and focuses on the following theories in particular: the utilitarian approach, the public benefit theory, the natural rights theory, and the moral rights theory.

The theories lay the foundation for an examination of authors' roles within the current Australian copyright structure and tie in the expectations of authors from a natural right and moral rights point of view with the broader utilitarian principles followed in copyright legislation. Furthermore, this chapter provides a basis for further discussion of authors' sphere within the public sphere and how authors function in relation to other competing subaltern spheres. In the next chapter, the focus shifts to the subject of authorship, dealing specifically with the concept, definition, and rights of the "author."

The chapter concludes by comparing the theories and noting their alignment and divergences.

CHAPTER 4: AUTHORSHIP – FROM QUILL TO KEYBOARD AND CYBERSPACE

The role of the author and the meaning of authorship is examined, first, in the context of legislation and case law and, second, as seen by critical theorists. The author's position as natural rights holder and moral rights holder within the ambit of the law is considered against existing legislation and case law. The discussion then moves to an account of the author as creator, first in the 21st century and, thereafter, in the digital era. New challenges to authorship and changes in the perceptions of readers are highlighted and discussed.

Evidently, the definition of "author" is an ever-expanding and evolving concept, influenced by a changing public sphere and, more specifically, by technological advances. The dual nature of the author's persona as creator and rights holder has also been emphasised by the changing role of authorship in the new technology. One may validly observe that the effects of hypertext, reader participation, and increased collaboration have created a new breed of writer: the digital author. However, the quality and quantity of creative content and the identity of the writer remain distinguishing factors in this electronic sphere, separating the author from the reader/commentator. As with most things, change is inevitable and survival depends on the timely recognition of changing circumstance. Readers are becoming writers, writers are turning into authors, and authors have to rise to the challenge of distinguishing themselves on the World Wide Web.

CHAPTER 5: COPYRIGHT SUPPORT STRUCTURES

This chapter deals with government and other support structures available to authors internationally and nationally in relation to the enforcement of their copyright and funding. It provides an overview of how the Australian government support structures interact with equivalent global structures and how these mechanisms are utilised to supplement authors' incomes. These structures rely on the premise that copyright law creates incentives for people to invest their time, talent, and other resources in the creation of new material that benefits society and includes government support structures such as grants as well as licensing schemes such as the Copyright Agency Limited (CAL), Public Lending Rights (PLR), and Educational Lending Rights (ELR).

This chapter, thus, provides a bird's eye view of international copyright structures as well as Australian government agencies and schemes that support authors in their creative work. The benefits provided to authors by these programmes, such as the CAL, PLR, and ELR licensing schemes, are evident and signify an effort on the part of government to recognise the importance of financial rewards for creators. Chapters 8 and 10 will investigate how authors have benefited from these resources, and whether they regard the support structures as adequate for their needs.

CHAPTER 6: THE PUBLISHING INDUSTRY

This chapter examines the current evolving publishing framework in Australia and the relationship between authors and their publishers, noting the competing interests of the various subaltern spheres (such as the "author sphere" and "publisher sphere") within the greater public sphere. A comparison between a standard publisher's contract and the model contract recommended by the Australian Society of Authors (ASA) provides a source for analysis and discussion, which relevantly reflects the nature of the relationship between author and publisher. The issue of digital publishing is investigated to ascertain what constitutes an equitable arrangement for authors. Finally, new business models in publishing are considered and observations are made on copyright protection measures on the Internet, alternative licensing models such as the Creative Commons, and the "honesty box" model used by some authors. A brief discussion of the anti-copyright actions of Google is also included, and in conclusion, the author-publisher power balance is addressed, taking into account the different characteristics of print books and ebooks.

The chapter makes the point that some may argue that the author has gained and the publisher has lost traction in the copyright balance, as authors are able to self-publish their ebooks or do so through online publishers without reliance on traditional print publishers. Others point towards the discrepancy in the terms of existing publishing agreements as opposed to those proposed by authors' societies and argue the opposite, namely that authors remain in a weak position vis-a-vis publishers. Publishing on the Internet may be easier, they would say, but the marketing of the book remains an issue, as some authors point out. It appears that, to a great degree, this is why some authors give their ebooks away for free – in order to gain exposure and develop a following of readers, which in turn assists them with selling their printed books in bookstores. This new breed of author uses the Internet to their advantage and employs new technology to publish and market their books.

It concludes that digital technology has brought new challenges and may demand a wider range of skills from authors who wish to benefit from the increased opportunities. It has become apparent that authors who cannot or will not master these skill sets will continue to be reliant on publishers to publish and market their work—whether online or in print—to the reading public.

CHAPTER 7: RESEARCH AND METHODOLOGY

As an inter-disciplinary project, the research underlying the book—discussed in this chapter—employs a multi-method research methodology. The research design is characterised by a qualitative/quantitative research model, incorporating survey data and in-depth interviews. Purposive sampling has been employed to secure in-depth interviews with published authors and to involve qualified respondents in an online survey. The data obtained in this manner provides the basis for the findings and conclusions in chapters 8, 9, 10, and 11. This chapter considers the purpose and scope of the research and discusses the two-stage strategy used to obtain the data, acknowledging the limitations of the research strategy, on the one hand, and the purposeful nature of the information obtained in this manner, on the other. By implementing this process and utilising these two "purposeful samples" of published authors, this research aims to provide a window into the collective viewpoints of a group of Australian authors on various copyright issues, and to investigate how these viewpoints affected their creative practice.

CHAPTERS 8 AND 9: RESEARCH FINDINGS

Chapter 8 deals with the findings in relation to the first two research topics, whilst chapter 9 deals with the third topic. Specifically, chapter 8 records the findings and preliminary observations in relation to authors' perceptions of copyright and the copyright framework, whereas chapter 9 considers authors and publishers in a changing publishing industry. Chapter 8 also includes a description of the demographics of the survey respondents and information on their incomes. Further issues canvassed in chapter 8 are: whether authors see copyright as an incentive to create, how they view moral rights, their thoughts on existing copyright structures such as CAL, perceived problem areas in the field of copyright, and whether they regard authors as adequately protected by copyright legislation. Chapter 9 focuses on the relationship between authors and publishers, publishing contracts, ebooks, Google, and publishing options for authors in the digital world. Preliminary conclusions regarding authors' views on these issues lay the foundation for an in-depth discussion and analysis in the next chapter.

During the second part of the investigation, it becomes evident that copyright and copyright legislation are not viewed by the author participants as something localised, to be seen only in an Australian context, but rather in the wider context of global copyright. The reasons for this perception appeared to be two-fold: firstly, many of the interviewees and respondents have published books in other countries and have to contend with international copyright issues and regional considerations, and secondly, with wider application, media platforms and structures such as the Internet and a variety of electronic devices provide increased forums for publication on an international level. These factors prompt authors to contemplate a departure from traditional copyright frameworks and, in many cases, to embrace alternative frameworks that allowed them to function creatively. These alternative structures, such as the Creative Commons and various forms of online publishing, as discussed more fully in chapter 6, provide increasing options for authors and publishers.

Once the enquiry shifts from traditional publishing models and their supporting legislative structures to the wider options offered by new technology, it also becomes clear that the majority of interviewees and survey respondents acknowledge that most preconceived ideas of copyright legislation would have to adjust in keeping with public expectations and the needs of copyright creators. As evidenced by both the interviews and the online survey results, many authors support a need for change and are intent upon making technological innovations work for, rather than against them.

These findings also highlight some discrepancies in authors' perceptions and levels of knowledge in relation to copyright and the current copyright structures.

CHAPTER 10: DISCUSSION AND ANALYSIS

A discussion and analysis of the key aspects emerging during the course of the research comprise the basis of this chapter. It addresses, *inter alia*, the effect of the parallel importing debate on authors' rights, the issue of publishing contracts, the idea of a "heavenly library," and copyright protection on the Internet, including a discussion on how existing territorial copyright structures may be affected by electronic publishing. This chapter also considers the Google initiatives and possible new business models for authors. The emerging theme of resale royalties for authors is examined and compared with the Resale Royalty Right for Visual Artists Act 2009. In conclusion, observations are made on the role of the author in the changing publishing landscape, situating the author as member of the "author sphere" in the context of the public sphere.

It shows that the Internet has expanded the boundaries of copyright protection that current legislative structures may not offer authors the necessary protection. Several authors mention the need for new copyright solutions, although the findings showed divergent views on the subject. While some suggest that authors should be more proactive in their approach to copyright, others are of the view that the existing copyright structure is insufficiently suited to copyright use in the digital domain. The Internet has created a stronger focus on public benefit considerations by providing free access to information. The chapter proposes that this trend has, to an extent, eroded both authors' private creative rights and the utilitarian model. In order to remain competitive and gain acceptance in the marketplace, they have to be flexible in their copyright approach and embrace new business models. Conversely, in order to remain creative, they require reward. This dichotomy has resulted in some uncertainty in the author ranks about future copyright models, despite opportunities for new publishing and licencing opportunities.

CHAPTER 11: CONCLUSION AND RECOMMENDATIONS

This chapter addresses the research topics based on the discussion and analysis of the findings in chapter 10. It considers, first, what authors' views are on copyright and how these perceptions influence them in their creative work. Second, it examines the role of copyright support structures and the legis-lative framework in order to ascertain how they are perceived by authors. Third, it discusses how authors have been affected by changes in publishing and, more specifically, the impact of electronic publishing. This discussion includes observations on the author-publisher relationship, publishing con-tracts, and future business models for authors. Finally, the research topics are considered against the backdrop of philosophical theory with consideration of the author's place in the literary and public spheres.

Factors such as developments in technology, parallel importing concerns, and changing trends in publishing and marketing are prompting authors to cultivate a greater awareness of issues that affect their livelihood. Google's unauthorised digitalisation of copyrighted work and the resulting legal issues that arose from this action are one such example. The conviction of Apple for anti-trust collusion with five large publishers to increase the price of e-books will also have repercussions for authors and traditional publishers. These developments imply a movement towards a global awareness of copyright issues – rather than relying on territorial copyright law alone, authors have to consider how their copyright is being impacted on an international scale.

The recommendations included in this chapter reflect an examination of the views, opinions, and impressions of authors with regard to copyright, copyright structures, and the changing publishing industry at a critical moment in history. They suggest changes that will invigorate and empower the often marginalised subaltern sphere of authors who are caught at the crossroads of change in the publishing industry. The chapter concludes that copyright perceptions of Australian authors in the literary sphere are subject not only to current legislative provisions but also encompassed by the expanding digital sphere within the broader public sphere envisaged by Habermas. In considering these findings on both a functional and philosophical level, against the backdrop of existing legislation, policy, and theory, it is shown that authors will have to equip themselves to deal with the challenges of new media technology to ensure that they are adequately rewarded for their creative efforts. It suggests that this will require an increased familiarity with electronic licensing agreements and copyright protection measures, knowledge of publishing options, and a stronger awareness of royalty provisions. It will also require authors to assert their rights as creators and to be consistently proactive in addressing future copyright challenges.

Francina Cantatore
Bond University, Australia

Acknowledgment

I would like to thank everyone involved in the production of this book, without whose help the process would have been daunting. My thanks especially go to the publishing team at IGI Global, whose contributions throughout the whole process from inception of the initial proposal to final publication have been invaluable, in particular to Austin DeMarco, who assisted in keeping this project on schedule and providing me with motivation and encouragement throughout. I am also thankful to my Australian editors, Tersia Parsons and Catherine Karcher, whose professional editing abilities and creative suggestions contributed to the final format of the book. My thanks also go to the two anonymous reviewers who provided constructive and comprehensive reviews, informing the final contents of the book.

The research for this book culminated from a desire to marry my love of books and the law, and I am greatly indebted to those people who helped me on this journey of discovery. A very special thanks goes to my husband, Angelo, for his unwavering love and patience as I sat glued to the keyboard for days on end, and to both Angelo and my son, Matt, for their constant inspiration and support.

In particular, I am grateful to my PhD supervisors, Associate Professor Jane Johnston and Professor William van Caenegem of Bond University, for their advice and positive encouragement during the research. Their insightful recommendations and guidance throughout the development of the project—which formed the basis of this book—are very much appreciated. Finally, I would like to thank each and every author and publisher who generously gave of their time and energy during the research interview process, including the authors who took the time to complete the online survey. The project would not have been possible without their participation, and I thank them for their support.

Francina Cantatore
Bond University, Australia

Chapter 1
Introduction

ABSTRACT

The subject of "authorship and copyright" is an extensive field, encompassing a vast area of research possibilities, spanning areas of law and humanities. This book is situated at the intersection of copyright legislation and literary critical theory on the issue of authorship of written work. The writer, poised at this nexus, has drawn together data from a range of primary sources, namely Australian authors, publishers, and specialist academics, as well as secondary data analysis of legislation, case law, author contracts, and literature in this field. Significantly, it reflects the views of authors in a challenging transitional period that incorporates issues such as the Google initiatives, the parallel import debate, and the shift from traditional print to electronic publishing. The book aims to provide a snapshot of this purposive sample of Australian authors' perspectives on copyright issues at a pivotal point in history when authors find themselves between the old and the new, grappling with the realities of traditional expectations and digital advances in publishing. Furthermore, the book sets out to position Australian authors in the changing and expanding literary public sphere within which they find themselves, with reference to global considerations. There has been very little other research on Australian authors' views on copyright, and the changing copyright landscape brought about by the Internet provides an important, if unwieldy, environment in which to investigate authors' perceptions of this legal concept that impacts so intrinsically upon their creative rewards.

DOI: 10.4018/978-1-4666-5214-9.ch001

BACKGROUND

Issues that emerged whilst mapping the course of recent copyright developments included authors' changing perceptions of the value of copyright, problems associated with the current copyright structures and the changing inter-relationship between authors and the publishing industry. It was evident that the literature showed limited research on these issues, specifically as they pertained to the subaltern sphere* of authors, and how this group related to the broader public sphere of existing Government structures and the global publishing environment. A closer examination of these issues, specifically how the author sphere intersects with other competing spheres in this changing milieu and how the resulting tension between authors' interests, publishers' interests and the public interest impacts on the author's practice as creator, forms part of this book.

The 1999 Australian Copyright Council report, *Copyright in the New Communications Environment: Balancing Protection and Access* addressed 'the new communications environment and the future role within it of the main exceptions to copyright infringement'. It examined the balance struck in Australian copyright law between the protection afforded to copyright creators and owners and exceptions to infringement which provided access to copyright materials for certain uses and how that balance was being altered by developing digital communications technologies (McDonald, 1999). The study informed some of the 2000 and 2006 amendments to the *Copyright Act 1968* (Cth), discussed in Chapter 2.

Other examples of copyright research undertaken in recent years include reports such as the *Economic perspectives on Copyright law* by The Centre for Copyright Studies Limited (The Allen Consulting Group, 2003) and the *Productivity Commission Report on Copyright Restrictions on the Parallel Importation of Books*, (Productivity Commission, 2009). Previous reports such as the *Report of the Copyright law Committee on Reprographic Reproduction* (Franki, 1976) and the *Review of Intellectual Property Legislation under the Competition Principles Agreement* (Ergas, 2000), which are discussed in Chapter 2, dealt with Australian copyright legislation and provided insight into the grounds and justification of Australian copyright law.

A more recent study, *Do you really expect to get paid: An economic study of professional artists in Australia* (Throsby & Zednik, 2010), concerned the income of Australian artists. The study, an extensive research project funded by the Australia Council, involved 120 occupations, including writers, dancers, musicians and visual artists. Another study, *What's your other job? A census analysis of arts employment in Australia* (Cunningham & Higgs, 2010) dealt with the employment of artists from different occupations in Australia. However, these reports focussed on the arts industry as a whole and not the writing industry specifically.

In May 2008, the Queensland University of Technology conducted a survey, limited to academics, on *Academic authorship, publishing agreements and open access*. The study was designed to provide evidence of the attitudes and practices of academic authors in Australia in relation to publication and dissemination of their research, in order to inform the effective management of copyright in the Australian research sector (Austin, Heffernan, & David, 2008).

A further study funded by the Australia Council, *A case for literature: the effectiveness of subsidies to Australian publishers 1995-2005,* dealt with the extent to which the Literature Board's publishing subsidy program had been effective in supporting the publication of Australian literary titles (McLean, Poland, & Van den Berg, 2010). It assessed the contribution this publishing subsidy program made to Australian literary culture during the period 1995-2005; however, it did not address the issue of subsidies made specifically to authors.

In February 2010, the Australian Government's Department of Innovation, Industry, Science and Research announced the establishment of the Book Industry Strategy Group (BISG), with the aim of developing viable strategies for the Australian book industry in the digital age. A research report, *Digital Technologies in Australia's Book Industry*, provided an overview of digital technologies used in the Australian book industry as at July 2010 (Lee, 2010). The BISG also obtained 138 submissions from individuals and industry operators that contributed to the debate on the future of books in Australia (Lee, 2010). Just prior to the submission of this book, the BISG released a *Final Report to Government* on the Australian book industry (Jones, 2011), after considering submissions from the industry. Where relevant, their recommendations have been referred to in the final chapters of this book. The recommendations affecting authors in the BISG's *Final Report to Government* were largely informed by a Submission of the Australian Society of Authors (Loukakis, 2011). Subsequently, on the eve of submission of this book, Loukakis released a further paper, *The author as producer, the author as business* (2011), which deals with authors' incomes and authorship as a business model. His observations are highly relevant to the findings in this book, discussed in Chapters 10 and 11.

Also in 2011, The Copyright Council Expert Group released a paper on *Directions in Copyright Reforms in Australia* dealing with various issues in relation to copyright, namely optional copyright registration, orphan works, liability of online service providers and exceptions for non-commercial transformative copyright use (Brennan, De Zwart, Fraser, Lindsay, & Ricketson, 2011). The report contains useful recommendations on these topics, some of which are beneficial to authors, particularly with regard to copyright registration and alternative solutions to the Creative Commons licensing options (2011, pp. 4, 11).

These reports are referred to in future chapters where relevant. However, there are no studies available on the specific subject of copyright as viewed by Australian authors, except in relation to the issue of the parallel importation of books, where a number of authors made submissions on the topic. In that instance, the Productivity Commission conducted the *Productivity Commission Study on the Parallel Importation of Books* (2009), relating to proposed legislative changes, eventually rejected by the Australian Government, which are discussed in Chapter 2.

COPYRIGHT: AN EVOLVING CONCEPT

Copyright law has been constantly evolving in response to economic demands, in an attempt to balance utilitarian principles with the changing times and technological advances. However, unprecedented advances in technology have challenged legislature globally and are having a disruptive effect on traditional publishing models and the copyright provisions that underpin them. It is in this unchartered terrain that both authors and publishers find themselves, with the legislature adopting a reactive position, trying to deal with copyright infringement problems as they present themselves on the one hand and accommodating public demand for access to creative works on the other.

As the 20th century drew to a close, the Internet and digital publishing were relatively unknown concepts to authors as a creative group, the ereader was a future possibility and digital libraries existed only in the realms of science fiction. To most authors, terminology such as ePub files, digital rights management (DRM) and ebooks have only entered their vocabulary in the last five to ten years.

The Internet, apart from providing access to previously unparalleled levels of information, also heralded a new era in publishing and literary creativity. This evolution can be described as a movement of technical advancement with strong undercurrents, pulling the author involuntarily into an ocean of information and opportunity. Authors, who previously functioned in a specific, geographically determined area, subject to regional publishing boundaries, have now transcended those barriers to find themselves in the vastly expanded literary or creative sphere offered by the Internet.

Although territorial copyright still exists, and countries such as Australia, the United States of America and the United Kingdom maintain their parallel import restrictions on books, booksellers such as Amazon have rendered such protection measures virtually pointless from a copyright perspective, as will be discussed in Chapter 6. Having said that, the Booksellers Association of Australia has blamed the demise of bookstores Borders and Angus and Robertson in Australia partly on parallel import restrictions and booksellers' resultant inability to benefit from cheaper imports (Carr, 2011, p. 3). This book, however, is less concerned with the plight of booksellers and publishers; rather, it is squarely focussed on authors and their views of copyright in the digital era.

Additionally, territorial copyright has been impacted by US Supreme Court decisions such *Kirtsaeng v. John Wiley & Sons* (2013). This case illustrates the implications of applying the 'first sale doctrine' to books imported from another country and then sold in the country of origin, which puts paid to the idea that territorial rights will necessarily protect US rights holders from the impact of cross-border sales. The far-reaching effect of this approach is highlighted in Chapter 2.

Globally copyright law is facing challenging times. In his book, *The book is dead – long live the book*, Australian author Sherman Young compares the infrastructure of the changing book industry with the car industry, pointing out that change in the industry will necessitate a new copyright infrastructure. He criticises current copyright legislation as 'copyright laws that speak to a nineteenth-century mindset, and set up barriers to access' (Young, 2007, pp. 158-159). These comments mirror those of many critics of copyright laws who recognise the burdens of national and regional boundaries in copyright law. In an online debate held by *The Economist* in May 2009, 71% of participants voted in favour of the proposition that existing copyright laws 'do more harm than good' (Fisher & Hughes, 2009). Although debaters relied on a variety of arguments in support of this proposition, the results indicated that there was a marked public perception that some kind of copyright reform was imperative, if not inevitable.

For authors, the Internet has caused a perceived loss of copyright protection (such as in the case of Google's unauthorised copying of books in American libraries, discussed in Chapter 6) and the concomitant need of *having* to adapt to a changing publishing environment. Furthermore, the conviction of

Apple in the case of *United States of America et al v. Apple Inc et al* (2013) for anti-trust collusion with five large publishers to increase the price of e-books, illustrates the power wielded by large online publishers to control ebook prices and ebook libraries of readers. This is not an issue confined to the United States. In 2012, Apple settled a separate ebook price-fixing case with the European Commission, without admitting wrongdoing (Flood, 2012).

However, the Internet has also brought with it a vast increase in publishing options, more accessibility to publishing for new authors and possibilities of international exposure that would previously have been difficult to implement.

Some historicists argue, as noted in Chapter 3, that the changes produced by the advent of the Internet are, on the whole, not as ground-breaking as the radical changes effected by the invention of the printing press in the fifteenth century and no different from the inevitable changing business models that were adopted from time to time over the centuries in response to new technology. Whilst it is true that the emergence of print literature precipitated the basis for current copyright law, it is argued here that the development of a digital environment has materially impacted on copyright considerations for Australian authors. A discussion of these changes forms a significant part of this research.

The following issues are addressed in this book:

1. How do Australian authors perceive copyright affecting them, and does it have any impact on how they practise?
2. Do Australian authors believe that the existing copyright framework supports and encourages them in their creative efforts?
3. What are Australian authors' views on the changing nature of the publishing industry, and how have they been affected by changes/advances in this area?

These questions are investigated in depth and discussed during the course of the research methodology (discussed in Chapter 7) and over the following chapters. In the final chapter, tentative conclusions are drawn in respect of these topics, based on the discussion and analysis of the findings in Chapter 10. The final chapter considers, first, what authors' views are on copyright and how these perceptions influence them in their creative work. Second, it examines the role of copyright support structures and the legislative framework in order to ascertain how they are perceived by authors. Third, it discusses how authors have been affected by changes in publishing, and more specifically, the impact of electronic publishing. This discussion includes observations on the author-publisher relationship, publishing contracts and future business models for authors. Finally, these issues are considered against the backdrop of philosophical theory with consideration of the author's place in the literary and public spheres.

CONCLUSION

Factors such as developments in technology, parallel importing concerns and changing trends in publishing and marketing are prompting authors to cultivate a greater awareness of issues which affect their livelihood. Google's unauthorised digitalisation of copyrighted work and the resulting legal issues that arose from this action are one such example. These developments imply a movement towards a global awareness of copyright issues – rather than relying on Australian copyright law alone, authors have to consider how their copyright is being impacted on an international scale. This chapter commences the discussion on the way in which authors are navigating their copyright in the expanded literary sphere and how they are dealing with digital technology in their creative work and publishing contracts. On a deeper level, it also introduces the discussion of the author's role in the literary and the greater public sphere and the relationship between the competing groups in the publishing industry.

REFERENCES

Allen Consulting Group. (2003). *Economic perspectives on copyright law*. Strawberry Hills, Australia: The Centre for Copyright Studies Limited.

Austin, A., Heffernan, M., & David, N. (2008). *Academic authorship, publishing agreements and open access (Research Report)*. Brisbane, Australia: The OAK Law Project, Queensland University of Technology.

Australian Copyright Council. (2011, May 23). *Digital opportunity – The Hargreaves report*. Retrieved May 24, 2011, from http://www.copyright.org.au/news-and-policy/details/id/1958/

Brennan, D., De Zwart, M., Fraser, M., Lindsay, D., & Ricketson, S. (2011). *Directions in copyright reform in Australia (Report)*. Canberra, Australia: Copyright Council Expert Group.

Carr, B. (2011, February 19-20). It's the lunacy of protectionism writ large. *The Weekend Australian*, p. 3.

Cunningham, S., & Higgs, P. (2010). *What's your other job? A census analysis of arts employment in Australia (Research Report)*. Sydney: Australia Council for the Arts.

Ergas, H. (2000). *Review of intellectual property legislation under the competition principles agreement (Final Report)*. Canberra, Australia: Intellectual Property and Competition Review Committee.

Fisher, W., & Hughes, J. (2009, May 5-15). Copyright and wrongs. *The Economist*. Retrieved May 17, 2009, from http://www.economist.com/debate/overview/144

Flood, A. (2012). European Commission and Apple reach settlement over ebook price-fixing. *The Guardian*. Retrieved November 10, 2013, from http://www.theguardian.com/books/2012/dec/14/european-commission-apple-ebook

Franki, R. (1976). *Report of the copyright law committee on reprographic reproduction (Research Report)*. Canberra, Australia: Government of Australia.

Fraser, N. (1992). Rethinking the public sphere: A contribution to the critique of actually existing democracy. In C. Calhoun (Ed.), *Habermas and the public sphere*. Cambridge, MA: MIT Press.

Jones, B. (2011). *Book industry strategy group report (Research Report)*. Canberra, Australia: Government of Australia.

Lee, J. (2010). *Digital technologies in Australia's book industry* (Book Industry Strategy Group Research Report). Retrieved April 29, 2010, from http://www.innovation.gov.au

Loukakis, A. (2011a, January). *Submission to the book industry strategy group.*

Loukakis, A. (2011b). *The author as producer, the author as business.* Canberra, Australia: Australian Society of Authors.

McDonald, I. (1999). *Copyright in the new communications environment: Balancing protection and access (Research Report).* Redfern, Australia: The Australian Copyright Council for The Centre for Copyright Studies Limited.

McLean, K., Poland, L., & Van den Berg, J. (2010). *A case for literature: The effectiveness of subsidies to Australian publishers 1995-2005.* Sydney, Australia: Australia Council for the Arts.

Productivity Commission. (2009). *Restrictions on the parallel importation of books (Research Report).* Canberra, Australia: Author.

Throsby, D., & Zednik, A. (2010). *Do you really expect to get paid? An economic study of professional artists in Australia (Research Report).* Strawberry Hills, Australia: Australia Council for the Arts.

Young, S. (2007). *The book is dead: Long live the book.* Sydney: University of New South Wales Press.

TABLE OF CASES

Kirtsaeng v. John Wiley & Sons 568 U.S. WL 1104736 (U.S. Mar. 19, 2013)

United States of America et al v. Apple Inc et al, US District Court for the Southern District of New York, 10 July 2013 (US)

ENDNOTES

[1] As one of the parallel arenas within the public sphere as proposed by Fraser (1992, p. 131).

Chapter 2
History and Development
of Copyright

ABSTRACT

This chapter deals firstly with the history and development of copyright law internationally and secondly with Australian copyright legislation and legislative objectives. The discussion considers the meaning of copyright and, thereafter, studies the development of the copyright framework in Australia. Recent and current copyright issues, such as the parallel importing debate, are discussed, with reference to recent USA case law. Lastly, the chapter reflects on current moral rights provisions in Australian law and concludes with reference to the 2011 Hargreaves Report and possible future implications for Australian copyright law.

INTRODUCTION

In order to contextualise the findings of this research, it is necessary to provide an historical overview of the birth and development of copyright, current Australian copyright law and the philosophical arguments which seek to justify its existence. It is also useful to consider the socio-economic circumstances within which the concept developed, in particular, its application and perception in the public sphere as understood through the work of Jurgen Habermas, which will be discussed in the next chapter. In this regard, the historical development of the copyright concept and the evolution of the public sphere as it relates to authors are parallel issues that have

DOI: 10.4018/978-1-4666-5214-9.ch002

significantly impacted on authors' current perceptions of copyright. This chapter lays the foundation for the research questions, dealing firstly with the history and development of copyright law and secondly, with Australian copyright legislation.

THE ORIGINS OF COPYRIGHT LAW

In contrast to the accepted norm and belief today that copyright law exists to promote a balance between the public interest and the creator's rights, the beginnings of copyright law germinated largely as a result of early European printers' efforts to protect their investments. Although commercial printing started in Europe in the 15th century, it was unregulated with no protection afforded to either author or publisher. In the early 16th century, the printing industry was flourishing and competitive, with nothing preventing the copying and distribution of printed work without any regard for the rights of authors or original publishers (Armstrong, 1990, p. 21).

In British common law, the germination of copyright can be traced back to 1476 with the founding of the first printing establishment in England by Caxton and the English Crown's efforts to regulate the revolutionary new technology (Goldstein, 2001, p. 5).

Publishers in Europe started gaining protection when, in 1507, Paris publisher Antoine Verard obtained a grant from Louis XII, which covered Verard for three years for any book he was the first to publish. Other French publishers and booksellers followed suit and applied for grants from the State or the Crown, effectively protecting their publishing rights for a certain period of time. Economic considerations were cited as the most pressing reasons for obtaining such grants. Some authors also applied for and gained grants, such as Dr Jean Falcon for *Les notables sur le Guidon* (CH 1515, 1A), his main argument of persuasion being his fear that any merchant or bookseller could reproduce his work unless he received protection (Armstrong, 1990, p. 80).

In the United Kingdom, copyright advances were slower due to the smaller number of printers and the fact that books were often imported from the European mainland. Again, the printing industry prompted the first legislative steps. In an attempt to prevent unregulated copying of books, Charles II enacted the *Licensing Act 1662*, which required 'licensed books' to be entered into a registry. The Government, however, allowed this Act to lapse in 1694 when it expired, due to its restrictive nature.

The issue of copyright was the concern of publishers rather than authors. Although authors were recognised as having some rights in their work, they did not have ownership of the work. Milton in *Areopagitica* (1644) first mentions the idea of ownership of copyright. However, his discourse was centred on publishers and not authors, and this view prevailed until late in the 18th century, despite legislative advances such as the promulgation of the British *Statute of Anne* in 1709 (also known as the *Copyright Act* of 1710).

As Saunders points out, the principal agent in the copyright field was not an individual but a corporate entity: the Stationers' Company. The term 'copy right' appeared for the first time in their records in 1701, introduced in their by-laws in order to protect stationers' ownership of printing rights (rather than reflecting any common law rights of authors) (1992, pp. 47-48).

Until the *Statute of Anne*, which referred to the rights of the author in some depth and formalised certain copyright provisions, it was apparent that not a great deal of thought had been given to authorial ownership of property prior to that piece of legislation (Rose, 1993, p. 48). Copyright given to publishers under this Act expired after a fixed period of 14 years unless it was renewed for a further 14 years, to a maximum period of 28 years (provided the author was still living). Copyright on books already in print was limited to 21 years. It was evident that the Act had been promulgated not so much for the benefit of authors, as for the purpose of restricting London booksellers' control of valuable copyrights (Rose, 1988, pp. 51-56).

Although the author's right to control and benefit financially from the work was recognised, the Statute became the subject of a dispute between booksellers. It was relied on, for example, by certain booksellers, such as the Scottish bookseller Donaldson, to start publishing books after the 28-year period of copyright held by the original publishers had expired. London booksellers opposed his actions and asserted that copyright was a 'perpetual right,' based in common law, which was supplemented by the operation of the Act [*Donaldson v. Beckett* (1774)].

That view had previously been expressed in *Millar v. Taylor* (1769), where the Court affirmed the principle of perpetual copyright and the common law right of literary property (Rose, 1988, p. 52). The booksellers relied there on the Lockean theory of possessive individualism, that authors were the owners of their property and should be allowed to dispose of the rights in their property. The author was thus entitled to sell them the copyright, which they would hold in perpetuity (like any other property).

However, in the 1774 landmark case of *Donaldson v. Beckett*, the House of Lords on appeal disagreed with the approach in *Millar v. Taylor* and overruled Millar's case in favour of the principle that copyright should be limited in time. The Court held that authors had the exclusive right to the first publication indefinitely, but the right was annulled once the work was published. Thereafter a limited right would apply in accordance with Statute (Rose, 1988, p. 53).

Rose describes the 'modern proprietary author' as a 'weapon' invented by the London booksellers to do battle with the provincial booksellers. Whilst the London booksellers focussed on the author's labour to support their 'natural rights' argument, the opponents of the perpetual rights argument relied on the actual creative work, which, they argued, was subject to the time limits prescribed in the Statute, similar to other patent rights (Rose, 1988, p. 55).

The Court agreed with the provincial booksellers and treated copyright in the same manner as any other patent right for a new manner of manufacture, approving the provisions of the *Statute of Anne*, based on the Jacobean *Statute of Monopolies*, which imposed the same time limitations to patents for a new manner of manufacture. Copyright was regarded as 'a collection of ideas,' no different from patents (Rose, 1988, p. 60), and the Statute was seen as effectively disposing of the common law right to copyright.

In the United States of America, enabling legislation as early as 1787 provided for the passing of copyright legislation. The legislation allowed American authors to benefit financially from their efforts for a certain period of time. In 1790, the *Copyright Act* was enacted, with similar provisions (14 plus 14 years) as the *Statute of Anne*. Amendments to this Act in 1909 extended the copyright period to 28 plus 28 years, to the benefit of both authors and publishers.

In the late 19th century, the 1886 Berne Convention for the Protection of Literary and Artistic Works (Berne Convention) signified a major step in copyright recognition worldwide and was regarded as the key copyright agreement between nations. The Berne Convention progressively globalised previous bilateral agreements between nations (such as the United Kingdom's first *International Copyright Act* in 1838, which formed the basis for treaties with France and parts of Germany) to include all participating countries.

Australia became a signatory to the Berne Convention in 1928, with the United States only committing in 1988. The Berne Convention regulations were subsequently recognised by the World Trade Organisation's Trade-related

Aspects of Intellectual Property Rights (TRIPS) agreement (1995), giving it further international scope. It has been described as 'the most comprehensive multilateral agreement on intellectual property to date' by the World Trade Organisation.

However, commentators such as Ricketson are of the view that the emergence of international copyright was primarily a response to the piracy of German publishers and authors by the Dutch, of French publishers by the Belgians and of English publishers and authors by the Americans (Ricketson, 1987, p. 19). This viewpoint, according to Saunders, made the Berne Convention 'an occasion of mixing, not only of different national legal regimes but also of cultural ideals and styles of calculation' (Saunders, 1992, p. 181). Saunders further points out that article 6*bis* of the Berne Convention, which deals with the *droit moral* (moral rights) of the author, protects 'a highly specialised form of legal and aesthetic personality – that of the author – against the interests of the market' (1992, p. 185).

In the United States, the *Copyright Act* was amended in 1976 to extend the copyright term to the life of the author plus fifty years. The *Sonny Bono Copyright Term Extension Act* of 1998 further extended the term to the life of the author plus seventy years. This extension was only adopted in Australia in 2006 with the passing of the *Copyright Amendment Act*, after entering into the Free Trade Agreement with the United States in 2004 (Boymal & Davidson, 2004, p. 235).

In 1996, the World Intellectual Property Organization (WIPO) introduced the WIPO Copyright Treaty (WCT) in Geneva, which extended copyright protection to computer programmes and databases, which qualified as 'intellectual creations.' Further aims of the WCT included the promotion of acceptance of existing treaties, updating existing treaties, compiling international databases and provision of arbitration services. Australia ratified the WCT in July 2007. These changes were reflected in the *Digital Millennium Copyright Act 1998* (US), which provided for the criminalisation of the infringement of certain copyright provisions and recognised the necessity to regulate digitally based creation.

Since then, US legislation has been modified continually to accommodate new technological trends, and in 2005, the *Family Entertainment and Copyright Act* was promulgated to address further breaches of copyright in the digital technology sphere. United States copyright continues to be regulated by the Berne Convention and the TRIPS agreement, as is the case with

Australian copyright. International copyright law is seen to be constantly evolving to incorporate new technologies. As the Court stated in the 1984 US case *Sony Corporation v. Universal Studios, Inc.*: 'From its beginning, the law of copyright has developed in response to significant changes in technology' (at 225).

Inevitably, Australian law has been influenced and shaped by international copyright legislation, especially British law. In the recent UK Hargreaves Report, Professor Hargreaves admitted that the UK's existing intellectual property framework was impeding national innovation and economic growth (2011, p. 1). A digital copyright exchange – providing greater transparency in the marketplace – and the licensing of orphan works were two recommendations put forward by the Report. The fact that the UK Government has since accepted all of the Report's recommendations indicates a substantial transformation of the copyright industry in the UK in the near future. These recommendations are relevant as they may impact on Australian authors and Australian copyright law in the future.

According to the Australian Copyright Council, this Report would be of significance in the future review of Australian copyright law planned by the Australian Attorney General in 2011/2012. The Copyright Council Expert Group have subsequently released a paper, *Directions in Copyright Reforms in Australia,* which made recommendations in relation to copyright with regard to some of the issues covered by the Hargreaves Report, including optional copyright registration, orphan works, liability of online service providers and exceptions for non-commercial transformative copyright use (Brennan, De Zwart, Fraser, Lindsay, & Ricketson, 2011).

COPYRIGHT LAW IN AUSTRALIA

The Australian Constitution empowers the Commonwealth Government to legislate on matters of copyright, patents and trademarks [Section 51 (xviii)]. Australian Copyright law is embodied in the *Copyright Act 1968* (Cth) ('the Act'), (as amended by the *Copyright Amendment (Digital Agenda) Act 2000*, the *Copyright Amendment (Moral Rights) Act 2000* and the *2006 Copyright Amendment Act*).

Section 31(1) of the Act defines copyright as follows:

For the purposes of this Act, unless the contrary intention appears, copyright, in relation to a work, is the exclusive right:

1. in the case of a literary, dramatic or musical work, to do all or any of the following acts:
   a. To reproduce the work in a material form.
   b. To publish the work.
   c. To perform the work in public.
   d. To communicate the work to the public.
   e. [sic] to make an adaptation of the work.
   f. To do, in relation to a work that is an adaptation of the first-mentioned work, any of the acts specified in relation to the first-mentioned work in subparagraphs (a) to (d), inclusive.
2. In the case of a literary work (other than a computer program) or a musical or dramatic work, to enter into a commercial rental arrangement in respect of the work reproduced in a sound recording...

The Act also protects the 'moral right' of authors as defined in Section 189 as:

1. A right of attribution of authorship.
2. A right not to have authorship falsely attributed.
3. A right of integrity of authorship.

It is therefore evident that the legislation defines copyright not only as an economic right, but it also accommodates the author's moral rights under the definition of the rights protected under the Act.

The history of Australian copyright must be viewed within the context of the parallel development of British copyright law. The first copyright legislation to be enacted in Australia was contained in the *Trade Marks Act 1903* and the *Copyright Act 1905*. However, in 1912 the *British Copyright Act 1911* was adopted in Australia, and this position continued up to 1956. From 1935 to 1954, committees such as the Knowles Committee and the Dean Committee prepared the groundwork for the 1952 *Patents Act* and the *Trade Marks Act 1955*, which further led to the *British Copyright Act 1911* being repealed in 1956 by the *Australian Copyright Act*.

In 1959, the Spicer Committee reviewed the copyright position in Australia and made recommendations that distinguished Australian copyright law from the British model in several respects. It described the purpose of copyright as follows:

The law of copyright is chiefly concerned with the protection of the author of a literary, musical, dramatic or artistic work from the unauthorized reproduction of such work or its performance in public (Spicer, 1959, p. 8).

In the report, the Committee addressed some discrepancies in the interpretation of British and Australian legislation. For example, in British legislation, the place of first publication was an essential element in determining the existence of copyright in a published work; whereas, under the 1956 Act the place of first publication could be the determining element, but there were also other determining factors, such as nationality, domicile and residence of the author [sections 2 (2) (a), (b)] (Spicer, p. 8).

It also considered copyright obligations under the 1948 revision of the Berne Convention and made recommendations regarding the amendments necessary to comply with the changes to the Berne Convention, which it regarded as beneficial to Australian copyright owners in an international context. A further report in 1973 by the Franki Committee, the *Report of the Copyright Law Committee on Reprographic Reproduction* (1976, p. 139) made recommendations on retaining the 'fair dealing' provisions in the 1968 *Copyright Act* and also addressed the issue of the copying of 'reasonable portions' of copyrighted works by students at educational institutions.

With regard to trademarks and patents, the 1979 *Patents Amendment Act* was later followed by the *Patents Act 1990*, reflecting the changing perceptions and the growing importance of economic considerations in intellectual property law. Technological advances caused further strides to be made from 1983 onwards, when the Copyright Law Review Committee was established to address copyright reform measures, taking cognisance of digital advancement in particular.

Significantly, in 1975 a judgment was obtained in favour of creators in the case of *University of NSW v. Moorhouse* (1975). In this case, a graduate of the University used a photocopy machine in the University library to make two copies of a story from a library copy of a book of short stories written by Moorhouse. The High Court of Australia held that the University had authorised an infringement of the author's copyright within the meaning of section 36(1) of the *Copyright Act 1968* (Cth), as it had not taken reasonable steps to prevent the infringement. The case resulted in creators lobbying the Government for changes to the *Copyright Act* and later led to the creation of the Copyright Agency Limited (CAL), a not-for-profit Australian organisation, in 1986.

CAL's function was to manage the copyright interests of writers and assist them to obtain payment for reproduction of their work by public institutions, including educational institutions, government and corporations. The organisation has been instrumental in setting guidelines for copying of copyright works on a commercial basis and promoted the compliant use of digital material. Though not a legislative body, the organisation has been able to provide financial returns to both authors and publishers who have registered with it, marking an important innovation in the application of copyright law. Additionally, in 1985 the *Public Lending Rights Act* was promulgated to compensate authors for the loss of potential sales due to their books being available for free use in public libraries ('the PLR scheme'). This Act was later complemented by the Educational Lending Rights scheme ('the ELR scheme'), which provided for similar compensation in the case of libraries in educational institutions. CAL, the PLR scheme and ELR scheme are discussed in more depth in Chapter 4.

In 1995, the *Trade Marks Act* repealed the 1955 Act and incorporated provisions of the World Trade Organisation agreement on Trade-related Aspects of Intellectual Property Law. The 1995 Simpson Report, *Review of Australian Collection Societies*, made further recommendations on issues such as the protection of authors' moral rights and limitations on parallel importing provisions. It recommended a multiplicity of collecting societies rather than one merged body, to provide authors with more power to negotiate licensing fees in a changing technological landscape. At present, CAL remains the major collecting agency dealing with authors' copyright payments. Collecting Agency relationships are regulated by the Copyright Tribunal of Australia, an independent body established under section 138 of the *Copyright Act 1968* and having jurisdiction with respect to statutory and voluntary licences, with its powers and procedures set out in the Copyright Tribunal (Procedure) Regulations 1969.

These gradual advances led to further copyright reforms in the form of the *Copyright Amendment (Digital Agenda) Act 2000*, which updated the 1968 *Copyright Act* and addressed some of the challenges posed by digital technology. For example, the definition of 'manuscript' was extended to include electronic publishing and defined as 'the document embodying the work as initially prepared by the author, whether the document is in hardcopy form, electronic form or any other form (*Copyright Act 1968*, s. 10(1)).

The *Copyright Amendment (Moral Rights) Act 2000* introduced legislative provisions to protect the moral rights of Australian creators within the ambits of the Berne Convention provisions. This was followed by the 2006 *Copyright Amendment Act,* which, in turn, favoured an economic-utilitarian approach, addressing *inter alia* the benefits of parallel importation and updating provisions regarding collecting agencies. Consequently, current Australian copyright legislation is characterised by economic considerations. Below follows a brief discussion on the objectives of Australian copyright law and how these objectives have been implemented and viewed by the courts.

Ironically, copyright has historically been characterised as a negative right. Australian courts have, for example, defined copyright as '... *a power to prevent the making of a physical thing by copying'* (*Pacific Film Laboratories Pty Ltd v. FCT* (1976)). This definition has been cited with approval in subsequent Federal Court decisions such as *Australasian performing Rights Association Ltd v. Commonwealth Bank of Australia* (1992) at 157.

From a theoretical perspective, Australian case law has followed the utilitarian approach evident in many US decisions, such as in the *Fox Film* case (*Fox Film Corp v. Doyal* (1932) 286 US). The later US case *Computer Associations International, Inc. v. Altai, Inc.* (1992) expressed the following policy considerations, which have since been endorsed by Australian courts:

The goal of copyright law is to award artistic creativity in a manner that permits the free use and development of non-protectable ideas and processes. The main goal of copyright law is not to reward the labour of authors (at 1241)

and further:

While incentive based arguments in favour of broad copyright protection are perhaps attractive from a pure policy perspective, they have a corrosive effect on certain fundamental tenets of copyright doctrine...copyright seeks to establish a delicate equilibrium. On the one hand, it affords protection to authors and an incentive to create, and on the other, it must appropriately limit the extent of that protection so as to avoid the effects of monopolistic stagnation (at 1241).

This decision has been followed in several Australian decisions, such as *Coogi Australia Pty Ltd v. Hysport International Pty Ltd. & Others* (1998), where Drummond J referred to the *Altai* case in his judgment, in support of the transformative use of copyright (at 1059). In the Australian Federal Court decision of *Hamm v. Middleton* (1999), Von Doussa J took a different approach and held that:

The monopoly of the copyright is intended to give the authors a fair return for their effort, and to provide market incentives for authors to create new works for the public benefit (at 656).

Public policy considerations have also featured in Australian copyright decisions, as discussed above. In the 2002 Australian case *Copyright Agency Ltd v. Queensland Department of Education & Others*, the Tribunal emphasised the importance of 'public benefit' in the consideration of statutory licensing rates, stating further that the rate set should not inhibit the use of the statutory licence (at 19).

The legislative approach in Australia has thus historically been seen to limit intellectual property rights in order to avoid the restriction of distributing creative material to the end user in accordance with the Competition Principles Agreement 1995 (CPA). The CPA provided in clause 5(1) that legislation should be reviewed as follows:

The guiding principle is that legislation (including Acts, enactments, Ordinances or regulations) should not restrict competition unless it can be demonstrated that:

1. The benefits of the restriction to the community as a whole outweigh the costs.
2. The objectives of the legislation can only be achieved by restricting competition.

This approach was justified in the Ergas Committee Report (ECR), where it was stated:

...conferring intellectual property rights, while encouraging investment in creative effort, can allow the owners of the rights to unduly restrict the diffusion and use of the results of these efforts (2000, p. 34).

This report consequently formed the foundation for the *Copyright Amendment Act 2006*, which incorporated the recommendations of the Ergas Committee of 2000 in relation to economic considerations. In the ECR, it was recognised that:

The general objective of the system of intellectual property law in Australia is utilitarian, and more specifically economic, rather than moral in character (Ergas, 2000, p. 33)

and further:

...the Australian tradition in intellectual property law is more explicitly utilitarian: in the sense of seeking to maximize social welfare, rather than focusing on IP as having intrinsic value and hence merit (2000, p. 43).

These comments are in contrast to the views expressed in the 1995 Simpson Report, commissioned by government on the role of Australian collecting societies. According to Simpson:

*If society is to recognise creativity, innovation and imagination, then copyright is the principal tool by which we accord that recognition. This is economically expressed by the award of a range of exclusive rights which grant the owner, the power of control and the right of commercial exploitation. At the end of the day, the rights of copyright are an **award** for innovation, creativity and risk taking (1995, p. 8).*

He goes on to say:

It is a recognition that both the culture and the economy of our community is dependent on encouraging and fostering these characteristics. So, fundamental to the existence of bodies established to grant and administer licences of copyrights, must be the belief:

1. That copyright is valuable, not merely in the sense of being worth money, but valuable in the sense that our community has chosen to confer on copyright a range of cultural, economic and personal values.
2. That the collective administration of some of those values is likely to contribute to the community's benefit (1995, p. 8).

Current Australian law is reflected in the provisions of the *Copyright Act 1968* as amended by the *Copyright Amendment (Digital Agenda) Act 2000*, the *Copyright Amendment (Moral Rights) Act 2000* and the *Copyright Amendment Act 2006*. The amendments came about pursuant to the ECR, which relied heavily on the CPA, hence with a firm grounding in economic considerations. Whereas authors such as Thomas asserted that 'the purpose of copyright is basically to ensure a continuing profit to the originator or creator of a copyrighted work' (1968, p. 27), legislative provisions have become more far-reaching in protecting the rights of other stake-holders and to serve broader economic purposes, as is evident from the legislative approach in current Australian copyright law.

The ECR expressed a distinct preference for a utilitarian approach, which seeks to balance the economic incentive policy in respect of the creator with the public benefit idea and dissemination of the material to the distributor and end user. This approach is in line with the theory that copyright should serve as an incentive to the author to create, whilst also ensuring the derivation of financial benefit to the author; however, it goes further by addressing public interest considerations.

When contemplating the basis of Australian legislation and provisions, such as the approval of parallel importing in the 2006 amendments, the approach appears to favour the doctrine of 'serving the greater good' and economic considerations, rather than concerning itself unduly with the protection of the creator's interests. Having said that, the *Copyright Act* has, to date, retained parallel importation restrictions on books, effectively protecting Australian publishers and authors against unauthorised imports (1968, s. 29(5)).

An analogy by Hansen visualises two disparate and irreconcilable viewpoints of copyright, namely: 'a secular priesthood of copyright lawyers all firmly believing that creators are entitled to copyright in their works; second, the "agnostics and atheists" imbued with a culture of the public domain' (1996, p. 579). This viewpoint emphasises the conflict between the 'moral rights' and 'public benefit' or social interest theories, discussed in the next chapter. Whilst Australian copyright law has incorporated 'moral rights' in the 2000 *Copyright Amendment (Moral Rights) Act*, the *Copyright Amendment Act 2006* has placed the emphasis on economic considerations, thereby continuing to provide for divergent interests and needs.

Moral rights were only formally recognised in Australian legislation in 2000, when the *Copyright Act 1968* was amended to incorporate provisions relating to the moral rights of authors. The *Copyright Amendment (Moral Rights) Act 2000* purported to introduce a system to protect authors' moral rights, but a discussion of these moral rights will, inevitably, involve a consideration of economic issues. The theory of moral rights (or personality rights) is discussed in chapter 3 and specifically addressed in the research and examined in Chapter 8.

Moral rights provisions protect the creator rather than the copyright holder. However, as pointed out by Elizabeth Adeney, the Australian system may be regarded as: 'a hybrid system with authorial moral rights grafted onto a framework that has developed to protect the economic interests, not of the author, but the copyright owner' (2002, p. 10). Whether this perception is an accurate reflection of the views of the author focus group involved in this research is examined further in Chapters 8 and 10.

The Parallel Import Debate

In Australia, and in particular since 2009, following the Productivity Commission study, *Copyright restrictions on the parallel importation of books* (2009), issues such as the parallel importing debate and concerns about digital rights protection have raised authors' awareness of the dilemma of territorial copyright, which relies on the enforcement of copyright law as a national prerogative. The digital sphere has made it increasingly difficult to cling to existing copyright models, and territorial copyright protection is in a state of flux, as is evidenced by the inevitable encroachment of online booksellers such as Amazon on these rights, by selling books across international borders.

Current parallel importation provisions allow a restriction on importation of printed copyright material into Australia, which provide Australian publishers with a 30-day window to distribute a local version of a book (and 90 days to resupply) before competing overseas publishers may distribute the same product in Australia (*Copyright Act 1968*, ss. 102 and 112A). However, section 44F of the *Copyright Act* provides that there are no restrictions on importation of electronic literary works, except that it must be a 'non-infringing copy' (i.e. made lawfully in the country of origin), thus significantly affording no parallel import protection on digital books.

The parallel import provisions were under review between 2006 and 2009, with lobbyists advocating the removal of such restrictive provisions in the legislation. The Australian Productivity Commission conducted an investigation into the nature, role and importance of intangibles, including intellectual property, to Australia's economic performance, as well as the effect of copyright restrictions on the parallel importation of books. Submissions were put forward during 2008 by well known authors such as Frank Moorhouse, Nick Earls and Kate Grenville, forming part of the 268 submissions to the Productivity Commission on the issue of parallel importing in 2008 (Productivity Commission, 2009).

In their submissions, many authors provided examples of how they felt the current parallel import restrictions (PIRs) had benefited them, or how the potential removal of the restrictions might affect them. Nick Earls commented as follows:

I can foresee no circumstance in which a sale of a parallel-imported edition of a book of mine would earn me the same as a sale of a local edition. Allowing parallel imports will undermine author's incomes ... Parallel imported copies undercutting the local edition could destroy the local market for that edition and send the book out of print ... Both the author and the publishing company would suffer. This risk would be a serious disincentive towards Australian publishers publishing new Australian books, and unearthing new talent (2008, pp. 8–9).

Another author stated:

I believe that the risk is that projected changes will lead to our publishing industry producing primarily books for the local market; as few authors would be able to make a living in this way, an author's choice would be to aim at having an overseas publisher as one's primary publisher (Orr, 2008, p. 1).

Author Garth Nix pointed out the advantages of territorial copyright and said:

... territorial copyright provides publishers with certainty to allow them to invest in Australian authors and Australian books. Without that certainty, the business case to invest in and publish Australian books is far weaker and consequently the opportunities for Australian authors to begin here would be fewer (2008, p. 7).

In addition, Thomas Keneally foresaw the gradual demise of the Australian publishing industry, cautioning:

...I fear it will be without the resources of marketing, distribution and visibility which the existing Australian publishing industry is able to provide to a wide range of such books under the guarantee of Australian copyright based on PIR. Both authors and literary agents, particularly those whose interest is explicitly Australian, would be facing shrinking resources and contracts (2008, pp. 4-5).

Many authors also felt that, in the absence of PIRs, they would lose control over the sales of their books. Once the rights to books were sold overseas, authors would no longer be able to control which edition of the book was sold in Australia, potentially impacting on their returns. Furthermore, some new or undiscovered authors could find it more difficult to gain attention in an open market (Earls, 2008).

Despite the large volume of submissions by authors, publishers and booksellers against the proposed abolition of the PIR, the Productivity Commission recommended that the Government repeal Australia's PIRs for books, such repeal to take effect three years after the date of announcement. Furthermore, they proposed that the Government should review and revise the current subsidies aimed at encouraging Australian writing and publishing, with a view to improve the application, and thereafter to monitor the outcome from these measures five years after implementation (Productivity Commission, 2009, p. xxv).

The final result of the investigation was that the Government, under pressure from the publishing industry, rejected the recommendations by the Productivity Commission to phase out parallel import control and retained the *status quo*. Whilst the brief euphoria in the midst of Australian publishers and authors was well founded, it has become evident that these protective provisions in section 102 of the *Copyright Act* would not protect authors and publishers from the evolution taking place in the digital sphere, as discussed in further chapters.

GLOBAL CHALLENGES

Due to digital advances, many aspects of copyright law are in a state of flux. For example, the issue of what constitutes 'fair use' in Australian copyright is no longer an issue confined to Australian courts. As a result of the Google initiatives (discussed in Chapter 6), and in response to the contemporaneous involvement of American research libraries in the unauthorised book scanning projects by Google as well as the HathiTrust (a partnership of 50 American research libraries), a number of Australian authors together with the Australian Society of Authors have joined a lawsuit against HathiTrust and five of the American universities involved in these book scanning projects (Reid, 2011).

The lawsuit, filed in September 2011 in the Southern District Court of New York, is based on the unlawful digital scanning and copying of books under copyright in violation of the rights of copyright holders. It describes the unlawful scanning and digitising of library databases as 'one of the largest copyright infringements in history' and seeks an injunction against the defendants as well as an order impounding all unauthorised digital copies under their control (*Authors Guild, Inc. et al. v. HathiTrust et al* (2011), pp. 4, 22-23) . One issue addressed in the complaint is the copying and distribution of 'orphan works' by the HathiTrust, of which the authors are erroneously claimed to be unknown.

Angelo Loukakis, one of the plaintiffs and executive director of the Australian Society of Authors, specifically claims that his copyright has been infringed by the unlawful reproduction, digitising and distribution of his book *Vernacular Dreams* by Michigan University, one of the defendants (*Authors Guild, Inc. et al. v. HathiTrust et al* (2011), p. 7). The case is ongoing and it remains to be seen what the outcome will be. Although the HathiTrust has since suspended its 'orphan works' programme, acknowledging that it was flawed (University of Michigan, 2011), the other issues remain unresolved, providing a stark reflection of the impact of digitisation on the rights of Australian copyright holders.

Additionally, the realities of applying the 'first sale doctrine' to books imported from another country and then sold in the country of origin, as was the case in *Kirtsaeng,* puts paid to the idea that territorial rights will necessarily protect US rights holders from the impact of cross-border sales.

In the recent US case of *Kirtsaeng v. John Wiley & Sons* (2013), Kirtsaeng, a Cornell University student, purchased mathematics text books from his home country Thailand (with the assistance of friends) and then resold them on eBay to students in the US. The texts were English foreign editions and only authorised for sale in Europe, Asia, Africa and the Middle East. The issue to be decided was how s 602 (which prohibits the importation of works into the US without the copyright owner's permission) and s 109 (dealing with the first sale doctrine) of the *Copyright Act* applied to copies of books made and legally acquired abroad, and then imported into the US. The Supreme Court held by a 6-3 majority that US copyright owners may not prevent importation and reselling of copyrighted content lawfully sold abroad, due to the application of the 'first sale doctrine' (2013, p. 2). The effect of the first sale doctrine (also referred to as an 'exhaustion of rights'), is that the publisher's copyright is exhausted once a book is lawfully purchased. The majority opinion in this case stated from the outset that the first sale doctrine applied to lawfully made copyright works, even when made in a foreign country (2013, p. 2).

It is significant that the Court read the Act as imposing no geographical limitation. This approach was in contrast to the Lower Court decision in the case *John Wiley & Sons, Inc. v Kirtsaeng* (2011). In the earlier decision the Court had found in favour of Wiley, who relied on s 602 of the Act and argued that Kirtsaeng could not rely on the first sale doctrine (s 109) as it only applied to works manufactured in the US. The 6-3 division in the Supreme Court decision is reflective of the controversy surrounding the interpretation and application of these two provisions in the Act. Previously, in the *Costco Wholesale* case (2010) the Court was divided 4-4 on this issue, and in the earlier decision *Quality King* (1998) the Court held that s 109 limited the scope of s 602, leaving open the question whether US copyright owners could retain control over the importation of copies manufactured and sold abroad (p. 135).

In her dissenting judgment in *Kirtsaeng* Justice Ginsburg criticised the reasoning of the majority, stating that the majority's interpretation of the *Copyright Act* was 'at odds with Congress' aim to protect copyright owners against the unauthorized importation of low-priced, foreign made copies of their copyrighted works (2013, p.10).' She also expressed the viewpoint that 'the Court embrace(d) an international-exhaustion rule that could benefit US consumers but would likely disadvantage foreign holders of US copyrights (2013, p. 28).'

The Supreme Court in *Kirtsaeng* thus resolved the case in favour of permitting parallel importation by relying on the first sale doctrine. Despite the argument that this interpretation favours consumers by providing them with cheaper options, the flipside is that rights holders in written work could be disadvantaged by the erosion of their territorial rights. Principally, this decision illustrates how easily territorial copyright provisions may be circumvented, and the potential far-reaching impact on authors and publishers globally in the future.

CONCLUSION

This chapter provided an overview of the development of copyright and copyright legislation, as well as reference to some current challenges in the field of copyright law facing Australian authors. It is evident that copyright law has been evolving to adapt to new technologies and that electronic publishing may require further changes. The UK has recognised the need for transformation pursuant to the Hargreaves Report (2011), and submissions by the Australian Copyright Council Expert Group (Brennan, De Zwart, Fraser, Lindsay, &

Ricketson, 2011) have subsequently addressed some of the issues covered by the Hargreaves Report. However, a review of the Australian copyright system is imminent in 2012. The *Authors Guild* case (2011) is illustrative of the transitional challenges faced by Australian authors in protecting their copyright in the digital domain. However, the proactive involvement of the Australian Society of Authors in this US case is a positive step for Australian authors in the ongoing protection of their digital copyright.

REFERENCES

Adeney, E. (2002). Moral rights and substantiality. *Australian Intellectual Property Journal, 13*, 5.

Armstrong, E. (1990). *Before copyright – The French book-privilege system 1498-1526.* Cambridge, UK: Cambridge University Press.

Australian Copyright Council. (2011, May 23). *Digital opportunity – The Hargreaves report.* Retrieved May 24, 2011, from http://www.copyright.org.au/news-and-policy/details/id/1958/

Boymal, J., & Davidson, S. (2004). Extending copyright duration in Australia. *Agenda (Durban, South Africa), 11*(3), 23–246.

Brennan, D., De Zwart, M., Fraser, M., Lindsay, D., & Ricketson, S. (2011). *Directions in copyright reform in Australia (Report).* Canberra, Australia: Copyright Council Expert Group.

Caslon Analytics Intellectual Property. (2003, June). *Caslon analytics.* Retrieved July 12, 2008 and October 9, 2010, from www.caslon.com.au/ipguide3.htm

Earls, N. (2008). *Submission to the productivity commission.*

Ergas, H. (2000). *Review of intellectual property legislation under the competition principles agreement (Final Report).* Canberra, Australia: Intellectual Property and Competition Review Committee.

Franki, R. (1976). *Report of the copyright law committee on reprographic reproduction (Research Report).* Canberra, Australia: Government of Australia.

Goldstein, P. (2001). *International copyright: Principles, law and practice.* Oxford, UK: Oxford University Press.

Hansen, H. (1996). International copyright: An unorthodox analysis. *Vanderbilt Journal of Transnational Law, 29*, 579.

Hargreaves, I. (2011). *Digital opportunity: A review of intellectual property and growth (Research Report).* London: Government of UK.

Keneally, T. (2008). *Submission to the productivity commission.*

Milton, J. (1644). *Areopagitica: A speech of Mr. John Milton for the Liberty of Unlicenc'd Printing, to the Parliament of England.* London, UK: Government of UK.

Nix, G. (2008). *Submission to the productivity commission.*

Orr, W. (2008). *Submission to the productivity commission.*

Productivity Commission. (2009). *Restrictions on the parallel importation of books* (Research Report). Retrieved February 19, 2011, from http://www.pc.gov.au/projects/study/books/submissions

Reid, M. A. (2011). Authors create a new sub-plot in the quest to digitise the world's books. *Australian Copyright Council.* Retrieved from http://copyright.org.au

Ricketson, S. (1987). *The Berne convention for the protection of literary and artistic works: 1886.* London: Kluwer.

Rose, M. (1988). The author as proprietor: Donaldson v Becket and the genealogy of modern authorship. *Representations (Berkeley, Calif.), 0*(23), 51–58. doi:10.2307/2928566

Rose, M. (1993). *Authors and owners.* Cambridge, MA: Harvard University Press.

Saunders, D. (1992). *Authorship and copyright.* London: Routledge.

Simpson, S. (1995). *Review of Australian collection societies report.* Canberra, Australia: Governemtn of Australia.

Spicer, J. (1959). *Report of the copyright law review committee (Research Report).* Canberra, Australia: Government of Australia.

Thomas, D. (1968). *Copyright and the creative artist.* London: Institute of Economic Affairs.

University of Michigan. (2011, September 16). *U-M library statement on the orphan works project.* Retrieved October 23, 2011, from http://www.lib.umich.edu/news/u-m-library-statement-orphan-works-project

TABLE OF CASES

Australasian performing Rights Association Ltd v. Commonwealth Bank of Australia (1992) 25 IPR 157 (Austl.)

Computer Associations International, Inc. v. Altai, Inc. 1241, 23 IPR 385 (2d Cir 1992) (US)

Coogi Australia Pty Ltd v. Hysport International Pty Ltd & Others (1998) 157 FCA 1059 (Austl.)

Copyright Agency Ltd v. Queensland Department of Education & Others (2002) 54 IPR 19 (Austl.)

Fox Film Corp v. Doyal (1932) 286 US 123, 127 (US)

Hamm v. Middleton (1999) 44 IPR 656 (Austl.)

Kirtsaeng v. John Wiley & Sons 568 U.S. WL 1104736 (U.S. Mar. 19, 2013)

Pacific Film Laboratories Pty Ltd v. FCT (1976) 121 CLR 154 at 167 (Austl.)

Sony Corporation of America v. Universal City Studios Inc. (1984) 2 IPR 225 (US)

The Authors Guild, Inc. et al. v. HathiTrust et al, US District Court, Southern District of New York, filed 12 September 2011, 11 CIV 6351 (US)

University of NSW v. Moorhouse (1975) HCA 26; (1975) 133 CLR 1 (Austl.)

TABLE OF STATUTES

British Copyright Act 1911 (UK)Commonwealth of Australia Constitution Act 1900 (Cth)

Copyright Act 1790 (US)

Copyright Act 1905 (Cth)

Copyright Act 1956 (Cth)

Copyright Act 1968 (Cth)

Copyright Amendment (Digital Agenda) Act 2000 (Cth)

Copyright Amendment (Moral Rights) Act 2000 (Cth)

Copyright Amendment Act 2006 (Cth)

Competition Principles Agreement 1995 (Cth)

Copyright Tribunal (Procedure) Regulations 1969

Digital Millennium Copyright Act 1998 (US)

Family Entertainment and Copyright Act 2005 (US)

International Copyright Act 1838 (UK)

Licensing Act 1662 (UK)

Patents Act 1952 (Cth)

Patents Act 1990 (Cth)

Patents Amendment Act 1979 (Cth)

Public Lending Rights Act 1985 (Cth)

Sonny Bono Copyright Term Extension Act 1998 (US)

Statute of Anne 1709 (UK)

Trade Marks Act 1903 (Cth)

Trade Marks Act 1955 (Cth)

Trade Marks Act 1995 (Cth)

Chapter 3
Theoretical and Philosophical Foundations

ABSTRACT

This chapter deals with the theoretical foundation of copyright law and considers the various philosophical theories in this regard. The link between copyright law and the philosophical ideals that underpin its theory and interpretation is noted and considered within the ambits of the public sphere as proposed by Habermas (1974, p. 49). The discussion also includes an explanation of the public domain and focuses on the following theories in particular: the utilitarian approach, the public benefit theory, the natural rights theory, and the moral rights theory. The chapter concludes by comparing the theories and noting their alignment and differences.

INTRODUCTION

In this chapter, the philosophical theories relating to copyright are discussed with reference to the public sphere and, more particularly, the literary public sphere within which authors as creators find themselves. A discussion of these issues is important in laying the foundation for the research questions in relation to the value of copyright to authors, how they are affected by the implementation of copyright laws and structures and the extent to which their perceptions of copyright are influenced by changing technology.

Whilst there has been some debate regarding the accepted underlying philosophical concepts justifying copyright law, Australia has followed a largely utilitarian approach, as is evident from current legislation and the reasons set

DOI: 10.4018/978-1-4666-5214-9.ch003

out in the Ergas Committee Report (2000, p. 34) (ECR). As discussed in the previous chapter, the ECR recognised that the general objective of the intellectual property law system in Australia was utilitarian and, more specifically, economic rather than moral in character (Ergas, 2000, p. 33). However, as copyright law represents something different to its varying member groups (i.e. authors, publishers and users), it is necessary to go beyond this theory and consider a range of philosophical concepts and frameworks, which might be seen to underpin copyright.

Saunders expressed the view that:

Historical diversities and internal discontinuities make the legal sphere a good obstacle to any global theory concerning authorship. They also suggest why, given its purposeful character, legal personality is not and does not need to be all of a piece. As an attribute of legal personality, ownership of a copyright is inseparable from a particular purpose or purposes; in this respect, as a personifying or person-forming mechanism, the law of copyright is not bound by the philosophical ideal of an absolute or unified right. Yet, as we shall see, in less positive accounts of authorship it is in the name of just such an ideal that copyright is charged with the narrowness of its concerns and the piecemeal nature of its rights, remedies and objects of protection that have come to be bundled under its provisions (1992, pp. 19-20).

Thus, although critical of the historical philosophical approach in interpreting authorship, Saunders implicitly recognises the inextricable link between copyright law and the philosophical ideals that underpin its theory and interpretation.

Goldstein distinguishes between copyright and 'author's right' as two separate legal traditions for protecting literary and artistic works and states:

Copyright's philosophical premise is utilitarian: the purpose of copyright is to stimulate production of the widest possible variety of creative goods at the lowest possible price. By contrast, author's right is rooted in the philosophy of natural rights: an author is entitled to protection of his work as a matter of right and justice (2001, p. 3).

He regards these two traditions as 'far more alike than they are unlike' and cites the Berne Convention as a bridging factor and reason for the merging of the two philosophies by recognising authors' moral rights (Article 6*bis*) and also providing for allowable uses of authors' work (Articles 8-14) (Goldstein, 2001, p. 4).

Australian author Frank Moorhouse describes the range of philosophical positions in the following interview:

...the first position being the Socialist or Totalitarian model – that copyright is based on the premise that the State has educated you and cultivated your talents and so what you do with those talents should belong to the State; the second being the Capitalist model – that copyright is simply a tradeable commodity; the third being the European position – that copyright is not only a tradeable commodity but it is an extension of the personality of the creator; and the fourth being the British model – that copyright is partly a commodity with a commercial nature but that it also has a social dimension to it, so that after a term of 50 years it should go into the public domain where the public can use it in many ways and not have to pay for its use (Sexton, 2007, p. 6).

From a philosophical perspective, Moorhouse favours the British model (partly commercial and partly social) with the incorporation of a moral rights dimension (Sexton, 2007, p. 6). Although current Australian law reflects vestiges of this interpretation, the legislative model is largely utilitarian. This perception has given rise to concerns by authors, especially in relation to issues such as parallel importing and the Google initiatives, which have the scope of affecting authors and publishers globally.

Some authors, such as William Fisher, cite four popular approaches, namely the utilitarian approach, the natural right (or Lockean) theory, the personality theory and the 'social planning (for the public good) theory' (2000, p. 1). Others such as Stokes divide the philosophical theories into three categories: the economic/utilitarian theory, public policy arguments and moral rights. Stokes distinguishes two major moral rights, namely 'natural rights' and 'personality rights.' He further proposes that the granting of exclusive rights to the author is an incentive for the author to create, but it is also an incentive to publishers who will benefit from the copyright protection given to the author (Stokes, 2001, pp. 10-11).

Although the labels and divisions vary, most authors recognise four concepts that form the basis of copyright justification: economic/utilitarian considerations, public benefit policies, natural rights attaching to the labour/ work and moral rights attaching to the creator/personality.

In addition to a discussion of these theories, it is important to consider the social and political culture within which they developed. In this regard, literature dealing with the concept of the 'public sphere,' and more specifically the 'literary public sphere,' is of relevance, not only to provide a milieu for the emergence of copyright issues, but also to recognise the position of authors as a sub-group within that sphere. Vaidhayanathan remarks on the connection between copyright and the public sphere as follows:

The eighteenth-century public sphere was essential to the establishment of copyright law, and copyright's subsequent transformations coincide with the general structural transformation of the public sphere (2001, p. 6).

These comments are expanded in the discussion below, which indicates the intersection of the different groups affected by copyright within the public sphere.

THE PUBLIC SPHERE

As literature and the publishing industry have historically been influenced by the socio-political and legal frameworks within which they flourish, the concept of the public sphere, which is central to theories of Jurgen Habermas (1974, 1989), focuses on the connective area between civil society and the state and postulates the emergence of a 'public sphere,' which is shaped by sociology, politics, economics and law. As such, it provides a worthwhile backdrop to any discussion of the emergence of modern copyright law. It has been suggested that such a sphere is capable of different incarnations depending on the population of the sphere (Fraser, 1992, p. 131), and it is postulated here that authors operate in one such sphere within the realms of the wider public sphere.

Apart from the influence of the public sphere on copyright issues, it is therefore important to consider the author as a member of the 'literary sphere' but also in an even more defined context as a member of the subaltern sphere of 'authors,' one of the 'private spheres' referred to by Fraser as 'competing counterpublics' (1992, p. 131). This contextualisation is central to a discussion of how authors function as a group in relation to other groups such as publishers. It also allows for an examination of the strengths and weaknesses of such a group and how they are affected by copyright, in particular in relation to digital copyright challenges. An illustration of the inter-relationship between the 'author sphere' and 'publisher sphere' within the 'literary public sphere,' as perceived in this book, is depicted below as *Figure 1*.

Within the public realm, the concept of the 'literary public sphere' has historically been regarded as 'exceedingly fruitful for sociological investigations of literature and criticism' (Hohendahl, 1974, p. 48). It allows the investigation of literary and related developments such as copyright, within

Figure 1.

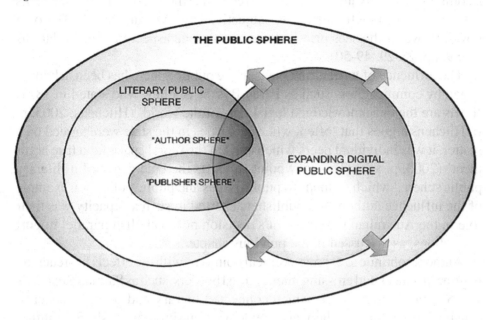

the social framework of a collective public opinion. Fraser refers to Habermas's conception of the public sphere as 'a theatre in modern societies in which political participation is enacted through the medium of talk' and 'the space in which citizens deliberate about their common affairs, hence an institutionalised arena of discursive interaction' (Fraser, 1992, p. 110).

In this way, the public sphere has been credited with the development of a new literary and political consciousness which reflects the public view on issues ranging from common political activity to public welfare concerns. McCarthy, in the introduction to Habermas's *The Structural Transformation of the Public Sphere: An Inquiry into a Category of Bourgeois Society* (1989, p. xi), describes Habermas's work as a 'historical-sociological account of the emergence, transformation and disintegration of the bourgeois public sphere.'

Habermas situates the emergence of this concept in the 18th century, stating: 'It was at that time that the distinction of "opinion" from "opinion publique" and "public opinion" came about' (1974, p. 50). He points out that literary and political opinions were debated in the coffee houses of the 17th and 18th centuries, which were regarded as centres of literary and political criticism (Habermas, 1989, pp. 30, 32). He further describes the literary sphere as a means of fostering a process of 'self-clarification' which enables a community of private individuals to recognise themselves as a public. This sphere includes practices such as subjective letter writing and the fictional novel. However, he sees print culture as only one aspect of social relations (1989, pp. 28-29, 49-50).

The influence of writers and poets in the public sphere has been acknowledged by commentators such as Percy Bysshe Shelley, who stated in 1821: 'Poets are the unacknowledged legislators of the world' (Hitchens, 2003, p. i). Hitchens argues that 'often, when all parties in the state were agreed on a matter, it was individual peers which created the moral space for a true argument' (2003, p. xiii). This viewpoint supports the emergence of a 'literary public sphere,' which influenced public issues and public policy. An example of the influence authors and publishers exerted in such a capacity was their role in the Australian Government's decision not to abolish parallel import restrictions, as discussed in the previous chapter.

Authors continue to express political opinions, with the effects far-reaching in some instances and crossing international borders, such as Salman Rushdie's *The Satanic Verses* (1989) which connected literary and political spheres, causing international acclaim and condemnation simultaneously. Schmittner comments that:

In the case of Rushdie...we see a new phenomenon, which only became possible with the end of the nineteenth century: the rapid production of a worldwide literary public sphere – which does not primarily consist of readers, but rather an audience which ignites itself on a book which it has not read and which it does not need to read... The western reader need not read The Satanic Verses in order to condemn the Fatwa, and the Muslim in Pakistan is not allowed and is possibly even unable to read this book... in order to demonstrate against the book and to threaten the author with death (1995, p. 155).

In this context, writers as a group historically played an important role in the development of copyright laws. It is the aim of this research to investigate the current position of authors as a distinct group in the evolving public sphere, particularly with regard to their views on copyright and the publishing industry and the effect of public interest pressures and government's economic measures on their creative copyright interests.

Habermas's theory has been criticised for its limited application by Fraser, who states that the bourgeois conception of the public sphere is not adequate for contemporary critical theory (Fraser 1992, p. 136). She criticises his analysis of the public sphere as failing to examine other competing public spheres and questions the assumption made by Habermas that a single public sphere is preferable to multiple spheres (1992, p. 115).

Fraser proposes a plurality of competing publics rather than a single public sphere and regards the emergence of 'private spheres' as often fixing the boundaries of the public sphere to the disadvantage of subordinate groups in the social structure. She further points out that the bourgeois public sphere was not the only public sphere in existence in the 18th century and proposes that there were many competing 'subaltern counterpublics,' including nationalist publics, popular peasant publics, elite women's publics and working-class publics' (1992, p. 131).

Social historians such as Geoff Eley support Fraser's criticism of Habermas's definition of the public sphere and recognise that the public sphere was always characterised by conflict. Eley states that 'the emergence of a bourgeois public was never defined solely by the struggle against absolutism and traditional authority, but necessarily addressed the problem of popular containment as well' (1994, p. 309). It follows that conflict will continue to arise not only between competing publics but also between popular publics and the state authorities. Two issues of interest emerge from these writings: first, the issue of private rights (such as 'moral rights') of authors as opposed to public rights and second, the concept of a subaltern sphere of creators, populated by authors.

This concept of separate public and private spheres or realms is also recognised by Hannah Arendt, a German-Jewish philosopher, in *The Human Condition* (1958). However, she treats human beings as members of the same natural species, to whom life on earth is given under certain conditions, namely those of political involvement, plurality, labour, work and action (Villa, 2000, p. 80). In her writing, she rethinks the hierarchy of modes of activity that originally characterised the active lives of human beings (Villa, 2000, p. 123). Her political philosophy envisages a 'recovery of the public realm' and sees the public sphere as being 'devoured' by 'household' concerns. She cites 'coercion-free communication' as a requirement for an effective public sphere (Villa, 1992, p. 712, 713). Habermas's endorsement of this premise is evident in his own conception of an 'ideal speech situation' (1984, p. 315).

Electronic media have transformed the public sphere by changing the models of public discourse. Carpignano, Anderson, Aronowitz, and DiFazio have regarded the mass media as the new public sphere, stating that public life has been transformed by a massive process of commodification of culture and of political culture (1993, p. 103). In a discussion of Habermas's discursive public sphere model, Gerhards and Schafer support the idea that the mass media constitute a third forum in the public sphere (along with the 'encounter public sphere' and 'public events') and recognise the significant impact of the mass media and, specifically, the Internet on society. After comparing the 'old' and 'new media' in the US and Germany and posing the question: *'Is the Internet a better public sphere?'* they conclude that Internet communication does not differ significantly from debates in the print media (2009, pp. 2-3).

The media and, more recently, the Internet have thus inevitably expanded the ambits of the public sphere within which the author creates, influenced by global perspectives instead of the limited public arenas of the 18th and 19th and most of the 20th century. The author has to navigate the changing landscape of technological change, an evolving public sphere in which the author's role (and even the concept of authorship) is not clearly defined. Not only have the online media created a revolution in journalism and literary expression, but they have also founded a new forum for political and social discourse on matters of public interest (Ward, 2006). Inevitably, authors' copyright has been affected by these technological advances, as discussed later in Chapter 6.

In the 21st century, the author has entered a decentralised literary public sphere where copyright issues, amongst other issues, have undergone a trans-formation. Copyright enforcement has become more onerous, with authors struggling to hold on to their ostensible moral rights in the face of political and economic motivations. It may be observed that the shifting of public debate from a national to a global forum has made the enforcement of per-sonal rights by creators more difficult due to a number of factors such as, for example, anti-copyright actions by Google and the difficulties associated with copyright enforcement on the Internet, as will be discussed in later chapters.

Furthermore, the sub-group or counter-public of which the author is a member has to compete not only with other groups, such as publishers, but also with the wider public sphere itself, within which it exists, as is evident from the previously mentioned parallel import debate. This dilemma raises questions about the balance of power between authors and other groups, such as publishers, which this research seeks to address.

Such an investigation is underpinned by the philosophical concepts of utilitarianism, natural rights, moral rights and public benefit, within which the concept of copyright developed. An examination of these theories follows after a brief discussion of the concept of the 'public domain.'

THE PUBLIC DOMAIN

Whereas the public sphere has its origins in philosophical discourse and reflects public opinion on politics, law, literature and socio-economics, the public domain is described by Habermas as a concept which is largely defined by legislation, denoting intellectual property which is not owned or controlled by anyone (1974, p. 49). While the public domain is accepted as a legislative environment rather than a philosophical one, it is still important to define it in the context of this research.

The *Butterworths Legal Dictionary* defines the 'public domain' as follows: 'In copyright law, the status of material which is not protected by copyright' (2003, p. 355). Rose states that the public domain has existed as long as copyright itself (2003, p. 75), a view which is endorsed by Johnson (2008, p. 587). He states further:

There is now, however, an expansive view of what constitutes the public domain. It is now said to include uses of works which do not require the author's permission (eg fair dealing with, or fair use of, a work) (Johnson, 2008, p. 588).

Lange sees the term 'public domain' as elastic and inexact and suggests that the public domain is perhaps most usefully seen as a commons, set off against the fences that delimit the interests of individual rights holders (2003, p. 463). This concept of 'enclosure' is expanded by Boyle in an essay entitled 'Fencing off ideas: Enclosure and the disappearance of the public domain' (2002, p. 13).

The creation of the modern day public domain is discussed in the parallel context of the English enclosure movement, which started in the 15th century. Boyle argues that, whilst intellectual property provisions were created in order to stimulate creativity and productivity, there are inherent dangers in delimiting property rights too severely. 'A large, leaky market may actually produce more revenue than a small, tightly controlled market,' he states in defence of this proposition (Boyle, 2002, p. 17).

It is evident that, however the public domain is perceived, it is today largely defined by intellectual property legislation, based on the common law and historic copyright developments. The public domain is of relevance in this research insofar as it relates to authors' copyright and the effects of copyright continuing after the author's death, which can have far-reaching effects. Examples of such instances are noted during the in-depth interviews discussed in Chapter 8. Moreover, the public domain is important as it provides a concrete foundation for discussion of the various philosophical approaches to copyright.

UTILITARIAN APPROACH

First proposed by Jeremy Bentham in 1776 as 'the greatest good to the greatest number of people' as a guiding principle of conduct, utilitarianism has since been promoted and applied as a legislative principle. Today it is regarded as the most widely accepted and recognised justification for copyright. This principle has been applied in Australian copyright law over the last century, along with considerable influence from early UK models since 1901. As noted in the previous chapter, the Ergas Committee Report of 2000 specifically recognised that the general objective of the system of intellectual property law in Australia was utilitarian and, more specifically, economic rather than moral in character (2000, p. 33).

The legislature, through this approach, has striven towards balancing the rights of creators with public benefit, i.e. the use and enjoyment of their creations (*Competition Principles Agreement 1995*, Clause 5(1)). This view militates against situations where too much emphasis is placed on either side of the scale, creating a risk of loss of the creative incentive to the author or, conversely, a risk of too much copyright control, which may stifle economic utility. Whether such a balance, from authors' perspectives, is in fact achieved in current Australian copyright legislation and structures is investigated as a key part of this research.

Proponents of the utilitarian theory, such as Landes and Posner, suggest that creators should be given the exclusive right, for a limited period of time, to make copies of their creations. This would enable them to recoup their 'costs of expression,' whilst consumers would have access to the products at a cost which takes into account the reward to the creators (Landes & Posner, 1989, p. 325). This approach would thus provide an economic incentive to creators and prevent them being undercut by copyists.

In their earlier work, Landes and Posner explored the dual perspective of copyright: the positive benefit to the owner as a result of the property right and the incentive purpose of the right which causes the author to create (1987, p. 265). Although expressed as a utilitarian viewpoint, this approach showed strong elements of the natural right approach followed by John Locke. In *The*

Economic Structure of Intellectual Property Law, Landes and Posner concede, however, in discussing the economics of property rights in intellectual property, that 'it is unclear to what extent an intellectual property right can realistically be considered the exclusive fruit of its owner's labour' (2003, p. 4).

The utilitarian approach has historically been favoured in the United States, causing legislation to be been interpreted in favour of public benefit considerations in United States case law. An example is the 1932 case of *Fox Film Corp v. Doyal* where copyright was regarded as a 'limited grant,' with reward to the author a secondary consideration. In his judgment, Hughes CJ held as follows: '*...the primary object in conferring the monopoly lie(s) in the general benefit derived by the public from the labors of authors*' (at 123).

This case has since been followed in a number of decisions in the United States such as *Eldred and Others v. Ashcroft* (2003), where the Supreme Court referred to the legislative approach to copyright in the USA as follows:

Under the US Constitution, the primary objective of copyright law is not the reward of the author, but rather to secure for the public the benefits derived from authors' labours. By giving authors an incentive to create, the public benefits in two ways: when the original expression is created and...when the limited term...expires and the creation is added to the public domain (at 608).

This judgment was based on the extended copyright term to seventy years after the creator's death, introduced by the United States Congress in 1998. The same extended copyright term was adopted in the European Union (EU) in 2006 through Directive 2006/116/EC (2006, p. 13). As a result of this approach, many major works such as James Joyce's *Ulysses* have continued to cause copyright disputes after the death of the author through protective efforts by heirs. Stephen James Joyce, the grandson of James Joyce, has consistently opposed the use of any aspect of his grandfather's work, even, for example, the community 'ownership' of Bloomsbury and any public readings or productions of his work. Joyce's first unpublished writings will enter the public domain in 2012 (Max, 2006). The publicity afforded to this issue has illustrated the practical effect of copyright legislation being purposefully enforced to the disadvantage of academics, performing artists and society as a whole.

In the Australian context, the current system of copyright law, which provides for aspects such as 'moral rights' recognition, the same seventy year copyright term as applied in the United States and EU and the establishment of licensing bodies such as Copyright Agency Limited (CAL), appears to embody the Landes and Posner ideal. However, there has been meagre research on the viewpoints of non-academic authors on this issue. It is suggested that Landes and Posner represent an academic rather than 'grass roots' viewpoint and do not necessarily represent that of authors in general. This research focuses on the perceived value, ambits and limitations of copyright from such 'grass roots' authors' viewpoints.

NATURAL RIGHT THEORY

This approach originates from the writings of John Locke, who believed that property ownership was a natural right derived from labour. His famous statement reads:

Though the earth and all inferior creatures be common to all men, yet every man has a property in his own person; this nobody has any right to but himself. The labour of his body and the work of his hands we may say are properly his (Locke, 1689, ch. IX, par.123).

Supporters of this theory hold the belief that a creator has a natural right to the fruit of his or her labour or an exclusive right of property in one's own labour. It requires the common resources to be 'unowned' or 'held in common,' as opposed to those that have been utilised or transformed by the labourer. The Lockean argument relies on the theory that the resources derived from one's labour are owned by the labourer, provided 'there is enough and as good left in common for others' (Locke 1689, ch. V, par. 31).

In the United Kingdom during the 18th century, booksellers relied on the Lockean discourse of possessive individualism to emphasise the author's common law right to ownership of the fruits of their labour. According to this argument, the property was transferred to the bookseller when the copyright was purchased, and continued perpetually thereafter. This approach served the purposes of the booksellers rather than the authors. Their argument was subsequently challenged and defeated by the verdict in *Donaldson v. Beckett* (1774), when the argument of perpetuity was rejected and a time limit imposed on copyright.

However, some authors have questioned Locke's original rationale for his property rights theory and especially his argument that 'labour upon a resource held 'in common' should entitle the labourer to a property right in the resource itself' (Fisher, 2000, p. 10). As Rose aptly states: 'We are the heirs of the institution of literary property that emerged in the eighteenth century and of the problems and paradoxes that treating literary texts as private property involves' (1988, p. 76).

Whilst utilitarianism strives to marry the conflicting interests of public benefit and creators' protection, based on economic considerations, the natural rights theory can be viewed as somewhat idealistic in its application of proprietary rights to works created through the labour of the creator. There is difficulty with the interpretation of what can be regarded as 'a resource in common' and further problems with allowing the person who 'labours on the resource' a right in the property itself. Although an edited compilation of work may be cited as the obvious example of such a resource, in instances where a number of people are involved in a project, this theory creates scope for several persons to assert a right in such resource, and considerations such as the extent to which a person laboured on a resource, conflicting claims and the extent of transformation become relevant. The natural rights theory, despite its equitable character, remains problematic for these reasons and does not offer sound resolutions to the creator/public interest conflicts; nor does it properly address the intangible nature of creative effort, its focus being limited to the tangible end result, the written work itself.

Some theorists, such as Epstein, argue that the Lockean theory should be observed in more 'consequentialist terms' and that, once this is done, the gulf between tangible and intangible property rights will be much narrower (2004, p. 1). He suggests that the strength of the natural law theories rests on their implicit utilitarian (broadly conceived) foundations, which are evident from Locke's concern with the protection of the lives, liberties and property of individuals in general (1689, ch. V, par. 26). It follows then that if a utilitarian (and consequentialist) outcome is sought, it may be applied to suit the requirements of both tangible and intangible intellectual property rights, which would include the recognition of natural rights.

Theoretically, the concept proposes unlimited creative resources for all, on the basis that copyright does not diminish the available creative expression. Suzor argues that 'each appropriation is a limitation on the ability of future creators to work,' which devalues the substance of the 'no harm' argument in the realms of an ideal limitless creative environment (2006, p. 106).

This approach is in contrast with Macpherson's earlier observations in his book *The Political Theory of Possessive Individualism*, where he states: 'The individual is proprietor of his own person, for which he owes nothing to society' (1962, p. 269). He defines possessive individualism as the basic assumption 'that man is free and human by virtue of his sole proprietorship of his own person' and can alienate his work but not his person (Macpherson, 1962, p. 270).

Rose later comments: 'As long as society was and is organised around the principles of possessive individualism, the notion that the author has the same kind of property right in his work as any other labourer must and will recur' (1993, p. 45). This understanding is shared by Stokes, who sees natural rights as part of the 'moral rights' theory, based on the idea of a 'just reward' for labour (2001, p. 12). Although this approach recognises the intrinsic right of the creator, it does not go further in addressing the rights of middle or end users who may have invested financially in the product. In this sense, the natural rights theory has limitations, which are only addressed to a limited extent by Locke's 'no harm' provisions.

Although the Lockean approach does not feature prominently in the history of United States copyright law, it has been favoured in the United Kingdom and in Europe. It is justified on the basis that a creator's reputation is established by his/her entire body of work and that the right of integrity is important to preserve this reputation and, thus, the value of the work (Stokes, 2001, p. 66).

In Australia, there has been some measure of recognition of this theory, evidenced by the inclusion of a 'moral rights' provision in the legislation, which seeks to acknowledge the creator's right to derive a benefit from and have control over his creative work (*Copyright Amendment (Moral Rights) Act 2000*), incorporated in section 189 of the *Copyright Act 1968*. The concept of 'natural rights' may therefore be regarded as a close relation of the 'moral rights' theory discussed in the following section. In this context, the book investigates, as part of the research, how Australian authors perceive copyright affecting them and whether this perception has any impact on how they practise.

MORAL RIGHTS THEORY

Also described as the personality theory and derived from the writings of Kant and Hegel, this theory is premised upon the idea that private property rights are crucial to the satisfaction of some fundamental human needs. This viewpoint justifies copyright on the ground that it protects the piece of work created by the author or on the basis that it creates conditions conducive to 'creative intellectual activity,' which in turn meets the creator's needs (Fisher, 2000, p. 4).

Hegel, in his 1820 document, *Philosophy of Right,* identifies the requirements for an effective intellectual property system. These guidelines are summarised as follows by Hughes (1988, p. 330-350):

1. The fruits of highly creative intellectual activities, such as writing novels, deserve more legal protection than less creative activities, such as research.
2. A person's public image or 'persona' should be given extensive legal protection, even though it is not brought about through labour.
3. Authors should be allowed to sell or give away copies of their work in return for money or public respect and admiration, but should not be allowed to give away their right to prevent the destruction or misappropriation of their work. (In this respect Kant differed from Hegel in that he reasoned that an author's creative expression is part of his personality, and thus inalienable).

Hegel's proposition is in alignment with the idea of moral rights for creators and the moral rights provisions incorporated into the Australian law in 2000 by way of the *Copyright Amendment (Moral Rights) Act.*

Kant makes a distinction between the book as an object (a property right) and the contents of a book (the author's personal right) in a section titled 'Was ist ein Buch?' in his paper, *The metaphysical elements of justice* (1797, *Section 31*):

The book, on the one hand, is a material product (opus mecanicum) which can be imitated (by he who legitimately possesses a copy of it) and, consequently, there is a right in rem; on the other hand, the book is a discourse from publisher to public, and this no one can reproduce publicly, without first having from the author the authority to do so, such that it is a matter of personal right. The error consists in confusing these two rights (1907, p. 240).

The personal rights of the author are thus acknowledged by Kant as the right to grant permission for reproduction or copying of the book, a right which extends beyond the mere right of ownership of a book.

Whilst France was the first country to recognise 'moral rights,' both France and Germany claimed to balance moral rights and economic rights (Ricketson, 1987, p. 457). The difference was that in France 'moral rights' were seen as perpetual rights, whereas in Germany both moral and economic rights were limited (Cornish, 1999, p. 444). Saunders points out that 'the notion of property as the source of authorial right was to recede before the advance of the *droit moral*' (rights of personality) in France, causing the *droit moral* to be a distinctive feature of French law (1992, pp. 167-185).

This approach is a departure from the natural right theory in that it does not rely on labour as a necessary requirement, nor does it give extensive consideration to the 'public good' aspect of copyright justification. Instead, it focuses solely on the protection of the personality of the creator. The recognition of personality rights may pose a problem for the objective observer: How does one define the ambits of a 'moral right,' and how is it administered? In this regard, legislative provisions are necessary to enforce such rights, and the overlap between moral rights and intellectual property rights may become indistinguishable upon closer examination.

Of interest in this research is the author's perception of 'moral rights' in copyright, and whether, in the author's view, legislative provisions succeed in protecting his/her rights. According to Stokes, moral rights can be justified on economic and public policy grounds for the following reasons: consumer interest is served by establishing the authenticity of products and, further, the value of a product will be increased if it is shown to be original (2001, p. 65). Whilst particularly true in the field of art, this line of reasoning is applicable to all forms of creative endeavour, especially when viewed within the ambits of transformative capabilities.

Woodmansee points out that authors have lamented the lack of historical analysis of the relationship between legal-economic and creative discourse in the discussion of copyright (1984, pp. 425-448). It is evident, however, that in the modern utilitarian based approach, both of these aspects are present. Woodmansee regards the interplay of the two levels as the reason for the modern perception of authorship. Other authors regard the current system as 'dualist,' with notions of property on the one hand and personality on the other (Adeney, 2002, p. 9).

Although cases such as *Donaldson v. Beckett* (1774) played an important part in the recognition of the rights of authors, the issue of 'moral rights' was not given any consideration in the Court's decision. Arguments were based on the concepts of 'property' (and the nature of the property), 'author' (the 'creator') and the 'work' (a tangible thing) and hinged on the proprietary rights of authors, rather than personality or moral rights.

Inclusion of moral rights provisions in legislation, such as the amendments implemented by the *Copyright Amendment (Moral Rights) Act 2000*, shows a move towards legal recognition of author's personality rights. However, whilst the legislature attempts to formulate the ambits of moral rights, these rights remain firmly subject to the economic-utilitarian provisions of the amendments in the *Copyright Amendment Act 2006*. This research also investigates how authors perceive these inclusions.

PUBLIC BENEFIT THEORY

This approach favours the widest possible application of knowledge and culture in the interest of the public good. It has also been described as a 'social planning theory' (Fisher, 2000, p. 3), whereas Stokes refers to it as 'public policy arguments' (2001, p. 10). Early proponents of this doctrine include Jefferson and Marx who have as their ideal a just and desirable society, rather than the utilitarian aim of 'social welfare' (Fisher, 2000, p. 3).

Some authors regard copyright as a contributing factor to the creation of a democratic civil society. Netanel claims that copyright has a two-fold purpose in this context. First, it provides an incentive for creative expression of a variety of issues, including political and social issues, i.e. a productive function. Second, it has a structural function in that it supports a sector of creative activity, which (usually) does not rely on state subsidy and cultural hierarchy (Netanel, 1996, p. 283).

Theorists such as Netanel favour a shortened copyright term, extension of the 'public domain' for the purpose of creative manipulation and less power of control over derivative works by copyright owners, which would benefit the public interest (1996, p. 283). However, whether this viewpoint is shared by Australian authors is an issue which would benefit from further investigation and is illuminated by the views of authors in later chapters.

In Australia, the Courts have shown an underlying regard for public policy arguments in many of the cases dealing with copyright issues. This was evident in their treatment of satire in the 2001 case *TNC Channel Nine Pty Ltd & Others v. Network Ten Pty Ltd,* where Conti J found at first instance that Network Ten ('Ten') had not re-broadcast a substantial part of any of the 20 segments pleaded by Channel Nine ('Nine') in its television programme *The*

Panel. In relation to the first claim that Ten had made a cinematographic film, his Honour interpreted section 25(4) of the Act as incorporating a requirement of substantiality which had not been made out by Nine.

As the excerpts used comprised matters of public interest, their use for satirical purposes fell within the fair dealing defence. The Court distinguished between satire (allowable) and the use of parody or burlesque, which would not avoid copyright infringement (at 15). However, on appeal the Court found that Ten had contravened Nine's copyright in the source broadcasts by making a cinematographic film of them. The Court also found that the re-broadcast of extracts from nine programmes was an infringement of Nine's copyright under sections 87(c) and 101 of the Act. Ten's liability was subject to the availability of 'fair dealing defences,' which the Court found to apply in nine of the segments so that infringement was made out in relation to 11 of the segments.

This position has now been altered by the provisions of the *Copyright Amendment Act 2006* which determine that the fair dealing use of neither parody nor satire will constitute copyright infringement (Schedule 6). Sections 40-42 of the *Copyright Act* now provide for examples of fair dealing such as research or study, criticism or review, parody or satire and reporting news.

McCutcheon argues that the new provisions in the *Copyright Amendment Act 2006* dealing with parody and satire defences will enhance the copyright regime by striking a better balance between the interests of authors and parodists, but that a broader defence of 'transformative use' is warranted (2008, p. 163). This viewpoint has been expressed by other academics such as Suzor, who claims that the transformative use of existing expression is beneficial for society (2006, p. 2). These arguments support the proposal that copyright should be observed within the broader context of public benefit considerations and not solely as an advantage to the creator or originator.

The issue has become more pertinent with digitisation and the electronic media, raising the argument that copyright restrictions prevent the proper utilisation of creative expression for broader use in the interest of the public benefit. Transformative use such as parody and animation are lauded as creative re-expression, and it is suggested that transformative use of existing expression is beneficial for society (Suzor, 2006, pp. 2-3). Whilst the advantages of a public benefit approach are undeniable, there is some difficulty in formulating guidelines as to what constitutes 'the public good' or 'public benefit.' Fisher suggests various considerations, such as consumer welfare, access to information and ideas and a rich artistic tradition (2000, p. 16). Whilst some authors may agree with these considerations and value the transformative benefits gained by the limitation of copyright, others may disagree.

The challenge lies in reconciling these (sometimes) conflicting ideologies. An example is the legislative protection of the use of parody, which may be seen to promote symbolic democracy on the one hand, by facilitating creative expression, and eroding the personal interests of a copyright holder on the other hand.

It is suggested here that this dualistic approach to parody may be likened to the utilitarian 'left wing,' where authors' moral and natural rights occupy the right. The danger of placing undue emphasis on public interest considerations in limiting the scope of copyright (and maximising public benefit) is that those very limitations imposed to provide freedom of use by the public may be responsible for the demise of creative efforts, due to a lack of creative or financial incentive to the author.

Paradoxically, this result of an excessively robust public interest focus may be more likely to harm than benefit the public interest if creativity is stifled as a result, a consequence often ignored by proponents of a strong public benefit pursuit. The views of authors on publishing options such as the Creative Commons (discussed in Chapter 6) are an indication of the willingness to accommodate the public interest as opposed to the personal interests of authors.

However, contrary to the public interest perspective, in the recent case of *Larrikin Music Publishing Pty Ltd v. EMI Songs Australia Pty Limited* [2010] FCA 29, the Court applied the fair dealing principle strictly, in favour of the copyright holder. Larrikin Music succeeded in a case against EMI and the band Men at Work in the Federal Court, claiming that their use of two of the four bars of the 1934 children's song 'Kookaburra Sits in the Old Gum Tree' in their song 'Land Down Under' constituted an infringement of their copyright in the song. The judge held two of the four bars reproduced from the song amounted to a substantial part, thereby constituting breach of Larrikin Music's copyright, and ordered that EMI pay damages in respect of the breach. EMI appealed the findings, but the appeal was dismissed in March 2011. It would appear that the Court, in this instance, favoured the protection of the copyright holder's interest over that of the public interest, in spite of Justice Emmet's comment: 'One may wonder whether the framers of the *Statute of Anne* and its descendants would have regarded the taking of the melody of *Kookaburra* in the impugned recordings as an infringement, rather than as fair use that did not in any way detract from the benefit given to Miss Sinclair for her intellectual effort in producing *Kookaburra*' (*EMI v. Larrikin*, at 101).

CONCLUSION

This chapter, in dealing with the philosophical theories underpinning copyright, has also provided a brief overview of the public sphere as it relates to this book. The theories lay the foundation for an examination of authors' roles within the current Australian copyright structure and tie in the expectations of authors from a natural right and moral rights point of view with the broader utilitarian principles followed in copyright legislation. Furthermore, this chapter provided a basis for further discussion of authors' sphere within the public sphere and how authors function in relation to other competing subaltern spheres. In the next chapter, the focus shifts to the subject of authorship, dealing specifically with the concept, definition and rights of the 'author.'

REFERENCES

Adeney, E. (2002). Moral rights and substantiality. *Australian Intellectual Property Journal, 13*, 5.

Boyle, J. (2002). Fencing off ideas: Enclosure and the disappearance of the public domain. *Daedalus, 131*(2), 13.

Carpignano, P., Anderson, R., Aronowitz, S., & DiFazio, W. (1993). Chatter in the age of electronic reproduction: Talk, television and the 'public mind. In B. Robbins (Ed.), *The phantom public sphere*. Minneapolis, MN: University of Minnesota Press.

Cornish, W. R. (1999). *Intellectual property*. London: Sweet & Maxwell.

Eley, G. (1994). Nations, publics, and political cultures: Placing Habermas in the nineteenth century. In N. B. Dirks, G. Eley, & S. B. Otner (Eds.), *Culture/ power/history*. Princeton, NJ: Princeton University Press.

Epstein, R. A. (2004). Liberty versus property? Cracks in the foundations of copyright law. *IPCentral Review, 1*, 1.

Ergas, H. (2000). *Review of intellectual property legislation under the competition principles agreement (Final Report)*. Canberra, Australia: Intellectual Property and Competition Review Committee.

Fisher, W. (2000). Theories of intellectual property. In S. Munzer (Ed.), *New essays in the legal and political theory of property*. Cambridge, UK: Cambridge University Press.

Fraser, N. (1992). Rethinking the public sphere: A contribution to the critique of actually existing democracy. In C. Calhoun (Ed.), *Habermas and the public sphere*. Cambridge, MA: MIT Press.

Gerhards, J., & Schafer, M. S. (2009). Is the internet a better public sphere? Comparing old and new media in the US and Germany. *New Media & Society*, 1–18. Retrieved from http://nms.sagepub.com

Goldstein, P. (2001). *International copyright: Principles, law and practice*. Oxford, UK: Oxford University Press.

Habermas, J. (1974). The public sphere: An encyclopedia article (1964). *New German Critique*, (3), 49-55.

Habermas, J. (1984). *The theory of communicative action*. Boston: Beacon Press.

Habermas, J. (1989). *The structural transformation of the public sphere.* Cambridge, MA: MIT Press.

Hitchens, C. (2003). *Unacknowledged legislation: Writers in the public sphere.* Washington, DC: Verso.

Hohendahl, P. (1974). Jurgen Habermas: The public sphere (1964). *New German Critique,* (3), 45-48.

Hughes, J. (1988). The philosophy of intellectual property. *The Georgetown Law Journal, 77,* 330–350.

Johnson, P. (2008). Dedicating copyright to the public domain. *The Modern Law Review, 71*(4), 587. doi:10.1111/j.1468-2230.2008.00707.x

Kant, I. (1907). Metaphysische anfangsgrunde der rechtslehre (The metaphysical elements of justice, 1797), Kants werke, vol.6. Berlin: Druck und verlag von Georg Reimer.

Landes, W. M., & Posner, R. A. (1987). Trademark Law: An economic perspective. *The Journal of Law & Economics, 30,* 265. doi:10.1086/467138

Landes, W. M., & Posner, R. A. (1989). An economic analysis of copyright law. *The Journal of Legal Studies, 18,* 325. doi:10.1086/468150

Landes, W. M., & Posner, R. A. (2003). *The economic structure of intellectual property law.* Cambridge, MA: Harvard University Press.

Lange, D. M. (2003, Winter/Spring). Reimagining the public domain. *Law and Contemporary Problems,* 463.

Locke, J. (1689). *Of civil government: Second treatise,* ch. IX, par. 123, ch. V, par. 26, 31.

Macpherson, C. B. (1962). *The political theory of possessive individualism.* Oxford, UK: Oxford University Press.

Max, D. T. (2006, June 19). The injustice collector: Is James Joyce's grandson suppressing scholarship? *The New Yorker.* Retrieved from www.newyorker.com/archive/2006

McCutcheon, J. (2008). The new defence of parody or satire under Australian copyright law. *Intellectual Property Quarterly, 2,* 163.

Netanel, N. (1996). Copyright and a democratic civil society. *The Yale Law Journal, 106*, 283. doi:10.2307/797212

Nygh, P., & Butt, P. (Eds.). (1997). *Butterworths concise Australian legal dictionary*. Sydney: Butterworths.

Ricketson, S. (1987). *The Berne convention for the protection of literary and artistic works: 1886*. London: Kluwer.

Rose, M. (1988). The author as proprietor: Donaldson v Becket and the genealogy of modern authorship. *Representations (Berkeley, Calif.), 0*(23), 51–58. doi:10.2307/2928566

Rose, M. (1993). *Authors and owners*. Cambridge, MA: Harvard University Press.

Rose, M. (2003, Winter/Spring). Nine-tenths of the law: The English copyright debates and the rhetoric of the public domain. *Law and Contemporary Problems, 75*.

Rushdie, S. (1989). *The Satanic verses*. New York: Penguin.

Saunders, D. (1992). *Authorship and copyright*. London: Routledge.

Schmitter, E. (1995, September). Boycott Lufthansa: Literature and publicity today – A few ruminations and a suggestion. *TriQuarterly, 155*.

Sexton, C. (2007). In conversation with Frank Moorhouse. *IPSANZ IP Forum, 68*, 6.

Stokes, S. (2001). *Art and copyright*. Oxford, UK: Hart Publishing.

Suzor, N. (2006). *Transformative use of copyright material*. (Thesis). Queensland University of Technology, Brisbane, Australia.

Vaidhayanathan, S. (2001). *Copyrights & copywrongs: The rise of intellectual property and how it threatens creativity*. New York: NYU Press.

Villa, D. R. (1992). Postmodernism and the public sphere. *The American Political Science Review, 86*(3), 712–721. doi:10.2307/1964133

Villa, D. R. (Ed.). (2000). *The Cambridge companion to Arendt*. Cambridge, UK: Cambridge University Press. doi:10.1017/CCOL0521641985

Ward, S. (2006, May 6). Educating global journalists. *The Toronto Star.* Retrieved December 29, 2008, from http://www.global.factiva.com.library-proxy.griffith.edu.au

Woodmansee, M. (1984). The genius and the copyright: Economic and legal conditions of the emergence of the 'author'. *Eighteenth-Century Studies, 17,* 425–448. doi:10.2307/2738129

TABLE OF CASES

Donaldson v. Beckett (1774) 2 Bro.P.C. 129 (UK)

Eldred & others v. Ashcroft (2003) 56 IPR 608 (US)

EMI Songs Australia Pty Limited v. Larrikin Music Publishing Pty Limited [2011] FCAFC 47 (Austl.)

Fox Film Corp v. Doyal (1932) 286 US 123, 127 (US)

TNC Channel Nine Pty Ltd & Others v. Network Ten Pty Ltd (2001) 184 ALR1 (Austl.)

TABLE OF STATUTES

Copyright Act 1968 (Cth)

Copyright Amendment (Moral Rights) Act 2000 (Cth)

Copyright Amendment Act 2006 (Cth)

Directive 2006/116/EC of the European Parliament and of the Council on the term of protection of copyright and certain related rights

Statute of Anne 1709 (UK)

Chapter 4
Authorship:
From Quill to Keyboard and Cyberspace

ABSTRACT

The role of the author and the meaning of authorship is examined first in the context of legislation and case law and second as seen by critical theorists. The author's position as natural rights holder and moral rights holder within the ambit of the law is considered against existing legislation and case law. The discussion then moves to an account of the author as creator, first in the 21st century and, thereafter, in the digital era. New challenges to authorship and changes in the perceptions of readers are highlighted and discussed.

INTRODUCTION

It is only the unimaginative who ever invents. The true artist is known by what he annexes, and he annexes everything.-Oscar Wilde

The concepts of 'the author' and 'authorship' are central to this research. This chapter deals with the traditional and contemporary definitions of what an author is. The 'author' referred to in this research can be more specifically described as a 'literary,' 'fiction,' 'non fiction' or 'academic' author, rather than related groups such as journalists, poets, composers, song writers, artists and performers. The term is further defined later in the chapter.

DOI: 10.4018/978-1-4666-5214-9.ch004

This enquiry will first consider the legal position of the author and his/her legal rights, which include the proprietary rights of the author as natural rights holder and moral rights owner (Rose, 1988, p. 64). Second, it will examine some of the critical theories that provided the foundation for the current perception of authorship, and third, it will investigate who and what the author is today.

In doing so, this chapter examines the evolving perception of authorship and argues that the definition of 'author' is an ever expanding concept, influenced by a changing literary public sphere and, more specifically, technological advances. It further shows that the understanding of what an author is in the early 21st is inextricably linked with the perception of authorship that developed through the course of critical theory of the 20th century and the recognition of the author's legal status. Much as the invention of the printing press signalled an irrevocable change in the status and recognition of authorship, so too has digital technology precipitated a different perspective on the subject of authorship.

This investigation requires an acknowledgement of the close link between the philosophical theories of copyright (as discussed in the last chapter) and the critical theories relating to the concept of authorship, discussed in this chapter. Furthermore, these theories have to be considered within the ambits of the broader public sphere, within which the rights of the author as creator is recognised through various protective legislative structures, such as The Berne Convention of 1886 ('the Berne Convention') and the Australian *Copyright Act 1968* (as amended) ('the *Copyright Act*').

AUTHORSHIP AND THE LAW

As discussed in Chapter 2, Part III of the *Copyright Act* protects authors' copyright in their original work, while Part IX defines and protects authors' moral rights. Authors further enjoy specific protection of their moral rights under Article 6*bis* of the Berne Convention.

However, the question of how the legislation has interpreted the concept of authorship and whether authors' rights are sufficiently protected merits further investigation. It is further necessary to consider the 20th century critical theory on authorship, as well as current perceptions of authorship, against the backdrop of the moral rights and natural rights theories relating to copyright ownership. This chapter takes into account the dual nature of the author's persona: the author as both creator and rights holder, as well as the various factors that impact on the perception of authorship in a digital era.

Recognition of Authorship

It has been noted that authors had limited rights, if any, in the early 16th century (Armstrong, 1990, p. 21). Authorship attracted no special privileges and the concept of copyright remained unexplored. Although publishers started gaining protection after 1507, with the emergence of the State grant schemes, and authors followed suit in limited numbers, these measures were insufficient to protect the rights of authors and only allowed for limited licensing of books. Eventually the British *Licensing Act 1662* required 'licensed books' to be entered into a registry.

Authors were generally sponsored by benefactors or patrons who supported the arts, such as noblemen and clergy, who enjoyed recognition for the author's work. During the mid-17th century, noble patronage was well established in Europe with many nobles regarding the production of literary works such as poems, plays, works of criticism and moral reflection as a necessary practice (Viala, 1985, pp. 145-146).

At this point, the issue of copyright was the concern of publishers rather than authors, and no legal protection was afforded to authors. Until the *Statute of Anne*, the authorial ownership of property had not been considered in the legislature. This Act referred to the rights of authors in some depth and formalised certain copyright provisions legislation, however, it was not until the late 18th century that the Courts formally acknowledged authors' rights (Rose, 1993, p. 48).

The landmark case of *Donaldson v. Beckett* (1774) signalled a change in that early perception by elevating the status of the author to a previously unattained plane. In *Donaldson v. Beckett,* the court considered not only the issue of whether literary property was a statutory or a common law right, but also the ideological dimension of values such as 'property' and 'freedom' and the changing role of the author in society. Rose comments that Lord Camden, in considering the *Donaldson* appeal, expressed a profound distaste for the conception of the author as a professional who wrote for money, by stating:

Glory is the Reward of Science, and those who deserve it, scorn all meaner Views: I speak not of the Scribblers for bread, who teize the Press with their wretched Productions; fourteen Years is too long a Privilege for their perishable Trash. It was not for Gain that Bacon, Newton, Milton, Locke instructed and delighted the World; it would be unworthy such Men to traffic with a dirty Bookseller for so much as a Sheet of Letter-press. When the Bookseller offered

Milton Five Pound for his Paradise Lost, he did not reject it, and commit his poem to Flames, nor did he accept the miserable Pittance as the Reward of his Labor; he knew that the real price of his Work was Immortality, and that Posterity would pay for it (Rose, 1988, p. 53).

However, his Lordship's impassioned view was not shared by others, such as the publishers of the *Monthly Review* (in 1774) who regarded the case as empowering authors, who would now be able to 'repay themselves for their labours, without the humiliating idea of receiving a favour, where they had the right to claim a debt' (Rose, 1988, p. 53). Significantly, the case acknowledged the natural right of authors as proprietors of their work, a view which is still supported and recognised in the legislature today.

Rose regards the distinguishing feature of the modern author as that of proprietorship, based on the perception that the author is the originator and, therefore, the owner of 'the work' (Rose, 1988, p. 53).

This view had also been expressed earlier by Eisenstein, who stated:

From the very first, authorship was closely linked to the new technology.... Partly because copyists had, after all, never paid whose works they copied, partly because new books were a small part of the early book trade, and partly because divisions of literary labour remained blurred, the author retained a quasi-amateur status until the eighteenth century (1979, pp. 153-154).

Since the *Donaldson* judgment, the concept of proprietorship originating in the author's copyright has been widely accepted, to the extent that it is protected by legislation and regarded as an asset to be bequeathed in the event of the author's death (*Copyright Act 1968*, s. 33). It therefore accounts for the present day recognition of authors' copyright in the legislation, which is balanced by a utilitarian application of economic considerations and the public interest.

Another theory which was instrumental in determining the current view of authorship as a right to be protected in the legislation was the concept of moral rights. As seen in Chapter 2, authors such as Kant and Hegel argued that writers held moral rights or personality rights in their creative work. Fisher points out that the moral rights viewpoint not only protects the author's personality rights, but also the piece of work created by the author (Fisher, 2000, p. 4).

The inclusion of Part IX of the *Copyright Act 1968,* dealing exclusively with moral rights, signified the legal recognition of Australian authors' personality rights and reflected the philosophies of these 19th and 20th century theorists. Its aim was, however, not only to protect the personality of authors, but also to incentivise creators to continue to create for the public benefit. It is therefore evident that the recognition of moral rights was closely connected to economic incentives (See also Ergas, 2000, p. 33).

With digital technology and ebooks, there has been some concern about protecting authors' moral rights. In a recent article on the Australian Society of Authors (ASA) Website, Loukakis points out that it is usually a contractual obligation for print publishers to show authors the final edited version of their work before it is printed, to ensure there has been no 'derogation' of their work (which he refers to as a critical right according to the moral rights provisions of the *Copyright Act*). 'It appears, however, that with ebooks, publishers are ignoring this vital responsibility,' he says. The ASA argues that 'the publisher is obliged – under the moral rights clause, as a common courtesy, and for sound commercial reasons – to show a digitized version of the text to their author before the "send to e-tailer" button is pushed' (Loukakis, 2010).

Authorship and the Courts

The issue of authorship was considered in the landmark Australian case of *Ice TV v. Nine Network* (2009). In this case, Nine Network claimed that its weekly television program schedules were protected by copyright as compilations and that IceTV had infringed on its copyright by reproducing a substantial part of the schedules in its own electronic program guide, the *IceGuide.*

The High Court, overturning the decision of the Full Federal Court, held that any reproduction of the time and title information in the *IceGuide* contained little originality and could not be regarded as a reproduction of a substantial part of any of Nine's Weekly Schedules or the Nine database. In their judgment, their Honours stated that: 'The "author" of a literary work and the concept of "authorship" are central to the statutory protection given by copyright legislation, including the Act' (2009 HCA 14 at 22).

The Court regarded 'authorship' and 'material form' as two fundamental principles underpinning copyright law:

The first principle concerns the significance of 'authorship.' The subject matter of the Act now extends well beyond the traditional categories of original works of authorship, but the essential source of original works remains the activities of authors. While, by assignment or by other operation of law, a party other than the author may be owner of the copyright from time to time, original works emanate from authors (2009 HCA at 95 - 96).

It was further acknowledged that, like the *Copyright Act 1956* (UK) ('the 1956 Act') in its original form, the Act did not define the term 'author' beyond the statement that, in relation to a photograph, it was the person who took that photograph. As a result of changes made by the 1988 UK Copyright, Designs and Patents Act (in relation to a work 'author' meant the person 'who creates it'), in the case of a 'computer-generated' work this was taken to be 'the person by whom the arrangements necessary for the creation of the work are undertaken.' No such provision was made in the Australian statute, but the notion of 'creation' conveyed the earlier understanding of an 'author' as 'the person who brings the copyright work into existence in its material form' (2009 HCA at 98).

The High Court also recognised the importance of balancing the reward to the author of an original work with public benefit considerations, and acknowledged the influence of the Statute of Anne on present Australian copyright law:

In assessing the centrality of an author and authorship to the overall scheme of the Act, it is worth recollecting the longstanding theoretical underpinnings of copyright legislation. Copyright legislation strikes a balance of competing interests and competing policy considerations. Relevantly, it is concerned with rewarding authors of original literary works with commercial benefits having regard to the fact that literary works in turn benefit the reading public (2009 HCA at 24).

In both its title and opening recitals, the *Statute of Anne* of 1709 echoed explicitly the emphasis on the practical or utilitarian importance that certain 17th century philosophers attached to knowledge and its encouragement in the scheme of human progress. The 'social contract' envisaged by the Statute of Anne, and still underlying the present Act, was that an author could obtain a monopoly, limited in time, in return for making a work available to the reading public.

Whilst judicial and academic writers may differ on the precise nature of the balance struck in copyright legislation in different places, there can be no doubt that copyright is given in respect of 'the particular form of expression in which an author convey[s] ideas or information to the world' (2009 HCA at 24-26).

The Court further held that a literary work will only be 'original' if it had been created by some 'independent intellectual effort' or 'sufficient effort of a literary nature' (2009 CLR at 458).

The case signalled a move away from the Court's approach in the *Desktop Marketing Systems Pty Ltd v. Telstra Corporation Ltd* (2003) case, where the Court found that the names and telephone numbers from Telstra's *White Pages* and *Yellow Pages* were protected by copyright. In the *IceTV* case, the Court considered the information reproduced as not sufficiently substantial to constitute an infringement of the skill and labour expended by Nine Network's employees. Significantly, the Court also agreed with the proposition that 'IceTV adopted its own form of presentation of the time and title information and drafted its own synopses and thus had not taken sufficient of Nine's skill and labour so as to have infringed by copying "slivers" of time and title information' (2009 HCA at 126).

In a more recent decision, *Telstra Corporation Limited v. Phone Directories Company Pty Ltd* (2010 FCA 44), the Federal Court held that copyright did not subsist in the *White* and *Yellow Pages* phone directories produced by Telstra. Her Honour Justice Gordon referred to the 2009 *IceTV* decision and stated that for copyright to subsist, it was necessary to identify authors and demonstrate that those authors directed their contribution to the particular form of expression of the work. Telstra subsequently appealed the judgment to the Full Federal Court, but in December 2010 the appeal was dismissed (2010 FCAFC 149).

Another Federal Court decision that focussed on the importance of authorship and the need to identify the authors who contributed to the work was *Acohs v. Ucorp* (2010). Significantly, it was held, amongst other things that copyright did not subsist in the source code of certain electronic files that were based on data entered into a computer program. The decision has been appealed and, at the time of the research, the Court had not yet handed down its judgment.

A recent case that dealt with the issues of joint authorship and copyright protection of headlines, *Fairfax Media Publications Pty Ltd v. Reed International Books Australia Pty Ltd* (2010), held that discrete items like titles, names and slogans were generally not substantial or original enough to be protected by copyright. The case dealt with allegations by Fairfax Media that Reed International had infringed its copyright in the *Australian Financial Review (AFR)*. Reed had reproduced elements of *AFR* articles in its ABIX service, which essentially provided subscribers with abstracts of already published articles together with the (often unaltered) headlines and by-lines of these articles.

The Court was satisfied that the compilation of articles, as well as the edition works, were capable of being protected as works of joint authorship, having been produced through the collaboration of a number of authors whose contribution was not separate from the contribution of the others. On the issue of identifying the authors, Justice Bennett noted that it was sufficient for Fairfax to establish which particular employees by role had contributed, as opposed to the specific identity of these employees.

Inevitably, proprietary issues arise where the author as creator depends on the use of his or her creation to earn a living. This copyright centred perspective, however, whilst addressing some of the philosophical arguments in favour of authors' rights in relation to copyright law, does not address the intrinsic meaning and value of the concept of 'authorship.' To examine who and what the perception of the author is in the context of this research, it is instructive to follow the development of critical theory on this issue and consider the writings of post-structuralist commentators such as Barthes and Foucault.

CRITICAL THEORY AND THE DEVELOPMENT OF AUTHORSHIP

Authorship in the 20th Century

If the 18th and 19th centuries can be regarded as having heralded and progressed the importance of the author in the public sphere (through copyright legislation), then it may be said that the 20th century produced a shift away from the author figure, with critical theory centring around concepts such as semiotics (the study of signs), structuralism, narrativism, reader-response criticism and post-structuralism. All these movements signalled a move away from the Romantic historical view that authorship was inseparable from the creative work and that the role of the author as creator was paramount.

The concept that a creative work should be studied with a view of discovering the intention of the author by having regard to the life of the author was first challenged by the 'New Critics' from 1930 to 1950 (Malpas & Wake, 2006). This movement proposed that the text itself was paramount and that it was a complete entity in and of itself. Its doctrine was one of semantic autonomy with little attention paid to the historical, psychological or autobiographical context of a creative work. In the 'New Criticism,' the text was attributed an immutable meaning to the exclusion of authorial considerations (Malpas & Wake, 2006, pp. 147, 232).

This approach paved the way for a greater adherence to structuralism in the late 1950s and a further move away from the author's importance in relation to the creative work. The concept of structuralism had its foundation in the work of Ferdinand de Saussure between 1907 and 1911, who proposed that language provided a foundational structure for the world around us. When applied in relation to literary theory, it provided that a focus on the structural properties of literary works was essential to an understanding of the work (McGowan, 2006, pp. 4, 12).

According to McGowan, this approach, used together with semiotics, could be regarded as having changed how readers engage with the specific meanings of texts and the practice of reading itself. She suggests that:

to read literature as a system of signs would be to open literary texts them-selves to a process of decoding capable of revealing not just its structures and forms but also the ideological implications of the very syntax and grammar from which it is composed (McGowan, 2006, p. 12).

This text specific approach was expanded by authors such as Roland Barthes, whose theories were reflective of the poststructuralist era, which also disregarded the author as the origin of meaning in a text but went even further in its textual focus. Poststructuralists argued that texts contained an inexhaustible multiplicity of meanings and that the reader played an impor-tant interpretative role in the creative process (Eco, 1979, p. 4). The positive emphasis on the text, rather than its creator, led to discourses such as *The death of the author* by Barthes (1977, p. 142) and Eco's *The Open Work* (1989), which will be discussed later in this chapter. Eco proposed that, even from a structuralist perspective, the sender (author), addressee (reader) and context were indispensable to the understanding of any act of communica-tion (reading) (1979, p. 4).

Barthes argued for the removal of the author figure, stating that 'the birth of the reader must be at the cost of the death of the Author,' thereby empowering the reader to ascribe different meanings to the text not neces-sarily envisaged by the author (1977, p. 148). He described a text as 'not a line of words releasing a single "theological" meaning (the "message" of the Author-God) but a multi-dimensional space, in which a variety of writings, none of them original, blend and clash' (1977, p. 146). With the 'death' of the author, he envisaged a 'rebirth' of the reader:

Thus is revealed the total existence of writing: a text is made up of multiple writing, drawn from many cultures and entering into a mutual relations of dialogue, parody, contestation, but there is the reader, not, as was hitherto said, the author. The reader is the space on which all the quotations that make up a writing are inscribed without any of them being lost; a text's unity lies not in its origin but in its destination! (Barthes, 1977, p. 147).

Saunders is critical of how Barthes makes no mention of actual laws and legal systems, noting: 'by contrast with this transcendental aesthetic primacy... the law is depicted as having to differentiate (*between the intent and result of art*) at a much more mundane level' (1992, pp. 227, 229, *my parenbook*). Saunders' approach significantly recognises the inevitable impact of positive law, which he regards as a determining factor in an interpretation of the concept of authorship (1992, p. 7).

He approaches the issue of authorship in conjunction with copyright and takes a different view of the concept by emphasising the importance of statutory and case law of copyright as a factor influencing the literary field (Saunders, 1992, p. 239). He rejects the romantic ideology of 'the birth of the author' (the historicist approach) as well as the opposing critical theories proposing 'the death of the author' (the poststructuralist approach) in favour of a different approach to the issue of authorship and copyright.

He suggests the use of three coordinates, namely, communications technologies (print literacy), the historical anthropology of personhood (rights of personality) and the determining role of positive law; he further points out that there exists a common characteristic of these determinates, namely 'the technical and technological character of authorial personality as it has been recognised in law' (Saunders, 1992, pp. 2-7).

His approach offers a different perspective of authorship, arguing that it is defined by positive law, assisted by technological change, such as the invention of the printing press, and, it could be further argued, by the widespread use of digital technology.

Saunders offers an historical account of the 'internationalisation of copyright and authorship' and argues that the Berne Convention affords an international generality to the authorial attributes protected by moral rights, which reflects the effectiveness of international law in protecting authors' interests (1992, pp. 167-185). However, his work precedes the later challenges presented to copyright legislation by digital technology, such as Google's unauthorised digital copying of books in American libraries. What emerges from his writing is the fact that the concept of authorship cannot be viewed from a purely literary or historic perspective, but that the legal implications of the term should be taken into consideration in determining its definition.

Michel Foucault in his 1977 essay 'What is an author?' includes the legal implications of the concept of 'author' by defining it as both a legal and cultural function significant to the understanding of a text. Foucault traced the historical role of the author-function in critical theory and concluded that the author concept as a function of discourse served only to limit the meaning of the text. He stated: 'We can easily imagine a culture where discourse would circulate without the need for an author' and ended his essay by quoting Beckett: 'What matter who's speaking?' (Foucault, 1977, pp. 113-138).

Foucault justified this argument *inter alia* by elucidating the difficulties associated with the meaning of an author's name, the fact that a proprietary/legal meaning had been ascribed to authorship in relation to books or texts, the lack of constancy of the author function (as some texts have not historically required authors) and the difficulties posed with the definition of 'author' (1977, pp. 121-130). His viewpoint put forth in that essay, namely that the principle of authorship exceeds the body of the text associated with him (Foucault, 1977, p. 131), is later borne out by the observations of late 20th century commentators such as Landow and Burke, discussed in the following section.

Postmodernists such as Umberto Eco argued that texts should be regarded as dynamic and open to numerous, but not limitless, interpretations. His semiotic theory sought to include the reader-response approach, by stating:

To organise a text, its author has to rely upon a series of codes that assign given contents to the expressions he uses. To make his text communicative, the author has to assume that the ensemble of codes he relies upon is the same as that shared by his possible reader (Eco, 1989, p. 7).

Eco elaborated on these theories in his works *The Role of the Reader* (1979) and *The Open Work* (1989), which examined the role of the author, the text and the reader (Malpas & Wake, 2006, p. 147, 178). Eco's postmodern view of alternate outcomes was expressed in his medieval crime novel, *The Name of the Rose* (1983), wherein he explored his 'open work' theory with regard to the roles of the author, the text and the 'model' reader (Malpas & Wake, 2006, p. 178). He did so by using the process of solving seven murders through involving the reader's interpretation of the text. The novel ends with uncertainty, leaving the reader to interpret the events (Butler, 2002, p. 126).

Poststructuralism thus saw a shift in significance towards the reader rather than reverting to the author figure as a source of interpretation. Belsey sees the main interest of poststructuralism (from a critical theory perspective) as an 'invitation to read differently' and a further proposition that the meanings of texts are not to be found in the mind of the author or anywhere else (2006, p. 43). Rather, textual meanings are 'unfixed, discontinuous and unstable' (Belsey, 2006, p. 43). She argues:

Poststructuralism offers the reader an overt awareness of the complex and unstable positions offered by specific modes of address, and a recognition that all texts – including advertisements, news stories, religious exhortations and internet chat, as well as fiction - may be enlisting us in both more and less than we bargained for (Belsey, 2006, p. 53).

However, poststructuralist theories were criticised by academics and theorists such as Burke, who were of the view that authorial subjectivity could 'not be practically circumvented' (1992, p. 191) and Saunders, who regarded poststructuralism as 'imposing an arbitrary philosophical direction on the history of authorship and the law of copyright' (1992, pp. 3-4).

Burke refers to the 'pragmatic intentionalist' movement of 1985, reflected in Knapp and Michaels' writing (1985), which challenged the poststructuralist view of an 'open text' and promoted a return to the concept of intention as reflected by textual meaning. As Burke points out, however:

The return to the author here is thus a return only to intention, and to a concept of intention that has no place either in the theoretical, critical or pragmatic enterprises. So far from forcefully unsettling the tradition of Anglo-American formalism, such a pragmatic gesture serves as one more way of keeping authorial subjectivity in abeyance. What the New Critics called 'objective meaning,' the poststructuralists 'textuality,' and Knapp and Michaels 'intention' – for all their differences in ethos – serve the common purpose of emptying out the author-problematic (1992, p. 187).

He argues that authorial subjectivity cannot be circumvented and sees all acts of authorship as springing from 'the distinctively human, that ever-singular place of desire,' which 'is the limit of an expressive world and the striving we make toward a beyond' (Burke, 1992, pp. 205-206). This viewpoint recognises the inherently personal nature of the act of creativity, and the fact that the author's intention is inevitably linked to the creative work.

Authorship in the Digital Era

It is significant that the writings of Barthes, Derrida, Foucault, Eco and Saunders were executed without considering the effects of digital technology on writing and authorship. Digital technology has seen the emergence of hypertext (short for hypertext mark-up language, or HTML), which denotes the relationship between nodes of text connected electronically in cyberspace. It allows for the linking of texts, diagrams and visual images in a non-linear fashion (Malpas & Wake, 2006, p. 203).

As Debray points out:

With data systems used for interactivity and geometrically variable hypertext, the reader is no longer simply a spectator, one who looks at meaning through the page's window in rectangle, from the outside, but co-author of what he reads, a second writer and active partner (1996, p. 145).

These comments appear to support Eco's earlier arguments on the importance of the reader and reader-response, referred to above. However, some authors such as Burke are critical of this movement towards reader empowerment. Burke discusses the efforts of 'technological visionaries' to eliminate the author in the epilogue of his book, *The death and return of the author* (1992). He refers to Landow, who argues that electronic linking facilitates the linking of texts, similar to the way in which Barthes, Derrida and Foucault stressed the interconnectedness of all written works. According to Landow, it further promotes active participation by the reader (for example, by clicking on a highlighted link to move to another Website or by adding links and comments) (Burke, 1992, pp. 192-193).

Landow regards hypertext as having a 'liberating and empowering quality' that provides the reader with power to write and link and 'which removes much of the gap in conventional status between reader and author' and 'permits readers to read actively in an even more powerful way – by annotating documents, arguing with them, leaving their own traces…The very open-endedness of the text also promotes empowering the reader' (1992, p. 178).

This viewpoint represents a paradigm shift in which the text revolves around the reader rather than the author. It concurs with the viewpoints of Barthes and Eco in the sense that the author is removed from the text once it is created, and reader interpretation becomes central to the reading experience.

Burke criticises it as an 'ultrademocratic' freedom which is awarded to the reader in opposition to a what he sardonically refers to as 'tyranically author-centred literature which forces the reader down a pre-determined and linear path imposed by authorial intention' (1992, p. 200). He is firm in his rejection of the reader empowerment argument proposed by Landow and states:

The argument for the political value of displacing the author fails to persuade... In associating itself with a politics of reading, the 'theorisation' of digital technology – something altogether different from the work of those who construct and refine technologies – disinters some of the most egregiously falsifying arguments for the removal of the author (Burke, 1992, p. 200).

It may be suggested that there is merit in Burke's criticism of the attempted 'removal of the author from the written work' and that the concept of authorship as it relates to authorial subjectivity and creative intention may be in danger of being significantly altered by digital interpretation and reader response.

It may be argued that the concept of authorship is constantly evolving in the public sphere, not only as a result of technological change or historical and legal developments, but also because of the changing perception of what an 'author' is in the digital era, as discussed below.

THE KEYBOARD AUTHOR

When everyone is somebody, then no one's anybody. -W. S. Gilbert

This then brings us to the third enquiry: Who and what is the *author* in the digital era? This leads to the further question: what does the future hold for the *author persona*? Such an investigation encompasses both aspects of the author, those of creator and rights holder, and requires consideration of how new media technology has impacted upon our perception of the author figure.

Writer or Author?

It may be argued that, with the increased opportunities for publication on the Internet, the definition of 'author' has become a fluid concept. Young, in his book *The book is dead – long live the book* (2007) describes the traditional transformation from *writer* to *author* as follows:

Everybody is a writer. Once written, getting a book published is the holy grail. When the book launch is done, and the book sits on shop shelves to be turned cover-out by family and friends, a writer becomes an author, they have been accepted into an elite club, their chosen path has been validated (2007, pp. 67-68).

Young further argues that 'book culture' depends on authority and that authors are the source of that authority, depicting books as 'creative acts whose only constraints are imposed by the author. Despite the alternative possibilities for validation created by new media technologies, he still maintains that 'only the publishing process turns writers into authors and ideas into books' (Young, 2007, pp. 82-83).

He regards the Internet as a 'social amplifier' which not only has 'provided a means of production to millions of writers, it has turned them into authors with significant readership' (Young, 2007, p. 71). He refers to content creators such as bloggers and the writers of 'fan-fiction' (writing based on existing stories or television series) and cites examples of popular blogs that have been published as books, so-called *'blooks,'* such as *Julia and Julia: 365 days, 524 recipes, 1 Tiny Kitchen Apartment'* (Young, 2007, p. 76). To Young, the new media forms allow for 'dynamic collaborative writing possibilities'; however, he acknowledges that 'for academics, journalists and others who write for a living, the blog is yet to gain required professional status' (2007, p. 80).

It is suggested here that the early 21st century author must of necessity be viewed in the context of the digital arena, an expanded 'literary sphere' within which the traditional concept of the author has been modified. This is largely due to the globalisation and diversification of the publishing industry and increased access to publication, but also to changes in the public perception of the value of creative work. Young's viewpoint that the new media technologies have blurred the lines between writing and publishing (2007, p. 83) is borne out by the ease with which anyone with an Internet connection can instantly write and publish content on the Internet. It is evident that, contrary to the distinct author-reader roles envisaged by theorists such as Foucault and Derrida, the blurring of the author-reader roles on the Internet has become a relevant consideration in the perception of what an author is, especially as authors are not always able to control the use of hypertext and linking on the Internet.

In 2009, Pelli and Bigelow provided a graph of the history of authorship, which took into account the number of published authors per year, since 1400, for books and, more recently, for social media, including blogs, Twitter and Facebook. They considered, for the purpose of the research, an author's text 'published' if 100 or more people had read it. The graph showed that, since 1400, book authorship had grown nearly tenfold each century and that, presently, authorship (according to their wider definition which included social media) was growing nearly tenfold each year. Their research revealed that new media authorship was growing 100 times faster than books (Pelli & Bigalow, 2009, p. 1). Their graph is included in *Figure 1.*

Taking into account Young's comments and the statistics provided by Pelli and Bigelow (2009), it could be argued that, whereas an author (in a literary context) was traditionally regarded as the writer of books, stories, articles or essays, the definition of an author today has been extended and is inextricably linked to the creative possibilities of new technology.

However, in the context of this research, the discussion of digital authorship focuses on eBooks and other creative works of significant length and the reader response to such works, rather than considering every 'blogger' or 'tweeter' to be an author. Thus, the Internet as a medium is viewed, in this context, as a platform for publication and comment, rather than a forum that affords all contributors the benefits of 'authorship' associated with traditional publishing.

Figure 1. The History of authorship: Number of authors who published in each year for various media since 1400 by century (left) and by year (right)

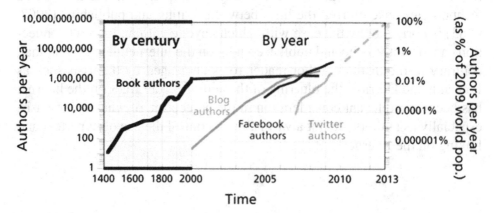

The Evolution of Authorship

If one considers the original Latin meaning of the word 'auctor,' 'author' means 'maker' or 'one who causes to grow' (Barnhart & Barnhart, 1981, p. 136). The Australian *Macquarie Dictionary* defines an author as '1. someone who writes a novel, poem, essay, etc.; the composer of a literary work, as distinguished from a compiler, translator, editor, or copyist' and '2. the originator, beginner, or creator of anything' (2003, p. 65). We have seen from the writings of Nunberg (1996, p. 105) and Young (2007, p. 71) referred to above that, in new media technology, this meaning has of necessity been extended to include the 'electronic content creator' or 'digital writer.'

Toschi earlier described the emergence of electronic text as a 'new and revolutionary' development for authors, but cautioned that:

Binary writing stands as an emblematic case of how the future we have yet to construct must needs [sic] have a mind and conscience which reflect ancient models. If it is a time when everything is changing, it is equally a time in order to build the new, and to defend it from the neobarbarism which every generation inevitably and invariably has to come to terms with, it is essential to have a clear idea of what has happened in the last centuries. This is why electronic writing needs, among other things, sound critical and philological knowledge (1996, p. 195).

More recent commentators such as Alexander argue that, although authors (as the recognised originator of written work) have to face fresh challenges in the digital environment, they are no more disadvantaged than their predecessors in the literary sphere (2010, p. 2). As previously discussed, earlier authors encountered, if not similar, at least as daunting obstacles in obtaining recognition for their work.

In discussing the impact of the digital economy in relation to copyright, Alexander argues that there has always been a struggle between competing economic interests as far copyright was concerned, since before the *Statute of Anne* was passed. She notes the fact that new innovations have historically been opposed through a 'backward-looking attitude' (Alexander, 2010, p. 20) and seen as a threat, rather than embraced. In her paper, she discusses decisions such as *Donaldson v. Becket (1774)* and refers to Paltry's book, *Moral Panic and Copyright Wars* (2009), which advances the book that copyright debates are essentially the product of outdated business models being threatened by innovators (Alexander, 2010, p. 20).

This argument is equally relevant when considering the parallel issues of authorship and the role of the author, if one accepts that new technology requires new business models. As discussed above, the invention of the printing press and subsequent proliferation of the printed word gave rise to an increased interest in and recognition of the author persona. However, literary critical theory of the twentieth century saw a move away from the author figure and a greater focus on the text itself, with the late 20th century shifting the focus onto the reader as an important participant in the creative process.

The latter change has been fuelled by technological advances around the turn of the century and an increased awareness of the reader in the creative process. In addition, thereto, the emergence and popularisation of ebooks and online publishing have contributed to altered perceptions of the role of the author.

Following on from commentators such as Barthes, Foucault, Eco and Landow, and taking into account the altered literary sphere in which authors function today, it is argued here that the emergence of the reader as participant has contributed to an expanded definition of who and what an author is today. In addition, the greater opportunity for transformative use of creative work has influenced the perception of authorship and required a repositioning of the author in relation to the creative work.

To fully appreciate the context within which the author finds him- or herself in the digital technology, cognisance must be taken of the surrounding influences of Web media such as blogging sites and virtual discussion forums where authors may receive feedback and commentary on their work. Nunberg points out its cyclic approach:

One of the most pervasive features of these media is how closely they seem to reproduce the conditions of discourse of the late seventeenth and eighteenth centuries, when the sense of the public was mediated through a series of transitive personal relationships – the friends of one's friends, and so on – and anchored in the immediate connections of clubs, coffee-houses, salons, and the rest (1996, p. 130).

In this sense, the Web resembles a new public sphere within which the participants share experiences, communicate and (as it is a visual medium) publish their viewpoints. This expanded reality is a move away from the printed word that Eco and Barthes considered, and reader-response takes on a more active role.

Landow points out that hypertext (electronic linking) had fundamentally changed the way we read and write. In his essay 'Twenty minutes into the future' he states:

By permitting readers to choose their ways through a particular set of lexias, hypertext in essence shifts some of the author's power to readers. Hypertext, which demands new forms of reading and writing, has the promise radically to reconceive our perceptions of text, author, intellectual property, and a host of other issues ranging from the nature of the self to education (Landow, 1996, p. 225).

Simone also acknowledges that anyone can add to or change a text on the Internet, causing the text to gradually lose its authorship and the perception that it is the product of an author to 'dwindle in the general consciousness.' 'Writing a book is quite another thing from commenting, copying or annotating it. However, in the near future it will be increasingly difficult – even impossible – to say who is the author of a text,' he comments (Simone, 1996, pp. 249-51).

In the mid-90s, these comments accurately projected the direction that authorship would take over the following 15 years. Today these observations are still extremely relevant, highlighting the issues faced by authors on the Web through reader participation and the loss of authorial control over the text. They further imply a shift towards collaborative creation and away from the Romantic notion of individual creation, which existed from the early 18th to the early 20th centuries.

Some may argue that, in a sense, the author is being returned to the pre-*Statute of Anne* era where an author was only useful insofar as he/she created 'useful work' and recorded history and folklore, little more than a commentator or collaborator with limited control over his/her work. However, such a view would ignore the copyright protection afforded to authors by legislative provisions and international conventions, which are evidence of the author's recognised standing in the public sphere today.

If one accepts that the scope of authorship is expanding to include Internet content creators, bloggers and contributors, it appears that the Internet may be changing the notion of an 'author.' Furthermore, it indicates that the author in the 21st century is moving away from the relatively passive role that he/she has traditionally occupied from a publishing and marketing perspective. The Internet writer requires a new set of skills, which include publishing and marketing, and a flexible approach to collaboration and reader-response.

CONCLUSION

Evidently the definition of 'author' is an ever expanding and evolving concept, influenced by a changing public sphere and more specifically, by technological advances. The dual nature of the author's persona as creator and rights holder has also been emphasised by the changing role of authorship in the new technology. One may validly observe that the effects of hypertext, reader participation and increased collaboration have created a new breed of writer: the digital author. However, the quality and quantity of creative content and the identity of the writer remain distinguishing factors in this electronic sphere, separating the author from the reader/commentator. As with most things, change is inevitable and survival depends on the timely recognition of changing circumstance. As Pelli and Bigelow observe: 'As readers we consume. As authors we create. Our society is changing from consumers to creators' (2009, p. 2). Readers are becoming writers, writers are turning into authors and authors have to rise to the challenge of distinguishing themselves on the worldwide Web.

REFERENCES

Alexander, I. (2010, May). *All change for the digital economy: Copyright and business models in the early eighteenth century.* Paper presented at University of Cambridge. Sydney, Australia.

Armstrong, E. (1990). *Before copyright – The French book-privilege system 1498-1526.* Cambridge, UK: Cambridge University Press.

Barnhart, C. L., & Barnhart, R. K. (Eds.). (1981). *The world book dictionary.* Chicago: Doubleday & Company.

Barthes, R. (1977). *Image music text* (S. Heath, Trans.). New York: The Noonday Press.

Belsey, C. (2006). Structuralism and semiotics. In S. Malpas, & P. Wake (Eds.), *The Routledge companion to critical theory* (pp. 43–54). Oxford, UK: Routledge.

Burke, S. (1992). *The death and return of the author.* Edinburgh, UK: Edinburgh University Press.

Butler, B. C. (2002). *Postmodernism: A very short introduction.* Oxford, UK: Oxford University Press.

Debray, R. (1996). The book as symbolic object. In G. Nunberg (Ed.), *The future of the book* (pp. 139–152). Berkeley, CA: University of California Press.

Eco, U. (1979). *The role of the reader: Explorations in the semiotics of texts.* London: Hutchinson.

Eco, U. (1989). *The open work.* Boston: Harvard University Press.

Eisenstein, E. L. (1979). *The printing press as an agent of change: Communications and cultural transformations in early-modern Europe* (Vol. 1). Cambridge, UK: Cambridge University Press.

Ergas, H. (2000). *Review of intellectual property legislation under the competition principles agreement (Final Report).* Canberra, Australia: Intellectual Property and Competition Review Committee.

Fisher, W. (2000). Theories of intellectual property. In S. Munzer (Ed.), *New essays in the legal and political theory of property.* Cambridge, UK: Cambridge University Press.

Foucault, M. (1997). What is an author? In D. F. Bouchard, & S. Simons (Eds.), *Language, counter-memory, practice*. New York: Cornell University Press.

Knapp, S., & Michaels, W. B. (1985). *Against theory: Literary studies and the new pragmatism* (pp. 19, 101, 104). Chicago: University of Chicago Press.

Landow, G. P. (1992). *Hypertext: The convergence of contemporary critical theory and technology*. Baltimore, MD: John Hopkins University Press. doi:10.1145/168466.168515

Landow, G. P. (1996). Twenty minutes into the future. In G. Nunberg (Ed.), *The future of the book* (pp. 209–238). Los Angeles, CA: University of California Press.

Loukakis, A. (2010, November 22). Warning: More ebook loopholes. *Australian Society of Authors*. Retrieved December 10, 2010, from https://asauthors.org/news/warning-more-ebook-loopholes

Toschi, L. (1996). Hypertext and authorship. In G. Nunberg (Ed.), *The future of the book* (pp. 169–208). Los Angeles, CA: University of California Press.

Macquarie Dictionary. (2003). *Macquarie: Australia's national dictionary*. Sydney: The Macquarie Library Publishers.

Malpas, S., & Wake, P. (Eds.). (2006). *The Routledge companion to critical theory*. Oxford, UK: Routledge.

McGowan, K. (2006). Structuralism and semiotics. In S. Malpas, & P. Wake (Eds.), *The Routledge companion to critical theory* (pp. 3–13). Oxford, UK: Routledge.

Moorhouse, F. (2007, June 3). From quill to keyboard. *Age*.

Nunberg, G. (1996). Farewell to the information age. In G. Nunberg (Ed.), *The future of the book* (pp. 103–138). Los Angeles, CA: University of California Press.

Paltry, W. (2009). *Moral panics and the copyright wars*. Oxford, UK: Oxford University Press.

Pelli, D. G., & Bigelow, C. (2009, October 20). A writing revolution. *Seed Magazine*. Retrieved September 19, 2010, from http://seedmagazine.com/content/article/a_writing_revolution/

Rose, M. (1988). The author as proprietor: Donaldson v Becket and the genealogy of modern authorship. *Representations (Berkeley, Calif.)*, *0*(23), 51–58. doi:10.2307/2928566

Rose, M. (1993). *Authors and owners*. Cambridge, MA: Harvard University Press.

Saunders, D. (1992). *Authorship and copyright*. London: Routledge.

Simone, R. (1996). The body of the text. In G. Nunberg (Ed.), *The future of the book* (pp. 239–252). Los Angeles, CA: University of California Press.

Viala, A. (1985). *Naissance de l'écrivain*. Paris: Éditions de Minuit.

Young, S. (2007). *The book is dead: long live the book*. Sydney: University of New South Wales Press.

ENDNOTE

[1]   With acknowledgement to Frank Moorhouse, 'From quill to keyboard,' *The Age,* June 3, 2007.

TABLE OF CASES

Acohs v. Ucorp (2010) FCA 577 (Austl.)

Desktop Marketing Systems Pty Ltd v. Telstra Corporation Ltd (2002) FCAFC 112; (2002) 119 FCR 491 (Austl.)

Donaldson v. Beckett (1774) 2 Bro.P.C. 129 (UK)

Fairfax Media Publications Pty Ltd v. Reed International Books Australia Pty Ltd (2010) FCA 984 (Austl.)

IceTV Pty Limited v. Nine Network Australia Pty Limited [2009] HCA 14 and [2009] 239 CLR (Austl.)

Telstra Corporation Limited v. Phone Directories Company Pty Ltd (2010) FCA 44 (Austl.)

Telstra Corporation Limited v. Phone Directories Company Pty Ltd (2010) FCAFC 149 (Austl.)

TABLE OF STATUTES

Berne Convention for the Protection of Literary and Artistic Works (9 September 1886, as amended on 28 September 1979)

Copyright Act 1968 (Cth)Copyright, Designs and Patents Act 1988 (UK)

Licensing Act 1662 (UK)

Statute of Anne 1709 (UK)

Chapter 5
Copyright Support Structures

ABSTRACT

This chapter deals with government and other support structures available to authors internationally and nationally in relation to the enforcement of their copyright and funding. It provides an overview of how the Australian government support structures interact with equivalent global structures and how these mechanisms are utilised to supplement authors' incomes. These structures rely on the premise that copyright law creates incentives for people to invest their time, talent, and other resources in the creation of new material that benefits society and include government support structures such as grants as well as licensing schemes such as the Copyright Agency Limited (CAL), Public Lending Rights (PLR), and Educational Lending Rights (ELR).

INTRODUCTION

The last chapter acknowledged the markedly changed public sphere compared with the creative environment of a century ago, when individualism was highly regarded and copyright protection paramount. In the 21st century authors face new challenges due to the borderless effect of the internet, especially with regard to copyright. This chapter deals briefly with support structures currently available to authors internationally and, on a national level, in relation to the enforcement of their copyright and funding. It provides an overview of how the Australian Government support structures interact with equivalent global structures and how these mechanisms are utilised to supplement authors' incomes.

DOI: 10.4018/978-1-4666-5214-9.ch005

INTERNATIONAL STRUCTURES

As discussed in Chapter 2, Australia is party to a number of international treaties that protect copyright material. The two most prominent of these are the Berne Convention for the Protection of Literary and Artistic Works (the Berne Convention) and the Universal Copyright Convention (UCC). The enforcement of rights under the Berne Convention and UCC is regulated by the Trade Related Aspects of Intellectual Property (TRIPS Agreement), which is managed by the World Trade Organisation (WTO).

The most relevant international organisations charged with upholding the provisions of these treaties in respect of Australian authors are the World Intellectual Property Organisation (WIPO) and the International Federation of Reproduction Rights Organisations (IFFRO) (Copyright Agency Limited, 2011). An outline of the functions of these organisations is provided below.

World Intellectual Property Organisation (WIPO)

WIPO is a specialised agency of the United Nations based in Geneva and charged with administering various international intellectual property instruments, which include the Berne Convention. It further establishes international norms and standards in respect of intellectual property, promotes the formation of new international treaties and the development of countries' intellectual property legislation (Copyright Agency Limited, 2011).

The WIPO agreements set minimum standards rather than prescribing optimal forms of copyright protection and membership is voluntary. Significantly, there are no formal mechanisms for the enforcement of WIPO agreements. Australia has been a member of WIPO since 1972 and is a signatory to a number of its treaties and conventions affecting copyright (Ergas, 2000). Whereas WIPO is primarily responsible for administering the Berne Convention, IFFRO plays a significant role in the promotion of reciprocal copyright licensing agreements between collecting agencies worldwide.

The Global Role of Collecting Agencies

Apart from the IFFRO's involvement, there is currently no international body dealing with the licensing of copyright use in different countries. However, reciprocal agreements exist between collecting agencies in Australia, New Zealand, the UK, the USA, South Africa and a number of other countries, whereby the licensing of copyright use is recognised and implemented (Nolan & Arcuili, 2010). In Australia the Copyright Agency Limited (CAL) is supportive of reciprocal recognition of licensing agreements with members of sister organisations in foreign countries (Copyright Agency Limited, 2011).

The role of collection agencies is essentially to license works for which they act as agents on behalf of their members for specific uses, monitor the use of those rights, collect revenue relating to use of the rights, distribute revenues as royalties to members and to enter into reciprocal arrangements with foreign collecting societies to collect and distribute local royalties to foreign rights holders and to receive and distribute royalties earned overseas to local rights holders. Reciprocity is also encouraged by international organisations such as the International Confederation of Societies of Authors and Composers (CISAC), the Bureau International des Sociétés Gérant les Droits D'Enregistrement et de Reproduction Mecanique (BIEM) (Caslon Analytics, 2003).

The increased recognition and protection of creators' rights, including those of authors, is regarded as a priority by CISAC. This organisation, a non-governmental, non-profit organization, with its headquarters in Paris and regional offices in Budapest, Santiago (Chile), Johannesburg and Singapore, was founded in 1926 (International Confederation of Societies of Authors and Composers (CISAC), 2010). Although the Australian Performing Rights Association (APRA – the Australian collection agency for the Performing Arts and Music), is a member of the CISAC, CAL is not a member of the organisation.

CAL is, however, a member of IFFRO, which has CAL's Chief Executive, Jim Alexander, as a member of its Board. The IFFRO's Mission Statement in respect of Reproduction Rights Organisations (RROs) promises to 'work to increase on an international basis the lawful use of text and image based copyright works and to eliminate unauthorised copying by promoting efficient Collective Management of rights through RROs to complement creators' and publishers' own activities' (International Federation of Reproductive Rights Organisations (IFFRO), 2010). In this regard, CAL, as the Australian RRO dealing with text based copyright work (including digital versions), represents Australian authors in respect of international licensing of their copyright.

GOVERNMENT SUPPORT STRUCTURES

In addition to the international structures and collecting agencies, various Australian Government support systems have been implemented to provide support for authors under the legislation.

The Australia Council

The Australia Council for the Arts (The Australia Council or The Council), an Australian Government statutory authority, was formed in 1968 as the Government's arts funding and advisory body (2013). The Council is regulated by the *Australia Council Act 1975*, which is administered by the Department of the Environment, Water, Heritage and the Arts. It is instrumental in funding various arts related organisations such as the Australian Copyright Council (ACC) and the Arts Law Centre, providing more than $158 million per annum for arts funding nationally. It supports Australian literature through the Literature Board, a division of the Australia Council, and invested in excess of $8.1 million into Australian literature during the 2008-2009 year in the form of grants to creators and financial support to operations that provide infrastructure to the sector (http://www.australiacouncil.gov.au).

The Council also researches and collects data on the arts and culture. In the Australia Council report *What's your other job? A census analysis of arts employment in Australia* (Cunningham & Higgs, 2010), dealing with the employment of artists (including authors) from different occupations in Australia, it was found that 'the arts have a much higher percentage of workers in part-time employment (44 per cent) compared to the workforce as a whole (32 per cent)' (Cunningham & Higgs, 2010, p. 5). It further stated: 'In real terms income levels within arts employment have risen. But this rise is not as great as the total workforce, which means that the 'negative income gap' between arts employment and the national average is now even greater.' Furthermore, average earnings in arts employment had remained constant from 1996-2006, at $37,000.00 per annum (Cunningham & Higgs, 2010, p. 4).

In a related study funded by the Australia Council, involving 120 occupations, including writers, dancers, musicians and visual artists, *Do you really expect to get paid: An economic study of professional artists in Australia* (Throsby & Zednik, 2010), it was acknowledged that 'the majority of artists cannot spend all their working time on their creative practice, and are obliged to seek income-earning work in other areas.' (Throsby & Zednik, 2010, p. 44). The study reported the mean earned income of writers in the financial year 2007/2008 as follows (2010, p. 45):

- Creative income (from principal artistic occupation): $11,100.
- Arts related income (from e.g. teaching): $8,100.
- Non-arts related income: $21,300.

These reports are discussed further in Chapter 10, within the context of the research findings.

The Council has been criticised by some commentators as having an 'archaic central role,' and there have been calls by these commentators to abolish the Council and focus on 'contemporary Australian culture' instead of 'heritage preservation.' Westbury argues that the Council 'has had little meaningful engagement with the digital cultural revolution' and that its structure and artistic focus is outdated (Westbury & Eltham, 2010, p. 41). In another article, Westbury argues that it should be the responsibility of the Australia Council to ensure that Australia is a nation of creators and not merely consumers of culture and to enable Australian creators to participate in an 'increasing globalised culture pool' (Westbury, 2010).

Cultural economist David Throsby agrees with this view and expresses the need for Australia Council to reform the way it operates and its funding responsibilities. He argues that Australia is in need of 'a new cultural agency that will fund the new and contemporary cultural expression the Australia Council won't' (Throsby & Zednik, 2010). These viewpoints take cognisance of the effects of digitalisation on the Australian arts and culture and seek to pursue Australian creativity as part of the greater public sphere of global arts and culture.

Australian Copyright Council (ACC)

The Australian Copyright Council, a non profit organisation also founded in 1968, provides information, publications and training on copyright in Australia, and makes submissions on copyright issues to Government based on its own research. The ACC is primarily funded by The Australia Council, deriving the balance of its funding from training programmes, publication sales, affiliation fees and consultancy fees. It describes its objectives as including assistance to creators to exercise their rights effectively, raising community awareness about the importance of copyright, researching and identifying areas of copyright law that are unfair, seeking changes to law to enhance the effectiveness of copyright and fostering cooperation amongst bodies representing creators and owners of copyright (Australian Copyright Council, 2011).

It aims to address topical issues and provides updates on copyright developments in its training seminars and addressed issues such as the Government 2.0 Taskforce Report of May 2010, the *Resale Royalty Rights for Visual Artists Act 2009*, the Government response to the Productivity Commission review of parallel importation of books and the Google Settlement at a seminar in June 2010 titled 'Hot Topics: Law, Policy and Business.' The seminar provided valuable insight into various contemporary copyright issues and considered copyright in a global, rather than a localised sphere (http://www.copyright.org.au). Its 2011 submissions have included submissions to the Book Industry Strategy Group and the Australian Government, regarding the National Cultural Policy and the role of copyright in the Australian Book Industry (Jones, 2011).

Arts Law Centre

Another body which provides assistance for authors is the not for profit Arts Law Centre of Australia, a national legal centre for the arts. This organisation was established with the support of the Australia Council in 1983 to provide specialised legal and business advice and professional development resources for creators and arts organisations (http://www.artslaw.com.au). It advises artists (including authors) on topics such as contracts, copyright, business structures, defamation, insurance and employment. For more complex enquiries, it provides referrals to a national referral panel. In addition, the Centre also publishes a range of materials for arts practitioners which include information sheets, sample contracts, seminar papers and booklets. An important function of the Arts Law Centre is to liaise with Government on the impact of Government policy on arts practice and to lobby for reform. Fundamentally, it aims to increase access to legal information about arts issues, with a special focus on advising indigenous artists on intellectual property issues and developing arts law expertise in the indigenous community (http://www.artslaw.com.au).

Copyright Agency Limited (CAL)

As noted above, CAL, a not-for-profit Australian organisation, commenced operations in 1986 to manage the copyright interests of authors (and other writers such as journalists) by assisting them to obtain payment for reproduction of their work by public institutions, including educational institutions, government and corporations. (Simpson, 1995, p. 19). Funded by the Australian Society of Authors and the Australian Book Publishers Association, two cases, namely *Moorhouse v. University of New South Wales* (1975) and *Haines v. Copyright Agency Ltd.* (1982) (and later also *CAL v. Department of Education* [1985]), were instrumental in establishing a rate of equitable remuneration for copying under the statutory licence for education in the *Copyright Act* and finally ensured compliance by educational institutions (Simpson, 1995, p. 19).

CAL offers voluntary membership to authors, who are invited to join the organisation free of charge, with the object of licensing the secondary (as opposed to primary) use of their work (Australian Copyright Council, 2011). CAL describes itself as 'a facilitator of access to content rather than a protector or enforcer,' a type of broker between users and creators. In May 2010, its membership stood at 16,000 members, which included 9,500 writers and artists and 6,500 publishers, evidencing a 300% growth since 1995 (Nolan & Arcuili, 2010).

CAL has been instrumental in setting guidelines for copying of copyright works on a commercial basis and promoting the compliant use of digital material, focussing mainly on non-fiction and educational content. Though not a legislative body, the organisation provides financial returns to both authors and publishers who have registered with it, marking an important innovation in the application of copyright law (Australian Copyright Council, 2011). Between 1989 and May 2010, CAL has paid over $650 million to members and received licensing income of $114 million in the 2009 financial year (Nolan & Arcuili, 2010).

Its monitoring system claims to provide a balance between accuracy, burden on staff and cost to CAL and operates by using sample surveys to monitor the use of material in electronic and hard copy form in schools and universities, by monitoring 4.2 million students (50,000 from universities). The university sampling includes eight universities per annum, six of which provide data on photocopying and electronic usage and two of which only provide electronic data. Each year 280 schools in urban and rural areas, 15 TAFEs and six community colleges are surveyed.

Internationally, CAL has relationships with sister collecting agencies in the USA, UK, South Africa and a host of non-English speaking countries. These arrangements allow members to distribute content worldwide without requiring foreign agents. CAL also supports a Cultural Fund locally, to which approximately $100,000.00 per annum is allocated. This fund supports individual creators and organisations in their creative efforts, as well as projects 'which enhance the economic and creative climate' (Nolan & Arcuili, 2010).

CAL does not regulate usage (copying) in public libraries, where section 40 of the *Copyright Act 1968* is applicable, allowing people to copy 10% or one chapter or article of a work. In the *Simpson Report*, the difficulties of achieving a balance between accuracy, burden on staff and cost to the collecting agency is explained as follows:

Until technology gives us this capability to capture all information, such processes will be imperfect. Until then, we will have to rely upon sampling techniques, approximation techniques; a balance between the absurd cost of obtaining perfect records and the aim of getting as much money to as many of the right people as possible. Collection too, is an expensive and inherently inefficient aspect of collecting societies (Simpson, 1995, p. 16).

According to Moorhouse the formation of CAL enhanced not only authors' economic base, but also their cultural base, due to its commitment to tie the writer's income not to a grant system but to the use of the book in the economy. He saw it as operating on an equitable basis, in measuring the ways a book was used in the economy, identifying the income derived from that use, collecting the income accordingly and returning it to the copyright owner (Sexton, 2007, p. 7).

Public Lending Rights (PLR) and Educational Lending Rights (ELR)

In 1985, the *Public Lending Rights Act* was promulgated to compensate authors for the loss of potential sales due to their books being available for free use in public libraries. This act was complemented by the Educational Lending Rights scheme which provided for similar compensation in the case of libraries in educational institutions. The schemes are administered by the Australian Government Department 'Environment, Water, Heritage and the Arts,' and came about as a result of the landmark case *University of NSW v. Moorhouse* (1975) and the Franki Report (1976), referred to above.

In the *Moorhouse* case, the UNSW was found liable for authorising the infringement of Moorhouse's copyright in an anthology of his short stories because it provided unsupervised photocopying machines in its libraries, which were used to make infringing copies. The case, together with the Franki Report (1976), caused the *Copyright Act 1968* to be amended and to include a provision in section 39A that all libraries should have a copyright notice prominently displayed (Sexton, 2007, p. 9).

Australia is one of 25 countries that operate a PLR programme. PLR payments are determined by the estimated number of copies of eligible books which are held in the Australian public lending libraries. Eligible books are those that have been allocated an International Standard Book Number (ISBN), been published and offered for sale, have an identifiable creator or creators, not exceeding five, and a catalogue record in a national bibliographic database. This information is obtained from an annual survey of the books held in a sample of public lending libraries selected by the Australian Bureau of Statistics. Payment is only made if 50 or more copies of an eligible book are estimated to be held in Australian public lending libraries (Ministry for the Arts, 2011).

Books are surveyed annually for three consecutive financial years following their year of publication. If, in the third year, a book is still held in sufficient numbers in public lending libraries, it will be resurveyed every three years. Books scoring less than 50 copies in the third or subsequent surveys are dropped from the survey cycle. The PLR payments are calculated as follows: separate payment rates are determined each year for creators and publishers, and these are published in the PLR scheme. If there is more than one eligible creator of a book, each receives a PLR payment in proportion to their share of the royalty payments. The scheme provides that amounts of less than $50.00 are not payable (Ministry for the Arts, 2011).

The amount of a PLR payment for a book is calculated by multiplying the relevant PLR rate of payment by the estimated number of copies of the book. The PLR rates of payment under the 2009-2010 PLR scheme were $1.66 per copy of each eligible book for creators and 41.5 cents per copy of each eligible book for publishers (Bell, 2010).

ELR complements the PLR scheme and allows for payments to eligible Australian creators and publishers whose books are held in educational libraries, such as school, TAFE and university libraries on the basis that income is lost from the availability of their books in these libraries. Eligible creators are defined as authors, editors, illustrators, translators and compilers who are Australian citizens, wherever they reside; or non-citizens who are normally resident in Australia. The Minister or his/her delegate may approve final payment in the financial year in which a creator died, after which books cease to be eligible (Ministry for the Arts, 2011). As in the case of PLR payments, where the payment is below the minimum of $50.00, no payment is made (Bell, 2010).

Eligible publishers are publishers whose business consists wholly or substantially of the publication of books and who regularly (at least once in the preceding two-year period) publish in Australia, Australian non-profit organisations or creators who self-publish. ELR payments only apply to books published in Australia, where an eligible creator is also entitled to payment for a book (Ministry for the Arts, 2011). The ELR rates of payment under the 2009-2010 ELR scheme are shown in Table 1.

Table 1. Total equivalent no. of book copies rates of payment (Bell, 2010)

	Creator	Publisher
First 50	$1.00	25 cents
51 – 500	58.5 cents	14.625 cents
501 – 5 000	38.5 cents	9.625 cents
5,001 – 50,000	15.886 cents	3.97155 cents
More than 50,000	9.24776 cents	2.31194 cents

Although the PLR and ELR schemes were not regarded as copyright-based schemes but rather as an Australian Government cultural program (Bell, 2010), they are relevant in examining the Government support structures available to authors to earn an income from their work. The fact that the payments are made to rights holders (authors and publishers), would indicate that copyright was a relevant consideration in the establishment of these schemes.

OTHER SUPPORT STRUCTURES

In addition to Government support structures, Australian authors have the benefit of a number of writers' organisations, which includes State based and regional Writers' Centres and informal writers' groups. The Australian Society of Authors' (ASA) website lists 17 Writers' Centres (Our partners, 2011); however, an internet search reveals approximately 52 Writers' Centres on record in Australia.

A discussion of these support structures falls outside the scope of this book; however, an organisation which merits some recognition here and played a pivotal role in this research process, is the Australian Society of Authors Limited, which is the professional association for Australia's literary creators. The ASA was formed in 1963 with the aim of promoting and protecting the rights of Australia's writers and illustrators, and now has approximately 3000 members across Australia. The ASA was also instrumental in setting up the Copyright Agency Limited and the Australian Copyright Council, and successfully campaigned for Public Lending Rights in 1975 and Educational Lending Rights in 2000 (Australian Society of Authors, *History*, 2011).

The ASA regards itself as an advocate for the rights of professional authors and is recognised as an important contributor to the Australian literary culture, campaigning for authors' rights on issues such as tax relief measures, public funding for authors and 'fair treatment and pay' (Loukakis, 2011, p. 2). Significantly, it provides free information sheets for authors on issues such as minimum rates, ebook royalties and contracts and guidelines on getting published, as well as precedent author/publisher contracts, which are discussed in Chapter 6.

CONCLUSION

This chapter has provided a brief overview of international copyright structures as well as Australian Government agencies and schemes which support authors in their creative work. The benefits provided to authors by these programmes, such as the CAL, PLR and ELR licensing schemes are evident and signify an effort on the part of government to recognise the importance of financial rewards for creators. Chapters 8 and 10 investigate how authors have benefited from these resources, and whether they regard the support structures as adequate for their needs.

REFERENCES

Australia Council for the Arts. (2013). *About*. Retrieved from http://www. australiacouncil.gov.au/about

Australian Copyright Council. (2011). *About us*. Retrieved from http://www. copyright.org.au/about-us/

Australian Society of Authors. (2011). [from https://asauthors.org/history]. *History (Historical Association (Great Britain))*, (January): 10. Retrieved December 10, 2010

Australian Society of Authors. (2011). *Our partners*. Retrieved December 10, 2010 & January 10, 2011, from https://asauthors.org/our-partners

Caslon Analytics. (2003, June). *Caslon analytics collecting societies*. Retrieved July 12, 2008 and October 9, 2010 from www.caslon.com.au/ipguide3.htm

Copyright Agency Limited. (2010). *International copyright: Treaties and organisations*. Retrieved September 16, 2010, from http://www.copyright. com.au/get-information/about-copyright/international-copyright-treaties-and-organisations

Cunningham, S., & Higgs, P. (2010). *What's your other job? A census analysis of arts employment in Australia (Research Report)*. Sydney: Australia Council for the Arts.

Ergas, H. (2000). *Review of intellectual property legislation under the competition principles agreement (Final Report)*. Canberra, Australia: Intellectual Property and Competition Review Committee.

Franki, R. (1976). *Report of the copyright law committee on reprographic reproduction (Research Report)*. Canberra, Australia: Government of Australia.

International Confederation of Societies of Authors and Composers (CISAC). (2010). *About CISAC*. Retrieved October 9, 2010, from http://www.cisac.org/ CisacPortal/page.do?name=rubrique.1.1

International Federation of Reproductive Rights Organisations (IFFRO). (2010). *Homepage*. Retrieved October 9, 2010, from http://www.ifrro.org

Jones, B. (2011). *Book industry strategy group report (Research Report)*. Canberra, Australia: Government of Australia.

Loukakis, A. (2011, June). ASA advocacy – 2011 and beyond. *ASA Newsletter*, 4.

Ministry for the Arts, Australian Government Attorney-General's Department. (2011). *Lending rights*. Retrieved June 5, 2011, from http://arts.gov.au/literature/lending-rights/guidelines

Nolan, E., & Arcuili, R. (2010, May 25). *CAL today*. Brisbane, Australia: CAL Seminar.

Sexton, C. (2007). In conversation with Frank Moorhouse. *IPSANZ IP Forum, 68,* 6.

Simpson, S. (1995). *Review of Australian collection societies report*. Canberra, Australia: Government of Australia.

Throsby, D., & Zednik, A. (2010). *Do you really expect to get paid? An economic study of professional artists in Australia (Research Report)*. Strawberry Hills, Australia: Australia Council for the Arts.

Westbury, M. (2010, July 26). Has the Australia council had its day? *The Age*. Retrieved September 12, 2010, from http://www.theage.com.au/entertainment/art-and-design/has-the-australia-council-had-its-day-20100725-10qgt.html

Westbury, M., & Eltham, B. (2010). Cultural policy in Australia. In M. Davis & M. Lyons (Eds.), *More than luck: Ideas Australia needs now* (pp. 103-110). Retrieved on September 12, 2010, from http://morethanluck.cpd.org.au/wp-content/uploads/2010/06/MTL_InHousePrint_webcopy2.pdf

TABLE OF CASES

Copyright Agency Ltd v. Queensland Department of Education & Others (2002) 54 IPR 19

Haines v. Copyright Agency Ltd [1982] FCA 137; 64 FLR 184

Moorhouse v. University of new South Wales (1975) HCA 26; (1975) 133 CLR 1

TABLE OF STATUTES

Australia Council Act 1975 (Cth)

Copyright Act 1968 (Cth)

Chapter 6
The Publishing Industry

ABSTRACT

This chapter examines the current evolving publishing framework in Australia and the relationship between authors and their publishers, noting the competing interests of the various subaltern spheres (such as the "author sphere" and "publisher sphere") within the greater public sphere. A comparison between a standard publisher's contract and the model contract recommended by the Australian Society of Authors (ASA) provides a source for analysis and discussion, which relevantly reflects the nature of the relationship between author and publisher. The issue of digital publishing is investigated to ascertain what constitutes an equitable arrangement for authors. Finally, new business models in publishing are considered and observations are made on copyright protection measures on the Internet, alternative licensing models such as the Creative Commons and the "honesty box" model used by some authors. A brief discussion of the anti-copyright actions of Google is also included, and in conclusion, the author-publisher power balance is addressed, taking into account the different characteristics of print books and ebooks.

DOI: 10.4018/978-1-4666-5214-9.ch006

INTRODUCTION

The book is dead. Long live the book. - Sherman Young

In addition to support structures available to Australian authors and the impact of the public sphere environment within which they function, issues such as the publishing industry and the business models used to monetise authors' copyright are important considerations when examining the third research question concerning Australian authors' views on the changing nature of the publishing industry and how they have been affected by advances in this area.

In this chapter the position of the author in relation to the publishing industry will be examined in three sections. The first part deals with publishing agreements and the relationship between author and publisher; the second part investigates current innovations in the publishing industry and the third section considers copyright options in emerging business models and the different ways in which copyright protection is being implemented electronically. It also considers whether the changing publishing models have brought about a shift of power in the author-publisher relationship.

Theorists have been examining the future of the book and have debated whether the book is in danger of being replaced by hypertext and digital technology for some years (Nunberg, 1996, p. 104; Young, 2007, p. 8). It is therefore important to investigate the changes that are occurring in the publishing industry as a result of the democratised space of the Internet, and consider how authors are being affected by these changes.

It is suggested that American writer Mark Twain's 1909 publishing contract was the first contract to make provision for electronic rights. The handwritten agreement provided that his publisher received the rights to publish his memoir 'in whatever mode should then be prevalent, that is by printing as at present or by use of phonographic cylinders, or by electrical methods, or by any other method which may be in use' (Jassin, 2010).

In the contemporary publishing environment there are many instances where publishers do not own the electronic rights to published novels and authors are self-publishing electronic versions of best-sellers. Examples are Ian Fleming's James Bond novels, which his estate is self-publishing in electronic form, and author Ian McEwan, who was able to utilise the digital rights to his back catalogue through Amazon.com, separately from previously negotiated publishing rights (Young, 2010).

PUBLISHING AGREEMENTS

The publishing agreement is generally regarded by authors as the author's means of protecting his/her copyright. Loukakis refers to it as 'a legal document that controls publication of a book,' pointing out that for a publishing contract to be meaningful, the most important word in this definition is 'control' (2011, p. 28). Publishers, however, generally view the publishing agreement as a means of outlining the terms and conditions of their contract with the author, as seen below. Historically the publishing agreement has been used to regulate the relationship between author and publisher, usually in respect of a printed book, article or other piece of written work, regulating the respective parties' rights and prescribing contractual issues such as royalty payments, reversionary rights and so forth.

This relationship still exists; however, technological change has caused a paradigm shift in the previously accepted norms and expectations of the publishing contract, as will be shown below. Electronic rights have become an important consideration in such contracts, whilst they previously merited a perfunctorily mention, or were entirely absent, in the case of older contracts. This issue will be discussed later in the chapter.

These changes have not only affected publishing contracts, but have also impacted on the publisher/author relationship. Authors now have access to a broader range of publishing options, no longer relying solely on mainstream print publishing, with access to electronic publishing through online publishers, small publishing houses and self-publishing, as discussed in the next section.

TRADITIONAL PUBLISHING AND THE AUTHOR/PUBLISHER RELATIONSHIP

The traditional publishing contract remains the main instrument of copyright regulation between authors and publishers. In this section the traditional publishing industry and copyright issues are discussed with reference to the author/publisher relationship. Loukakis states that 'authors have traditionally tended to be accommodating or naïve in their dealings over contracts, allowing much to slide away from them, seemingly in exchange for the guarantee of a publisher's advance and in the hope of further royalty payments' (2011, p. 28).

It is important to view the publishing agreement in context when undertaking a critical examination of this perception, and take into account the public sphere within which it is created, where the publisher (and financier) is in control and the author may be in a subordinate position. This may differ where a bestselling author is involved; however, in most instances the publisher provides the contract and stipulates the contract terms.

As pointed out in Chapter 3, the author functions in a literary sphere which is underpinned by economic and political considerations, which inevitably have a determining influence on the power of the author to negotiate publishing contracts. The publisher, on the one hand, is generally driven by economic forces and is required to profit from its endeavours, or perish. These circumstances inevitably influence the author/publisher relationship and provide the basis upon which a publishing contract is negotiated. As is evident from the examples discussed below, conflicts may arise between the interests of authors and publishers.

Authors such as Godwin point out that the copyright system was created, not to enrich authors or publishers, but to enrich the public sphere. He therefore notes that disputes between authors and publishers that take work out of the public sphere (irrespective of which party wins), cause the public to lose, and should thus be avoided (Godwin, 2001).

In examining the author-publisher relationship, a distinction may be made between different types of publishers. The Australian Society of Authors (ASA) distinguishes between three categories of publishers: commercial publishers (such as HarperCollins, Penguin, Allen & Unwin, Text, Scribe or UNSW Press); self-publishers such as authors or organisations taking on the role of publisher themselves, at their own cost: and vanity publishers, who take money from someone else (usually the author) in order to publish a book. The ASA Website cautions against the use of vanity publishers (who may call themselves 'partnership' or 'subsidy' publishers), who have no motivation to market and sell copies of a book as they exist on the fees charged to the payee author (2011).

In the present discussion the focus is on authors' relationships with commercial or mainstream publishers and how these relationships are managed, including a consideration of self publishing options.

TRADITIONAL PUBLISHING CONTRACTS

The authorial premise of the publishing contract has been described as 'a balance between the substantial investment of the writer's work and the financial and professional investment by the publisher' (Victoria Writers' Centre, 2011). This viewpoint takes into account the interests of both parties and is a valid basis on which to negotiate a mutually beneficial contract.

Publishers, however, often use standardised contracts, also known as 'boilerplate' contracts and are sometimes reluctant to change their standard provisions (Jassin, 2010). However, these contracts can be negotiated and negotiability will largely depend on the relationship between the publisher and author, the standing of the author and the contractual terms involved. It is understandable that a best-selling author will have considerably more scope to negotiate more favourable terms than a novice or unknown author.

Furthermore, in many cases standard contracts or clauses have been negotiated between publishers and professional associations and are practically non-negotiable as far as the author is concerned (Victoria Writers' Centre, 2011). To gain a better understanding of the terms of the 'standard publisher's contract' as opposed to the standard contract which the ASA recommends, a comparison between such a 'standard contract' and the template contract provided by the ASA, is drawn in the next section.

Standard Publisher's Contract vs. the ASA Recommended Contract

The comparison of a 'standard contract' (SC) of a mainstream publisher with a Model Publishing Agreement Template (ASAC) provided by the ASA, has revealed some discrepancies between what the ASA regards as a 'fair and equitable publishing agreement,' and the actual contents of a standard agreement. It must be noted that the 'standard contract' referred to in this discussion is an example of a standard contract used by a major Australian publisher and cannot be used to draw generalisations. Furthermore, it would be expected that the publisher's contract would favour the publisher and that the ASA contract would be pro-author, and the comparison is made on this premise. There are a number of clauses commonly used by mainstream publishers that merit discussion; however, this examination will focus on a few copyright related clauses which reflect the apparent conflict in the contractual approaches of the publisher and the representative author body, the ASA.

Rights/Licence

Significantly, the SC makes provision for the publisher to be granted the sole right and license to publish and sell the author's work, (including in ebook form or any abridgement), and to sublicense it **'for the legal period of copyright and throughout the World.'** In contrast, the ASAC suggests a clause that grants the publisher **a two year licence to publish and sell the work in the Territory**, which is specifically defined. The difference in approach is evident, especially as the legal period of copyright is usually until the death of the author plus seventy years.

Warranties and Indemnities

Whereas the ASAC include a clause to the effect that the author warrants that *'to the best of his/her knowledge the work contains nothing defamatory,'* the publisher's SC is much more far-reaching. It provides that the author warrants that *nothing in the work is defamatory or in breach of any law,* and that the author fully *indemnifies the publisher against all losses, damages, suits, claims, proceedings and expenses which may be made or taken against the publisher as a result of a breach of this warranty.*

From the publisher's perspective it could be argued that this is a reasonable protection; however, the author may argue that it is inequitable to require such an extensive warranty, which requires legal knowledge or advice. It is suggested that the publisher should be in a position to alert the author to any concerns about possible breaches of the law, and particularly, copyright in the work, before publication and afford him/her an opportunity to address any issues raised.

Remainders

Remainders can be defined as copies of the book sold at or below manufacturing price. The SC provides that the publisher may sell any surplus stock of the printed book as a remainder *after one year from first publication.* In contrast, the ASAC suggests that the period should be **t***wo years after first publication* and that the author should have the *right of first refusal to buy remainder stock.*

Because the author receives no income from books sold as at or below manufacturing price, authors would benefit from the longer period; however, publishers would argue that such an arrangement may impact negatively on their cash-flow.

Revision Clause

The ASAC advises that the contract should include a Revision Clause but does not provide a precedent (example) clause. In the publisher's SC a clause dealing with *'Revised Future Editions'* provides that the author agrees to update and correct the book should the publisher decide to publish a revised edition in the future. It goes further to say that, if the author declines or is unable to do so, the publisher *may employ someone else to do so and deduct the expense from any money due to the author under the agreement.*

It is suggested that this clause appears to be unreasonably onerous on the author, requiring an unspecified amount of work at the author's cost, especially in the case of academic textbooks or other books that require extensive updates.

Moral Rights

The issue of moral rights is regulated by Part IX of the *Copyright Act 1968* (Cth) *(as amended)*; however, in terms of Section 195AWA there is no infringement of the author's moral rights if the author has consented in writing to any acts or omissions relating to these rights. Such rights include the right to have the work attributed to the author, not to treat it in a derogatory manner, including not changing the work without the author's consent.

In the ASAC a *'Moral Rights'* clause is included which deals with these rights and in a further clause, *'Alterations,'* it is specifically provided that *no alterations be made to the title of the work without the author's consent.* There may be some difficulty reconciling this suggested clause with a clause in the SC which provides that, although the publisher agrees to consult with the author on the title, cover text, biographical note and cover design, *the publisher reserves the right to make the final decision on all such matters.* This means that the author, in signing the SC, is effectively consenting to the possible act of an involuntary title change, which otherwise would have been a breach of his/her moral rights.

Royalties

In respect of royalties it is significant that the ASA cautions against including a provision for royalties to be paid on the *'publisher's net receipts'* (which is the Recommended Retail Price (RRP) less the publisher's discount to booksellers), stating that royalties should be payable on the *RRP* instead.

However, the publisher's SC bases royalties on *'net receipts (being the actual sum received by the Publisher),'* and not on the RRP. This discrepancy means that, although both contracts make provision for royalties of 10% to be paid on the first 4,000 copies sold, the financial outcome to the author would be substantially lower in terms of the SC than the recommended ASAC.

Furthermore, the SC determines that a royalty of *10% of the publisher's net receipts will be payable on all electronic sales,* whereas the ASAC includes a provision that a royalty of *25% of the RRP be paid on all electronic sales (ebooks).* This appears to be a significant difference, and it is submitted that the ASAC provision is more equitable, considering the reduced printing costs to the publisher.

It is noted that royalties may be negotiable depending on the standing of the author and/or the tenacity of his/her agent in the negotiation process, as pointed out by some of the interviewees in Chapter 9. Furthermore, due to the increased publishing options for authors, it is likely that publishers will have to adapt to the marketplace and reconsider (and increase) electronic sales royalties for authors.

Publisher's Liability

The ASAC includes a clause holding the publisher *responsible for the safe-keeping of manuscripts in the publisher's possession* and insuring against the loss or damage of the manuscript, with an undertaking to pay the author the replacement costs in such event and the agreed royalties on any lost or destroyed copies.

In contrast the publisher's SC provides that the publisher will take reasonable care but *will not be responsible for any accidental loss or damage* to material provided by the author. It is submitted that this indemnification is unfair to the author who has entrusted the publisher with his/her manuscript and prompts questions about publishers' risk and insurance.

Minimum Print Run and Approximate Price

The ASA advises that a contract should make provision for a *minimum print run and approximate price* for the book; however, such a clause is absent from the SC, apart from the following provision: *'The Publisher shall be responsible for publication of the Work and all details concerning production, design, paper, printing, binding, jackets, covers, manner and extent of advertisements, price, terms of sale and methods and conditions of sale....'*

This clause appears to authorise the publisher to deal with printing and price in its own discretion, without consultation with the author. One would have anticipated that such crucial considerations would form part of a standard contract.

Accounting

The ASA militates against accounts (royalty payments) being rendered by publishers on an annual basis, instead proposing *six monthly statements and monthly sales reports*. However, the publisher's SC provides for the first two accounts of sales (royalty payments) to extend to 30 June and 31 December following the date of first publication, and thereafter *annually, with no monthly reports*. Furthermore, whilst the ASA recommended settlement time of such accounts to the author is *one month,* the SC provides for a *three-month* settlement period. This arrangement favours the publisher to the disadvantage of the author, who is then paid only once annually, three months in arrears.

In considering the two sample contracts with regard to the clauses discussed above, it is evident that there are some discrepancies between the ideal publishing contract terms promoted by the ASA and the actual standard contract terms used by mainstream publishers. It is significant that several of the clauses, such as the method of calculating royalties and the accounting methods, appear to be financially biased in favour of the publisher. In fact, in comparing the contracts it is submitted here that there is strong evidence to suggest that the expectations of authors are seldom, if ever, met, and that the standard publisher's contract favours the publisher in most, if not all respects. This trend suggests a lack of power on the part of authors vis-à-vis publishers.

It should further be acknowledged that book publishing is in a constant state of flux, especially with the introduction of new publishing models and licencing options, where other considerations (such as ease of self-publication, or conversely, a lack of technological skills on authors' part) may create a new set of considerations in setting up publishing agreements.

DIGITAL CONSIDERATIONS

Due to the significant increase in the distribution of ebooks, the ASA issued guidelines and suggested clauses for authors in relation to electronic book (ebook) royalty arrangements in its paper 'E-Books: Royalties and Contracts' (Loukakis, 2010) during November 2010. The paper dealt with ebook royalty clauses in digital publishing agreements, revision of current publishing agreements and advice for authors self-publishing ebook versions of their books. Whether authors have been able to implement these suggestions has varied, depending on authors' profiles and their digital literacy, as is evident from the author interviews discussed in future chapters.

As early as September 2009 Dan Brown's bestselling novel *The Lost Symbol* sold more electronic copies on Kindle than printed copies on Amazon (Associated Press, 2009). Significantly, on 20 May 2011 News Limited reported that ebook sales on Amazon had already surpassed hardcover sales in 2010 and that since 1 April 2011, it had sold 105 electronic Kindle books for every 100 physical books (NewsCore, 2011). According to unaudited figures released by the company in 2012, this figure increased to 114 ebooks for every 100 printed books by 6 August 2012 (Malik, 2012).

Loukakis predicted that, according to projections, ebooks would comprise 25-50% of all books sold within 15 years, and 20-25% of all books sold in Australia within 5 years. In July 2010, figures showed that ebooks comprised 5% of all books sold in Australia. Authors were cautioned to proceed carefully in contractual negotiations with publishers regarding ebooks (Loukakis, 2010, p. 1). Some of the salient issues raised by the ASA are examined below.

In respect of *royalties* the ASA pointed out that ebooks were cheaper to buy than print books, which meant lower revenues for publishers, and accordingly, less money for authors. The report further drew attention to the fact that there was a difference between the 'list' price (similar to the RRP) and the 'sell' price, i.e. the price to the consumer. A common 'sell' price for ebooks on Amazon (which accounted for 80% of ebook sales during 2009), would be US$9.99, instead of the higher 'list' price of the ebook (Loukakis, 2010, pp. 1-2).

Different companies favour different distribution models for ebooks. For example, currently the common royalty split between Amazon and publishers provides that 60% of the list price is paid to the publisher and 40% to Amazon. Apple, however, remits 70% of the list price to the publisher and retains 30%. The author then, in both instances, receives a fixed percentage of the publisher's share, which varies depending on the publisher (Loukakis, 2010, p. 3).

In their paper, the ASA recommended, for locally authored printed books also selling as ebooks, a minimum royalty return of (35% of 100%) to authors, of the publisher's 60% share of the list price. Alternatively, it was suggested that any return that was equivalent to the same dollar return on a printed book in a bookshop, would be acceptable. However, there was evidence of royalty rates for ebooks as low as 7% of the publisher's net receipts [i.e. 7% of (the publisher's 60% share minus expenses)], at the time of publication of the paper. This was regarded as unacceptably low, especially in view of the lower production costs associated with ebooks in comparison with printed versions.

According to Loukakis, it appeared that major publishers were generally offering authors 25% of their net receipts (2010, p. 5). However, the standard publisher's contract discussed above only allows for 10% of net receipts, considerably less than suggested by the ASA paper. The discrepancy might be accounted for by contracts which deal with ebooks *as part of the publishing deal* alongside print books, in which the percentage is the same for both versions (i.e. the standard 10%), and ebooks *as the only level of publication* (which was higher than 10% but still variable).

'Pay per view' options were also addressed, as publishers are able to display electronic contents in a variety of ways, such as PDF files (converted from a pre-existing Word document) and ePub files, and may make such files available for viewing online for a fee. The ASA proposed that the author should receive at least 50% of the proceeds as the PDF file would already be in existence for the printed book in any event, obviating the need to incur further format production costs, usually required for ePub files used for ebooks (Loukakis, 2010, p. 6). However, the publisher may argue that even though the cost of making the file available is lower than that of an ePub file, such 'rental' sales are the result of the publisher's negotiation and implementation, and should be viewed as an additional source of income for the author, which otherwise would not have occurred.

An important consideration for the ASA when dealing with *ebook royalties* was that ebook rights should be regarded as a 'primary right' and not a 'subsidiary right.' It was noted that the escalation of ebooks from a 'secondary' to a more prominent form of publication, should be reflected in the terms of existing publishing contracts, and that existing contracts should be amended to outline these rights specifically (Loukakis, 2010, p. 8). This is a valid concern, in view of the past treatment of electronic rights as evidenced in the sample agreement referred to above, in terms of which the publisher would only be paying a 10% royalty on net receipts for electronic versions of the work, although the production costs to the publisher are far lower than with printed books.

In recent years, the release pattern of a book has typically been that a print book would be issued first, to be followed by an ebook some 12-36 months later, once sales were reducing. However, it was evident that the ebook as the initial publication was becoming a more frequent occurrence, with indications of rapid growth. The ASA envisaged, from early patterns, that ebooks would constitute as much as 50% of all books sold in a generation, with Loukakis predicting - as noted above - that ebooks would comprise 25-50% of all books sold within 15 years (2010, p. 7). In its precedent draft contract the ASA made provision for the author to receive '50-80% of the list price OR the selling price (whichever is the higher) on each copy sold' (Loukakis, 2010, p. 11).

Loukakis conceded that there was presently insufficient data available to predict the life-span of 'born digital' book and the revenues to be generated by such a book: however, the ASA held firmly that authors should be 'paid adequately' for their work and that sufficient advances should be paid to authors, reflecting the reduced costs of ebook production as opposed to printed books (2010, pp. 7-8).

Significantly, for Australian authors (as in the case of the UK and USA), *territorial rights* are still in existence, as discussed in Chapter 2. The ASA cautioned authors to ensure these rights remained protected, and that ebook rights be managed in conjunction with print rights, so that the author's rights were not undermined in other territories (Loukakis, 2010, p. 9). However, it must be noted here that authors would find this advice more and more difficult to implement, considering the global reach of the online book market, which makes it unlikely for any publisher to accept a book for print without securing the world rights.

It was further suggested by Loukakis that the *moral rights* clause (or associated clause) in the publishing agreement should reflect the possible extraction and misuse of material in electronic download or ebook format. This would cover the unauthorised copying, re-arranging and reuse of an author's digital work, which could potentially infringe his/her moral rights by affecting the integrity of the work (Loukakis, 2010, p. 6). Such a clause would ensure that publishers remain alert to possible moral right infringements and guard against them when making the work available electronically.

It was noted that certain Australian-based 'trade' and 'print' publishers were paying insufficient attention to the quality of their electronic files, ignoring authors' rights regarding the integrity of their work by failing to provide authors with final copies of the work before these works were distributed (Loukakis, 2010, p. 1). According to Loukakis, this could lead to a 'derogation' of their work, which would be a breach of a critical provision in the *Copyright Act* (2010, p. 1).

The ASA paper levelled the following criticism at publishers:

Simply because a new process is being used to deliver a book to the public, this should not mean that publishers relax any of their usual standards. Having relinquished the control of this type of book (i.e. not doing it in-house), they seem to be ... losing essential quality control (Loukakis, 2010, p. 1).

It is suggested here that these complaints may be described as the result of a combination of 'teething problems' and a lack of control and sufficient motivation on the part of the publishers involved. It is quite possible that these difficulties will be resolved in the future, but that such resolution would be aided by including contractual terms binding the publisher specifically in respect of preserving the author's moral rights. Shortly before submission of this book, it was announced that the ASA will be releasing a *Model E-Publishing Agreement Template* late in 2011, which will greatly assist authors in assessing electronic contracts offered to them by publishers.

In this discussion, the recommendations of the ASA have been used as an example of the 'ideal' publishing contract from the author's point of view, in contrast with an actual standard contract used by a major publisher. It is noted that these 'standard contracts' may vary depending on the author, the publication and the publisher; however, the example used here represents an actual contract that is currently in use. Whilst this research is not primarily concerned with the viewpoints of publishers, a mainstream publisher's comments on these issues will be discussed in Chapter 9.

After examining the issues raised by the ASA, the further question then arises: What happens when a contract has not envisaged the possibility of electronic publication, or has dealt with it inadequately? As mentioned above, British authors such as McEwan have seized the opportunity to renegotiate their digital rights or (as in the case of the Fleming estate) self publish their ebooks.

Often, where a contract is ambiguous as to the intention of the parties, it may fall to the Court to decide what the parties intended. The Court, in such a case, will take into consideration industry practice and whether distribution of books in digital form was recognised by knowledgeable people in the industry when the contract was drafted. They will also look for limiting provisions regarding publication, but will not infer a grant of future technology rights unless the technology was known at the time of the agreement (Jassin, 2010). This approach is likely to be followed in Australia, being consistent with the principles applied in the construction of contracts in Australian Contract Law. Australian Contract Law requires that the contract is considered in context, taking into account the background knowledge available to the parties at the time the contract was concluded (Seddon & Ellinghaus, 2002, pp. 404-405).

There have also been emerging cases between authors and publishers as to who owned the digital rights in a work, the most relevant of which was the US *Random House Inc. v. Rosetta Books* (2002) case, where it was held that a licence to exploit a work in book form did not include ebook rights. In that case Random House had sued Rosetta Books, claiming that the defendant had infringed upon its rights by publishing electronic versions of the books of three authors contracted to Random House. The authors had granted Random House exclusive publishing rights in respect of their books, but then granted Rosetta Books the right to publish digital editions of their books. Random House failed in their application for a preliminary injunction, and on appeal, the judgment was confirmed. The Court found that the law which governed the scope of Random House's contracts, had 'adopted a restrictive view of the kinds of 'new uses' to which an exclusive licence may apply when the contracting parties do not expressly provide for coverage of such future forms' (2002 at 283). Whilst there is no Australian case law on the issue to date, it would be expected that Australian courts will follow a similar approach, in accordance with established Australian Contract Law principles (Seddon & Ellinghaus, 2002, pp. 404-405).

A CHANGING INDUSTRY: PUBLISHING OPTIONS FOR AUTHORS

The digital revolution has increased publishing options for authors but has brought with it its own unique challenges. As discussed in Chapter 4, the definition of authorship has been affected by these changes, adding to the challenges posed to copyright by the blurring of territorial borders, as noted in Chapter 2. Authors and publishers are having to revise traditional print expectations due to digital publication options, which have impacted on the printed book market. Furthermore, the cost of traditional printing and marketing has, in many instances, been replaced by electronic set-up costs and Internet marketing cost considerations.

Ebooks and Ereaders

With the emergence of ebooks there has been a corresponding interest in the use of ereaders such as Kindle, Kobo, Sony and various hand-held reading devices, as well as devices such as the iPad. As discussed above, the increasing popularity of electronic reading devices has given rise to a growing concern about the future existence of the printed book. However, some commentators are firmly of the view that new technologies will save and reinvigorate the book culture by capturing the essence of the book through computer-based creativity (Young, 2007, p. 9).

Other theorists express the viewpoint that the book is merely the vessel that contains the creative work, and that this vessel is interchangeable. John Perry Barlow states: '…one of the side effects of digital technology is that it makes those containers irrelevant…So whereas we thought we had been in the wine business, suddenly we realized that all along we've been in the bottling business' (1992). This viewpoint was supported by Nunberg, who viewed the printed book as an important part of the 'digital revolution' and saw no reason why the digital library should replace the brick-and-mortar library (1996, pp. 103-104). Young describes a book as a *technology* or a *system,* and argues that the publishing industry, by virtue of its creation of books, defines what a book is (2007, pp. 22-26). He also points out that *book culture* is what distinguishes the book from a mere printed object, and that the essence of the book is not grounded in the invention of the printing press and movable type, but in 'ideals like the democratization of ideas, of thinking and reflecting, of absorbing the thoughts of others, of creating one's own; of public conversation and discourse' (2007, pp. 28-29).

This perspective allows for books to be something other than a printed object, as, according to Young 'A book need not be printed. It does not require the resources of a publishing company to manufacture an object, ship it around the world and store it in warehouses. It does not have to be expressed as words on a page…. but it does require the peculiar form of interactivity which we call reading' (2007, p. 42). Thus, it may be perceived that, as long as the reading function is available, in whatever form, the reader has access to the contents of a book and is therefore reading a 'book.'

Landow also perceived the book as *technology*, and digital technology as a part of the developing technologies. He pointed out that information technology had permeated all known culture since the beginnings of human history, and that (with books) one should distinguish between the text itself and its physical embodiment in a particular delivery vehicle, reading site or machine (Landow, 1996, pp. 215-218).

Landow expressed the viewpoint as early as 1996 that we had moved beyond the book in various ways and observed that the books of today (as opposed to older, clothbound editions), embody 'ill-designed, fragile, short-lived objects.' Furthermore, many students were using 'cobbled-together compilations' of material for studying instead of books and even more significantly, many libraries were relying on electronic text to record numerous publications and databases. He stated further:

All the strengths of electronic text, including adaptability, infinite duplicability, and speed of transport, make these changes ultimately a means of saving time, energy, and other resources, particularly paper (1996, pp. 211-212).

This statement is still relevant today. Apart from these benefits, electronic text has also broadened publishing options from the author's and publisher's perspective, particularly in respect of economic considerations and ease of publication. Some authors have criticised the use of digital rights management (DRM) on many of the electronic devices, as discussed below and in Chapter 9. They argue that DRM is inconvenient and restrictive for readers, who cannot copy such restricted books onto other devices should they wish to do so. Certain devices such as Kindle, also limit the source of ebooks buying to their own ebook store, which limits the reader's ability to download any material from elsewhere.

It is evident that the electronic reading devices or the electronic files themselves may present some restrictions for authors and readers, due to ebook sellers' attempts to protect their own commercial interests. However, devices like the iPad allow a variety of files to be downloaded and read, as do the rival tablets of Nokia, Hewlett Packard, Dell and Android. A discussion of the restrictions on some of the reading devices follows in Chapters 9 and 10; however, the market changes constantly and new products are released frequently, offering more and better-developed functions.

The opening of Google's eBookstore in the USA in December 2010 signalled the introduction of a new type of ebook, which dispensed with the concept of the book as an electronic file and instead made it available on the Web in a 'cloud,' a type of virtual server available over the Internet (Knorr & Gruman, 2010). The same concept has been utilised by Australian company Booki.sh, which makes use of cloud technology and where an ebook is a Web link rather than an electronic file (Cunningham, 2013). Author Simon Groth sees this development as 'great news for anyone who doesn't want to be tied to a single device and solves a few problems around what happens to all your books if you lose or upgrade your ereader' (Groth, 2011, p. 17). It is also envisaged by some that the Google store will provide competition for the Amazon Kindle store and help to prevent Amazon from monopolising the marketplace (Cellan-Jones, 2010). However, this concept requires the reader to make a further leap away from book ownership, namely from electronic file licensing to Web link, thereby creating another dimension for authors to consider in the ongoing development of publishing and distribution.

Figures on the ebook market are difficult to ascertain as they are changing and growing constantly. Fisher quotes publisher Elizabeth Weiss of Allen & Unwin as saying of the ebook market:

Reliable data on ebook sales is hard to come by, and it's not unusual to see a variety of figures on the size of the US market. It's possible from the figures I see that the current e-book market is some 5 per cent of the whole US general book trade, while over the whole of the 2009 calendar year, ebook sales represented some 3 per cent of the market (Fisher, 2010).

Online Publishers and Self-Publishing

In the digital world authors have the opportunity of publishing through online publishers such as Smashwords at http://www.smashwords.com and Lulu at http://www.lulu.com, smaller online publishers such as Redhill Publishing at http://www.redhillpublishing.com, or self-publish and sell their ebooks through numerous sites such as Amazon at http://www.amazon.com or Clickbank at http://www.clickbank.com, to name but a few. Social publishing sites such as Scribd at http://www.scribd.com allow authors to upload and publish ebooks for free or for purchase on their Website.

Sites such as Smashwords provide online publishing services whereby authors can publish and distribute ebooks, by publishing to the Apple iPad, Barnes &Noble nook, SonyReader, Kobo reader and iPhone. They further offer author royalties of 85% net from sales at Smashwords and 60% of the 'list price' from major ebook retailers. These percentages are considerably higher than the percentages offered by mainstream publishers for ebooks, as discussed above (Smashwords, 2013).

Lulu offers similar services, enabling authors to self-publish and distribute their ebooks in EPUB format, which makes them compatible with the Apple iPad, Sony Reader, Stanza and Kobo reader. Authors earn approximately 56% of the list price for Lulu ebooks sold at the iBookstore, also higher than royalties paid by mainstream publishers. Authors are given instructions on publishing their own ebook to an ePub format, which makes it distributable on the electronic devices mentioned (Lulu, 2013).

Small publishers such as Red Hill Publishing (Red Hill) offer a different package for authors who wish to self publish. Authors carry the production costs of their work and then pay Red Hill 12.5% on all books sold, after all pre-print costs are recouped.

Authors retain their rights and control of the production process. Red Hill authors receive 87.5% of the selling price ($26 per copy on a $29.95 book) after the establishment costs are recouped through sales and earn 100% of all revenue until establishment costs are recouped. Red Hill offers the same percentage breakdown on net receipts for their digital distribution services into online stores such as Amazon's Kindle Store (http://www.redhillpublishing.com).

Scribd prides itself on being 'the largest social publishing and reading site in the world,' with 60 million readers each month. The site includes books, magazines and documents and its technology allows anyone to 'instantly upload and transform any file, including PDF, Word and PowerPoint, into a Web document that's discoverable through search engines, shared on social networks and read on billions of mobile devices' (Scribd, 2013).

Another option for authors selling digital products is Clickbank, which is an online retail outlet for more than 46,000 digital products. Clickbank has a one-off 'product activation fee' of US$49.50. In addition, they charge authors a $2.50 'pay period processing charge' for every payment that ClickBank issues to the author. Furthermore, Clickbank charges 7.5% plus US$1.00 on each sale. The author is also able to sell his/her ebook through 'affiliates' and pay them a commission through Clickbank (2013).

These are some examples of opportunities available for authors in the digital domain, which allow them to self publish and market their own work, free from the restrictions of traditional print publishing. New opportunities continue to arise in different formats, such as the Google eBookstore concept, which is discussed in the next section. It is noted, however, that in many instances authors do not have the support and exposure provided by traditional print publishers.

Hypertext and Online Publishing

The computer as writing tool is the very symbol of the open text. - Raffaele Simone

Another added dimension for authors in digital publication is the use of hypertext. It merits a brief discussion in this chapter as it signifies an important deviation from the traditional reading process. Landow referred to hypertext as 'another way of going beyond the book as we know it in print form.' He argued that hypertext shifted some of the author's power to readers and commented: 'Hypertext, which demands new forms of reading and writing, has the promise radically to reconceive our conceptions of text, author, intellectual property, and a host of other issues ranging from the nature of the self to education' (Landow, 1996, p. 225).

This viewpoint was echoed by Bazin, who expressed the view that the 'culture of the book' (was) 'fading a little further from view with every passing day' and was overshadowed by a metatextuality that extended progressively to the whole complex of modes representing the world, to all the different media. However, Bazin acknowledged that books would still 'proliferate for a long while yet' and that one of the major problems for librarians would be how to navigate a 'hybrid space of documents,' both printed and digital. (1996, p. 153). He described a printed book as a 'straitjacket' with a linear format which produced an argument, unlike digitised hypertext which 'simulates the complexity of things and behaves like a game of the world,' and argued that digitisation defied the boundaries of the text, preferring exchange and conversation to 'vertical' reading. He admitted however, that this shift in priority destabilised traditional institutions such as publishing houses and economic mechanisms such as authors' rights and copyright (1996, pp. 159-164).

Simone suggested that the idea of the text of a book as a closed and protected entity had changed, and predicted that 'the time (was) heralded when the protective membrane of the texts (would) decompose and they (would) once more become open texts as in the Middle Ages with all the standard concomitant presuppositions (of possible modification or manipulation) (1996, pp. 239-249).

These observations accord with those of Landow and Bazin and further support the comments in Chapter 4 regarding the changing notion of authorship. As Simone noted, 'in the near future it will be increasingly difficult – even impossible – to say who is the author of a text' (1996, p. 251). Authors, in utilising online publishing options, have to consider the fact their work may be linked to the comments of Internet users, and may also incorporate such hypertext links in their own work, thereby extending the scope of their publications.

The Google Initiatives

It may be argued that Google has pioneered various strategies such as Google Search, Google News, Google Books and YouTube, both criticised and applauded (John & James, 2011). However, this research is concerned only with their innovations with regard to books and the authors of written work, and how these actions impact upon authors' copyright. The views of the sample group of published Australian authors with regard to the Google Books initiatives are explored in Chapter 9.

Google, through Google Books, have been testing the boundaries of copyright in the digital arena, by digitising books in a number of libraries in the United States, and later providing copyright owners with an opportunity to 'opt out' of their proposed business model (John & James, 2011). The Amended Google Settlement Agreement, which was rejected by the Southern District Court of New York in March 2011 in *The Authors Guild et al v. Google, Inc* (2009), was the result of a copyright dispute which arose between authors and Google in 2009 with regard to this Google Library Project, which involved Google's digitisation of entire collections of participating libraries without the consent of the rights holders. Google's actions and subsequent claims of 'fair use' resulted in objections from the ranks of authors and publishers and legal action by their representative body against Google, which resulted in the Google Settlement Agreement which was later amended but subsequently rejected by Judge Chin.

These developments signified a major change in the application of copyright law on the part of Google, through the publication of electronic copies of work in which they held no copyright interests. The project affected Australian authors who had a United States copyright interest in their books and placed a burden on rights holders to opt out of the settlement proposed by Google, rather than allowing them to opt into the scheme.

The Google initiatives included three separate contracts, namely:

- The Google Book Settlement between Google and USA authors and publishers for out-of-print books.
- The contracts between Google and the libraries for the scanning of books whether public domain, out-of-print or in-print books (the Google Library Program.)
- The contracts between Google and the publishers for the in-print books (Google Partner Program) (Strowel, 2009, p. 5).

In terms of the settlement Google offered to pay US$125 million to create a Book Rights Registry, where authors and publishers would register works and be paid for books and other publications digitised by Google. Through Google's efforts many out of print books had been digitised, a step that made previously inaccessible works available to users.

If the book was in the public domain, then Google provided full access and even permitted users to download a digital copy of the book for free. If the book was presumptively under copyright, then at a minimum Google would grant 'snippet access' to the work, meaning users could see a few lines around the words searched and then would be given information about where they could buy or borrow the book. But if the work was still in print, publishers could authorize Google to make available as much of the book (beyond the snippets) as the publishers wanted (Lessig, 2010).

The Google project covered the rights owned by authors and publishers in books and inserts (such as book chapters) published on or before 5 January 2009. Google offered a one-off payment of around US$60 for each book scanned and US$15 for each insert digitised before this date. If rights holders opted into the settlement and allow Google to use the material for their own display purposes, they could benefit from a 63% payment of revenue received, which would be paid to the Google Book Registry. How much they receive would depend on the 'economic copyright usage terms' set out in the Google Settlement agreement, and on authors' agreements with their publishers.

On the positive side, through these initiatives Google created opportunities for authors to benefit from previously out of print publications, which would also benefit the public as a whole. The copyright owners would receive compensation for the use of their work and allowed control of future uses of their digital books (Strowel, 2009, p. 7).

However, Google's actions were conversely regarded as transgressing accepted copyright norms, due to the opt-out provisions (Strowel, 2009, p. 18). Another disadvantage was that these digitised books would only be accessible to libraries and users in the United States (§ 17.7(a) *Google Book Settlement*), which was a major restriction for universities and education institutions outside the USA, resulting in a negative impact on less developed countries and a comparative advantage for US universities (Strowel, 2009, p. 11).

Furthermore, there was a risk of Google acquiring a highly dominant position for the future delivery of new digital books which existing in a 'cloud' of digital files in Google's data centres. Strowel expressed the concern that '[c]ontrol over the past will translate into control over the future of books.' Google could discontinue the service, impose high fees for access, invade user privacy and censor books (Strowel, 2009, p. 15). Samuelson further commented that Google's commercial purpose and its systematic copying of whole books weighed against fair use considerations (2011, p. 6).

The presiding Judge Chin criticised the fact that, under the Amended Settlement Agreement, 'if copyright owners sit back and do nothing, they lose their rights' (*The Authors Guild et al v. Google Inc* (2009), p. 33). He further said: 'The Amended Settlement Agreement would give Google a significant advantage over competitors, rewarding it for engaging in wholesale copying of copyrighted works without permission, while releasing claims well beyond presented in this case' (*The Authors Guild et al v. Google Inc* (2009), pp. 1-2, 45). Judge Chin then encouraged the parties to consider a revision of the settlement, saying:

Many of the concerns raised in the objections would be ameliorated if the Amended Settlement Agreement were converted from an 'opt-out' settlement to an 'opt-in' settlement (The Authors Guild et al v. Google Inc (2009), p. 46).

The ultimate outcome of the matter will affect publishers and authors in the future. As will be seen in Chapter 9, some authors have expressed concerns about extracts of their books being shown on Google Books, which, in some cases, amount to a substantial portion of the book. (However, in many instances this issue has arisen due to publishers making such extracts available without consultation with the authors and can be addressed between the author and his/her publisher.) On the positive side, many authors recognise the benefits of having previously out-of-print books available for electronic use.

John and James (2011) speculate on the various options available in view of the judgment: the parties may appeal the judgment or seek a different outcome in a higher court, The Authors' Guild may decide to continue with the original action against Google and test Google's 'fair use' claim or the parties may renegotiate the agreement on the opt-in (instead of opt-out) basis suggested by presiding Judge Chin in the Google case. They further suggest that 'the decision may herald a drive for change at the legislative level' (John & James, 2011). At the conclusion of this research Judge Chin had rejected further proposed amendments to the Google Book Settlement at a status hearing on 15 September 2011 and adjourned the matter until July 2012 for the parties to renegotiate a settlement (Reid, 2011).

Samuelson suggests that, as an alternative to the Google Book Settlement, major research libraries should collaborate in the creation of a digital library of books from their collections, as such a digital library could greatly expand access to books, while avoiding certain risks to the public interest that the Google Book Settlement poses (2010, p. 1).

In a later paper, 'Legislative Alternatives to the Google Settlement,' she expands on the proposal, suggesting that the US Congress should authorise qualified entities to digitise in-copyright analog works for purposes of preserving their contents for future generations. As a basis for her argument she refers to the extended collective licensing (ECL) regime used in Norway, which authorises the grant of broad licenses to make specified uses of in-copyright works for which it would be unduly expensive to clear rights on a work-by-work basis (e.g. photocopying in-copyright articles in library settings) (Samuelson, 2011, p. 17). To facilitate an institutional subscription database (ISD) to make out-of-print but in-copyright books more broadly available to research communities, Samuelson proposes that the HathiTrust - a nonprofit organisation formed among a consortium of 50 American research libraries - be appointed as an intermediary through which to provide an appropriate ISD for use in institutions of higher education and nonprofit research communities. Although she admits that questions have arisen regarding the ECL's consistency with the strictures of the Berne Convention and U.S. obligations under the World Trade Organisation Agreements, she sees it as a viable and cost-effective alternative to the Google Settlement proposal (Samuelson, 2011, p. 25).

In 2011, following a number of Google initiatives, and in response to the contemporaneous involvement of American research libraries in the unauthorised book scanning projects by Google and the HathiTrust (a partnership of 50 American research libraries), a number of Australian authors together with the Australian Society of Authors (ASA) joined a lawsuit against HathiTrust and five of the American universities involved in these book scanning projects (*Authors Guild Inc v. HathiTrust, No. 11*). However, in a landmark decision Judge Baer ruled in October 2012 that the HathiTrust's actions were protected under the US 'fair use' legislation (Baer, J., 2012, p. 15), and the ASA and fellow Plaintiffs have filed an appeal, which is pending.

The distinction between the HathiTrust and Google cases appears to be the commercial nature of Google's digitisation project, which prevents them from relying on the same arguments as in the HathiTrust case. Whatever the final outcome of these matters, they are certain to significantly influence the future status and application of copyright to written works in the digital world.

Other Digital Copyright Concerns

In a recent article published by the Australian Copyright Council, the authors made the point that copyright license terms and conditions took on much greater importance in new subscription (and download for purchase) models than they did in the physical world (John & Reid, 2011, p. 2). These comments would also apply to ebooks which are 'purchased' from online stores such as Amazon and Google. As John and Reid pointed out:

In this sense, owners' and users' copying rights are determined somewhat less by provisions in copyright law and somewhat more by individual licenses than in the past. The overall effect is to deliver into the consumer sphere some of the complexity that has previously been restricted to the commercial sphere (2011, p. 2).

These authors acknowledged that copyright ownership had been devalued by online piracy and saw 'the subscription model' as a replacement for 'payment for individual pieces of content with immediate access to a vast content library that (could) be consumed on multiple platforms and devices' (John & Reid, 2011, p. 1). The article did not draw any firm conclusions on the viability of subscription based models, but the authors noted that cooperation between content providers (in this case authors) and new digital intermediaries (such as Google) was likely to be a key factor in how successful they were in persuading people to shift from unauthorised, free alternatives' (John & Reid, 2011, p. 2). These models have since found support with some online publishers and authors. Savikas, CEO of *Safari Books Online*, has described the benefits of running subscription-based ebook service models as similar to the cloud entertainment subscription services (Savikas, 2013). Services such as *Spotify, Rdio* and *Netflix* are widely used by consumers, and whether or not this will be feasible for digital books remains to be seen at the time of this publication. The willingness of readers to engage with digital books – as is evident from the Kindle figures above – would suggest a willingness to engage in alternative reading formats in the future.

The conviction of Apple in the case of *United States of America et al v Apple Inc et al* (2013) for anti-trust collusion with five large publishers to increase the price of e-books, will also have repercussions for authors and traditional publishers. Whilst regarded as a victory for the consumer, the lawsuit illustrates the power wielded by large online publishers to control ebook prices and ebook libraries of readers. Apple has indicated it will appeal the decision (Quain, 2013), raising further concerns for authors about the control exerted over their ebook sales by online publishers. This is not an issue confined to the United States. Relevantly, in 2012, Apple settled a separate ebook price-fixing case with the European Commission, without admitting wrongdoing (Flood, 2012).

NEW BUSINESS MODELS AND COPYRIGHT OPTIONS

This section focuses on copyright options in emerging business models and the different ways in which copyright protection is being implemented electronically. With the expansion of the public sphere of publishing, authors are being exposed to innovative ways of publishing. However, greater accessibility to publishing options may not be the solution for all authors, as Eltham pointed out by cautioning:

The author that can make a self-publishing project successful is the author who is an entrepreneur, a small business manager, a savvy marketer, a tireless communicator, and that's assuming effective distribution is in place (Eltham, 2009).

Australian author Sam Cooney refers to Smashwords as an example of such a new publishing option for authors, pointing out that the practice of giving away work for free is gaining momentum. 'The author can now also be the publisher, and the marketing team. Writers can wrestle back control of their work,' he says. He notes further that readers are demanding more from authors than in the past, expecting them to interact on social media and to be more accessible (Cooney, 2010, p. 11).

He criticises the traditional print model as being 'stacked against the majority of writers,' and states:

If you were fortunate enough to have a manuscript accepted by a publishing house and sign a contract, the whole process is then lengthy and complex.... And the actual chances of an author making a living from the book are remote. Some new movements, mostly finding their feet online, give power back to the author (Cooney, 2010, p. 10).

Cooney's viewpoint is reflective of the two publishing contracts discussed above, which show the disparate approaches by authors and publishers with regard to contract terms and conditions. However, Loukakis is sceptical that the ideal view of a 'balance of interests' is being achieved with publishing agreements. 'This might well be what happens in the ideal state of a stable industry and market environment,' he says. 'But it's debatable whether we have such a thing now or even will have in the future' (Loukakis, 2011, p. 28).

These comments take cognisance of the existing tensions between authors and publishers. Moreover, they recognise the tension inherent in a goal of achieving a balance between the private interests of authors, as advocated by the natural rights and moral rights theories, and the public interest on the other hand. These tensions remain characteristic of the utilitarian system of copyright usage when applied on the Internet. Authors who self publish have to consider copyright in their work and decide which approach to adopt in protecting their rights. Again, the tensions between interests emerge – whilst some opt for digital rights management (DRM) systems to protect copyright, resulting in stronger protection of their private interests, others favour more flexible models with a greater public benefit focus. These choices indicate a greater freedom on the part of authors to regulate the use of their work.

Digital Rights Management (DRM) and Other Protection Measures

DRM can be described as a system or technology used to place limitations onto digital content, including ebooks. The technology regulates access to or copying of the ebook and generally the publisher or author of the ebook determines the level of restrictions applied to it. This includes how many times an ebook can be downloaded for a single purchase, and the type of devices, such as computers and ebook readers, to which the ebook can be transferred.

Vaidhayanathan argues against 'electronic locks and gates' and for 'thin copyright protection: just strong enough to encourage and reward aspiring artists, writers, musicians and entrepreneurs, yet porous enough to allow full and rich democratic speech and the free flow of information' (2001, p. 5).

Some authors, such as Eltham argue that DRM technology restricts the use of creative work unnecessarily. Others, such as Corey Doctorow, a Canadian author, stated at a recent Melbourne Writers Festival: 'DRM is a bad deal for artists and financiers. It doesn't give authors what was promised. It doesn't protect authors' work sufficiently, it only benefits the companies that sell computers' (Doctorow, 2010). He further proposed new and innovative ways in which authors can circulate their work, which are discussed below.

Online publishers follow different approaches with regard to DRM systems such as Virtual Vault, a digital rights management system that prevents users from copying a document. Smashwords, on the other hand, promotes an 'open industry format,' with its books presented as DRM free, and advises authors to include a License Statement and Copyright Page (which designates the author as copyright holder) and to 'trust readers to honour your copyright' (http://www.smashwords.com). Lulu and Redhill Publishing offer a variety of publishing options, including the option to have DRM protection, should the author choose to do so (http://www.lulu.com; http://www.redhillpublishing.com).

Scribd uses a Copyright Management System (CMS) to prevent unauthorised uploading of documents, by comparing all uploaded documents to their existing CMS database and removing any copies. They also remove unauthorised documents if requested to do so by a copyright holder. However, the onus is on the author to upload his/her book to the CMS database (http://www.scribd.com). Ebook sellers such as Clickbank provide a delivery system which protects the author's work and regulates downloads (http://www.clickbank.com), whilst booksellers such as Amazon provide an option for authors and publishers to choose to enable DRM on their books. Once the book is published, it cannot be changed. Most of the books on Amazon's Kindle ereader are, however, DRM enabled and cannot be copied (Needleman, 2010).

Authors are also able to register their copyright on the Internet through professional service providers such as http://www.clickandcopy.com in the USA and http://www.wcauk.com in the United Kingdom, although the effectiveness of such registration is not known and may be difficult to enforce. Internet search engines such as Google (2013) and Internet Service Providers such as iiNet (2013) have made provision for the reporting of copyright infringements; however, it is difficult to determine what level of infringements occur on the Internet as only those reported can be quantified and tracked. Authors discuss this issue in Chapter 9.

The Creative Commons

The Creative Commons describes itself as 'a nonprofit organisation that develops, supports, and stewards legal and technical infrastructure that maximises digital creativity, sharing, and innovation.' The Australian version promises to increase sharing, collaboration and innovation worldwide at http://creativecommons.org.au. It is supported by creative artists, musicians and authors who wish to publish or make their work available for public use by way of an alternative license to the 'all rights reserved' paradigm of traditional copyright. The organisation also enables authors to choose the type of license they want to use, which allows authors to keep their copyright and prescribe how people may copy and distribute their work.

Six licenses are available for use through the Creative Commons, ranging from the 'Attribution' license (which allows the widest use of work, even for commercial purposes, as long as the creator is credited with the original work), to the most restrictive 'Attribution-NonCommercial-NoDerivs' license (which allows others to download works and share them with others noncommercially and without changing them, as long as they credit the creator).

As discussed in Chapter 9, several of the interviewees and respondents use one of these licenses in publishing their work. Kate Eltham, for example, uses the 'Attribution-NonCommercial-NoDerivs' license on her Website, http:// www.electricalphabet.com.

Australian author Lisa Dempster published her book *Neon Pilgrim* under an 'Attribution-Noncommercial' license, which means that anyone can copy and distribute her work for non-commercial purposes, as long as the original work is attributed to her. She states that she wants to be part of a creative community where people can engage with her ideas and experiences; in this respect the Creative Commons 'assists the flow of information rather than hold it up.' She further points out that the first Creative Common licensed book, *Stick this in your memory hole,* was published in Australia in 2007 by aduki independent press, which allowed free downloads of the book, yet print sales have remained robust (Dempster, 2010, p. 12). Dempster regards the premise of the Creative Commons as consistent with the Web 2.0 culture, which relies on sharing and exchanging of work and ideas. Although authors do not earn money directly under a Creative Commons license, they retain a measure of control of the copyright and stipulates how their work should be used.

Whilst this system provides authors with some protection of their private interests as creators, it also supports a significant public benefit interest, thereby contributing to a balanced utilitarian approach. However, some authors do not regard even the constrained limitations of the Creative Commons as warranted, proposing instead that creative work should be entirely free of copyright. In the section below, this more liberal and accommodating approach to copyright is discussed, predicated upon a 'copyright free' focus and a 'loss leader' strategy, as proposed by Doctorow (2010).

An Honesty Box Culture: The Donation Model and 'Loss Leader' Strategy

Obscurity is a far greater threat to authors and creative artists than piracy.
- Tim O'Reilly

Authors such as Doctorow use a Creative Commons license on their Websites and release their ebooks under this license. However, additionally, Doctorow gives the public an option to buy or download the books for free. Downloads are made available in a number of formats, all of which are DRM free. On the download page of his book *Makers,* Doctorow criticises ebook publishers who restrict the use of ebooks unnecessarily, as being 'anti-copyright activists,' his interpretation of copyright allowing for ownership of a book, and for a book to be given away, passed on or lent out to others. He accuses ebook publishers of double standards – whilst referring to 'book sales' they try to regulate the sale through a licensing agreement. Doctorow comments further:

Ebook publishers don't respect copyright law, and they don't believe in your right to own property. Instead, they say that when you 'buy' an ebook, you're really only licensing that book, and that copyright law is superseded by the thousands of farcical, abusive words in the license agreement you click through on the way to sealing the deal (2009).

In providing the free download of his book, he expresses further viewpoints on the copyright in his work: 'You bought it, you own it….So you own this ebook. The license agreement is from Creative Commons and it gives you even *more* rights than you get to a regular book. Every word of it is a gift, not a confiscation.' In return, he asks only that the book be read and shared with others, and explains his motivation as follows: 'Why am I doing this? Because my problem isn't piracy, it's obscurity … because free ebooks sell print books' (Doctorow, 2009).

Doctorow sees the relationship between author and reader as 'a social contract between creator and user' and is critical of companies such as Apple and Sony who refused to publish his books without DRM (Doctorow, 2010). Others, such as Babauta, 'uncopyright' their work, allowing anyone who buys their ebooks to copy, transform or use their work without attribution. Babauta states on his Website:

The uncopyright mindset is that of someone who gives without any guarantee of profit, who lets go of ownership and believes the world owns his creation. He hopes to contribute to the world in a small way, and if others benefit from this contribution, that's a good thing. And if others use his contribution to create something new and beautiful, that's a wonderful thing (2010).

McKenzie Wark proposes in his article 'Copyright, Copyleft, Copygift' that it is possible to sell books and give them away for free at the same time, thereby creating a 'gift economy' alongside the 'commodity economy.' He uses the example of his own book, *A hacker manifesto,* which has been sold in printed form and given away in electronic text files to those who want to copy it (Wark, 2010).

The approaches of these authors resemble an 'honesty box' expectation, where creators believe that there exists a social contract between readers and themselves, with the reader adhering to a certain 'code' or expectation of honest appreciation. On a theoretical level this concept attempts to marry the public benefit theory - through free access - with the natural rights theory: the expectation of eventual reward for creators through recognition of their work.

However, organisations such as the ASA caution their members against piracy and favour online protection of work. 'All digital editions should be protected by a publisher's own anti-piracy provisions in the first place. But authors must also request that their publisher satisfies them that the disctributors they intend using have adequate safeguards of their own,' warns Louka-kis. 'The ASA has never been happy with good faith, or "best endeavours" arrangements in the past, and even less so now' (Loukakis, 2011, p. 29). In the new digital publishing arena these views may need to be revised to accommodate the expectations of a digital reading culture, where 'free' content is often expected by readers who are used to unlimited access on the Internet.

Print Book vs. Ebook

Despite copyright concerns, it is evident that the changing nature of the book and reader expectations has necessitated the use of new business and copyright models. Like the invention of the printing press in the 15th century, the computer today is a technology that challenges the traditional definition of the book. Bolter aligned the future of the book with subtle interactions between changing technological constraints and changing cultural needs and commented that it was unwise to try to predict technological change more than a few years in advance. As he prophesised in the late 1990s:

We cannot know whether readers in the years 2000, 2010, or 2050 may come to prefer computers to printed books. Most readers today are not prepared to replace their books with computers, but they might change their minds in the future (Bolter, 1996, p. 255).

We know now that the figures provided by the ASA showed that, in July 2010, ebooks comprised 5% of all books sold in Australia (Loukakis, 2010, p. 1), thus leaving only the 2050 prediction a mystery. The Kindle figures also reflect the growing supremacy of ebook over print. Potts considered the fate of the book and predicted optimistically: 'The disciples of progress see only tomorrow; if the past is viewed at all, it is with distaste and impatience. But it's hard to dismiss the past of the book, which, like the wheel, has sheer longevity on its side' (Potts, 2010). Although Leslyn Thompson (2009) reported in *Australian Bookseller & Publisher* in October 2009 that 'Australian publishing output was up 12 per cent in 2008 (over calendar year 2007 levels),' including a total of 15,961 titles published, much has changed since 2009.

Fisher has relied on these statistics in arguing for the enduring nature of the printed book:

The printed book is showing no signs even of a death rattle. Book sales in the trade market have not decreased appreciably in the face of digital competition—in fact they have increased. Bookseller and Publisher Magazine's Weekly Book Newsletter reported trade sales of books in Australia in 2009, as recorded by Nielsen Bookscan (from 85 per cent of the trade market), increased 6 per cent over 2008 in both value and volume, totalling $1291 million in value and 64.8 million books...This is in large part because digital print-on-demand technology has meant that it is now easy for almost anyone to produce economically viable small print runs (Fisher, 2010).

The demise of a large number of Borders bookshops worldwide and Angus and Robertson in Australia, as well as the increase in ebook sales versus print sales, raised the question of the survival of the printed book again, as noted in Chapter 1. The reality that many readers today may prefer a hand-held reading device (whether an iPhone, a Kindle, an iPad or another device) to the option of a printed book, has to be acknowledged, as well as the shift of print book sales to online booksellers such as Amazon, the Book Depository and others.

CONCLUSION

How then has technological innovation in publishing affected the publisher-author relationship? Considering the increased options in publishing created by electronic publication, some may argue that the author has gained, and the publisher has lost traction in the copyright balance. Authors are able to self-publish their ebooks or do so through online publishers without reliance on traditional print publishers. Furthermore, online publishers such as www. lulu.com have made print on demand technology accessible for authors.

Others point towards the discrepancy in the terms of existing publishing agreements as opposed to those proposed by authors' societies and argue the opposite, namely that authors remain in a weak position vis-a-vis publishers. Publishing on the Internet may be easier, they would say, but the marketing of the book remains an issue, as Eltham points out (2009). It appears that, to a great degree, this is why authors such as Doctorow and Babauta give their ebooks away for free – in order to gain exposure and develop a following of readers, which in turn assists them with selling their printed books in bookstores. This new breed of author uses the Internet to their advantage and employs new technology to publish and market their books.

It is thus evident that digital technology has brought new challenges and may demand a wider range of skills from authors who wish to benefit from the increased opportunities. Authors who cannot or will not master these skill sets will continue to be reliant on publishers to publish and market their work - whether online or in print - to the reading public. Furthermore, publishers will continue to exert control over the terms of publishing agreements as they have done in the past.

REFERENCES

Associated Press. (2009, September 17). One million copies of Dan Brown's *The Lost Symbol* sold in one day. *Sydney Morning Herald.* Retrieved October 2, 2009, from http://www.smh.com.au/news/entertainment/books/1m-readers-find-lost-symbol/2009/09/17/1252780384841.html

Australian Society of Authors. (2011). *Types of publishers.* Retrieved December 10, 2010 & January 10, 2011, from https://asauthors.org/types-of-publishers

Babauta, L. (2010). Uncopyright. *Zenhabits.* Retrieved March 23, 2011, from http://zenhabits.net/uncopyright/

Barlow, J. P. (1992). *The economy of ideas: Selling wine without bottles on the global net.* Retrieved January 15, 2011, from https://projects.eff.org/~barlow/EconomyOfIdeas.html

Bazin, P. (1996). Towards metareading. In G. Nunberg (Ed.), *The future of the book* (pp. 153–168). Los Angeles, CA: University of California Press.

Bolter, J. D. (1996). Ekphrasis, virtual reality, and the future of writing. In G. Nunberg (Ed.), *The future of the book* (pp. 253–271). Los Angeles, CA: University of California Press.

Cellan-Jones, R. (2010, December 7). *Who's afraid of Google's book store?* Retrieved January 9, 2011, from http://www.bbc.co.uk/blogs/thereporters/rorycellanjones/2010/12/whos_afraid_of_googles_book_st.html

Clickbank. (2013). *Clickbank DIY.* Retrieved from http://www.clickbank.com/clickbankdiy/

Cooney, S. (2010, May). New publishing models: A shifting of power. *Writing Queensland, 196*, 10.

Cunningham, S. (2013, October 15). BOOKish. *Meanjin.* Retrieved from http://meanjin.com.au/blog/post/bookish/

Dempster, L. (2010, May). Creative commonsense. *Writing Queensland, 196*, 12.

Doctorow, C. (2009). Download for free. *Makers.* Retrieved March 23, 2011, from http://craphound.com/makers/download/

Doctorow, C. (2010, September 2). *Copyright versus creativity.* Paper presented at Melbourne Writers Festival. Melbourne, Australia.

Eltham, K. (2009, October 28). What do authors need? *Electric Alphabet: Writing and Publishing in the Digital Near-Future*. Retrieved January 10, 2011, from http://www.electricalphabet.net/2009/10/28/what-do-authors-need/

Fisher, J. (2010, September 27). Ebooks and the Australian publishing industry. *Meanjin, 69*(3). Retrieved March 23, 2011, from http://meanjin.com.au/blog/post/e-books-and-the-australian-publishing-industry/

Flood, A. (2012). European Commission and Apple reach settlement over ebook price-fixing. *The Guardian*. Retrieved November 10, 2013, from http://www.theguardian.com/books/2012/dec/14/european-commission-apple-ebook

Godwin, M. (2001). Book keeping. *American Lawyer Media*. Retrieved from http://global.factiva.com

Google. (2013). *Removing content from Google*. Retrieved from https://support.google.com/legal/troubleshooter/1114905?rd=2

Groth, S. (2011, March). Cloud atlas. *Writing Queensland, 205*, 17. iiNet. (2013). *Illegal content*. Retrieved from http://www.iinet.net.au/about/legal/illegal-content.html

Jassin, L. J. (2010, May 24). The publishing story behind Mark Twain's unpublished autobiography. *Copylaw*. Retrieved December 30, 2010, from http://www.copylaw.org/2010/05/mark-twains-unpublished-autobiography.html

John, J., & James, F. (2011, March 28). Copyrighting Google. *Australian Copyright Council*. Retrieved March 28, 2011, from http://www.copyright.org.au/news-and-policy/details/id/1907/

John, J., & Reid, M. A. (2011, April 28). Making content pay online. *Australian Copyright Council*. Retrieved 29 April 2011, from http://www.copyright.org.au/news-and-policy/details/id/1945/

Knorr, E., & Gruman, G. (2010). What cloud computing really means. *InfoWorld*. Retrieved March 16, 2011, from http://www.infoworld.com/d/cloud-computing/what-cloud-computing-really-means-031?page=0,0

Landow, G. P. (1996). Twenty minutes into the future. In G. Nunberg (Ed.), *The future of the book* (pp. 209–238). Los Angeles, CA: University of California Press.

Lessig, L. (2010, January 26). For the love of culture: Google, copyright and our future. *The New Republic*. Retrieved March 19, 2011, from http://www.newrepublic.com/article/the-love-culture

Loukakis, A. (2010, July 10). E-books: Royalties and contracts. *Australian Society of Authors*. Retrieved from https://asauthors.org/files/pages/ebooks_royalties_and_contracts.pdf

Loukakis, A. (2011). Giving contracts some clout. *Australian Author, 43*(1), 28–29.

Lulu. (2013). *eBook publishing*. Retrieved from http://www.lulu.com/publish/ebooks/free

Malik, S. (2012, August 6). Kindle ebook sales have overtaken Amazon print sales, says book seller. *The Guardian*. Retrieved from http://www.guardian.co.uk/books/2012/aug/06/amazon-kindle-ebook-sales-overtake-print

Needleman, R. (2010, January 22). Amazon adds optional DRM for Kindle publishers. *CNET News*. Retrieved March 16, 2011, from http://news.cnet.com/8301-19882_3-10439335-250.html

NewsCore. (2011, May 20). Kindle sales overtake paper books. *News Limited*. Retrieved June 5, 2011, from http://www.news.com.au/business/e-book-sales-overtake-paper-books/story-fn7mjon9-1226059335499

Nunberg, G. (1996). Farewell to the information age. In G. Nunberg (Ed.), *The future of the book* (pp. 103–138). Los Angeles, CA: University of California Press.

Potts, J. (2010). Book doomsday: The march of progress and the fate of the book. *Meanjin, 69*(3). Retrieved March 23, 2011, from http://meanjin.com.au/Ed.s/volume-69-number-3-2010/article/book-doomsday-the-march-of-progress-and-the-fate-of-the-book1/

Quain, J. R. (2013). *Apple loses e-book pricing lawsuit, but are consumers the real losers?* Retrieved November 13, 2013, from http://www.foxnews.com/tech/2013/07/11/

Reid, M. A. (2011). Authors create a new sub-plot in the quest to digitise the world's books. *Australian Copyright Council*. Retrieved from http://copyright.org.au

Samuelson, P. (2010). Google book search and the future of books in cyberspace (UC Berkeley Public Law Research Paper No. 1535067). *Minnesota Law Review, 94*, 1308.

Samuelson, P. (2011). Legislative alternatives to the Google book settlement (UC Berkeley Public Law Research Paper No. 1818126). *Columbia Journal of Law & the Arts, 34,* 697.

Scribd. (2013). *About.* Retrieved from http://www.scribd.com/about

Seddon, N. C., & Ellinghaus, M. P. (2002). *Chesire and Fifoot's law of contract.* Sydney: LexisNexis Butterworths.

Simone, R. (1996). The body of the text. In G. Nunberg (Ed.), *The future of the book* (pp. 239–252). Los Angeles, CA: University of California Press.

Smashwords. (2013). *How to create, publish, and distribute ebooks with Smashwords.* Retrieved from http://www.smashwords.com/about/how_to_publish_on_smashwords

Strowel, A. (2009, December). *The Google settlement: Towards a digital library or an inquisitive shopping mall?* Paper presented at Bond University. Gold Coast, Australia.

Thompson, L. (2009, October). Australian book publishing in 2008: Thriving in uncertain times. *Australian Bookseller & Publisher,* 12–13.

Vaidhayanathan, S. (2001). *Copyrights & copywrongs: The rise of intellectual property and how it threatens creativity.* New York: NYU Press.

Victoria Writers' Centre. (now Writers Victoria). (2011). Contracts. *Writers Victoria.* Retrieved January 10, 2011, from http://vwc.org.au/publishing/contracts

Wark, M. (2010, July 28). Copyright, copyleft, copygift. *Meanjin, 69*(1). Retrieved September 21, 2010, from http://meanland.com.au/articles/post/copyright-copyleft-copygift

Young, S. (2007). *The book is dead: Long live the book.* Sydney: University of New South Wales Press.

Young, S. (2010, November 26). Bond sidesteps Penguin. In *The book is dead.* Retrieved January 9, 2011, from http://shermanfyoung.wordpress.com/2010/11/26/bond-sidesteps-penguin/

TABLE OF CASES

Random House, Inc. v. Rosetta Books LLC, 283 F.3d 490, 62 U.S.P.Q.2d (BNA) 1063 (2d Cir. 2002) (US)

The Authors Guild et al v. Google, Inc, (2009) US District Court, Southern District of New York, No. 05-08136 at 1 (US)

The Authors Guild, Inc. et al. v. HathiTrust et al, US District Court, Southern District of New York, filed 12 September 2011, 11 CIV 6351 (US)

United States of America et al v. Apple Inc et al, US District Court for the Southern District of New York, 10 July 2013 (US)

TABLE OF STATUTES

Copyright Act 1968 (Cth)

Chapter 7
Research and Methodology

ABSTRACT

As an inter-disciplinary study, the research employs a multi-method methodology, with the focus on a Humanities-based approach. The research design is characterised by a qualitative/quantitative research model, incorporating survey data and in-depth interviews. Purposive sampling has been employed to secure in-depth interviews with published authors and to involve qualified respondents in an online survey. The data obtained in this manner provides the basis for the findings and conclusions in chapters 8, 9, 10, and 11. The chapter considers the purpose and scope of the research and discusses the two-stage strategy used to obtain the data, pointing out the limitations of the research strategy, on the one hand, and the purposeful nature of the information obtained in this manner, on the other.

INTRODUCTION: PURPOSE OF THE RESEARCH

In the preceding chapters the concept of authorship and the publishing industry itself have been shown to be constantly evolving. Amidst these changing frameworks, his research sought to address various areas of concern as they relate to Australian authors, who are influenced by Australian and international copyright legislation, the Australian and global publishing industry and by digital media.

In order to investigate authors' views on copyright and the writing profession in this climate of global economic advancement, various issues were examined, including publishing contracts and licensing agreements, copyright

DOI: 10.4018/978-1-4666-5214-9.ch007

restrictions and digital copyright enforcement. The research also focussed on authors' perceptions of the current legislative and Government structures, examining whether they sufficiently protected their copyright and provided an adequate framework in which they could be rewarded for their creative efforts.

As foreshadowed in Chapter 1, the research set out to address the following issues:

1. How do Australian authors perceive copyright affecting them and does it have any impact on how they practise?
2. Do Australian authors believe that the existing copyright framework supports and encourages them in their creative efforts?
3. What are Australian authors' views on the changing nature of the publishing industry and how have they been affected by changes/advances in this area?

By placing the author in the context of a 'literary sphere' of creators, a 'pool' of data was collected to reflect authors' views on these issues. Although Australian authors have a national body which promotes their interests in the Australian Society of Authors (ASA), their collective viewpoints remain largely unexamined. The nature of the writing profession as a solitary occupation provided the further incentive to assemble data on the combined perceptions of the author group on the issue of copyright. Did they perceive it to be a legal concept which effectively provided them with financial reward for their efforts, or was it an accepted and intrinsic right that creators had? How were they affected by copyright in their creative pursuits? And as far as digital media were concerned, how did the changes in the publishing industry affect them?

THE RESEARCH MODEL

A Multi-Method Approach

In order to address the research topics effectively, a multi-method approach was employed. Although strong elements of socio-legal research are present, the present research can be most accurately described as social research with a legal focus. The research design is characterised by a combination of qualitative and quantitative research methods, as discussed below.

In this task the use of multiple methods or triangulation (Denzin & Lincoln, 2005, pp. 5-6) assisted with an in-depth understanding of the research issues. In-depth face-to-face interviews with a group of authors, underpinned by qualitative data obtained through online survey questionnaires which were distributed through the Australian Society of Authors and Writers' Centres throughout Australia, formed the nucleus of the research. This information was supplemented by primary documents such as legislation and publishing contracts, a comprehensive literature review and background research on legislative and publishing issues.

The Denzin and Lincoln view of the qualitative researcher being described as 'bricoleur and quilt maker,' a person who assembles images into montages (a method of editing cinematic images), using a variety of methods, strategies and empirical materials (2005, p. 4), was a relevant consideration in structuring the research. The assembling of authors' viewpoints through in-depth interviews and online surveys, together with legal research, literature review and economic considerations, resembled such a 'quilt' as envisaged by these authors. This viewpoint also supported the idea of 'purposive sampling,' as described by Patton (2002, p. 235).

This approach proved an effective strategy to incorporate and relate the disparate, yet related areas of discourse, for example, Government support structures for authors, moral rights issues and digital publishing. Three important factors in particular merited consideration, described by Gray, Williamson, Karp and Dalphin as: 'the type of information to be gathered, the resources available for research and the access to individuals, groups and institutions' (2007, p. 43). These factors have been taken into account in both stages of the research model, and more particularly, in the construct of purposeful sampling, as proposed by Patton (2002, p. 45) and discussed below.

Purposeful Sampling

The strategy described by Patton as 'purposeful sampling' (2002, p. 40) has also been referred to as 'purposive sampling' (Stake, 2005, p. 451). Stake explains 'purposive sampling' as follows: 'For qualitative fieldwork, we draw a purposive sample, building in variety and acknowledging opportunities for intensive study' (Stake, 2005, p. 451). Patton regards such sampling as 'information rich and illuminative,' offering insight about the phenomenon studied rather than empirical generalisation from a sample to a population (2002, p. 40). In comparing the differences between 'qualitative purposeful sampling' and 'statistical probability sampling,' he describes purposeful sampling as follows: 'Qualitative enquiry typically focuses on a relatively small sample... selected purposefully to permit enquiry into and understanding of a phenomenon *in depth*' (Patton, 2002, p. 46).

The type of purposeful sampling used in this research can best be described as 'maximum variation sampling' as envisaged by Patton. This type of sampling aims to capture and describe central themes that cut across a great deal of variation (Patton, 2002, pp. 234-235). It relies on the identification of common patterns in the diversity of responses. In the case of authors and copyright, it would aim to recognise common themes emerging from the results of a diverse group of authors from different age groups, backgrounds and geographical areas.

Purposive sampling was implemented in two stages, namely: the first sample of face to face interviews with 17 published authors, including 'elite' interviews -as perceived by Marshall and Rossman (2010, p. 155) - who comprised more than half of the sample. A second sample of online surveys was completed by a larger group of 156 participants from the ranks of published Australian authors. I regarded elite authors as those who have been published over an extended period of time and have made continued contributions to the development of the book industry. Because of this naturalistic approach, it was envisaged that such a sample would provide an authentic and relevant result. The use of purposive sampling during the two stages of research is discussed in more depth later in this chapter.

STRATEGY

From a strategic viewpoint, the research was conducted bearing in mind that various types and sources of data have different strengths and weaknesses. As Marshall and Rossman state: 'The use of triangulation…increases the validity as the strengths of one approach can compensate for the weaknesses of another approach' (2006, pp. 79-111). This viewpoint is endorsed by Patton, who claims that '[m]ultiple sources of information are sought and used because no single source of information can be trusted to provide a comprehensive perspective on the program' (2002, p. 306).

In view of these considerations, the strategy to be implemented emerged as follows. First, historical background and theoretical research had to be carried out to place the current issues in context. This was achieved through a literature review dealing with important historical events in the field of copyright law and examining the theoretical basis of copyright, as well as the role of the author as creator. Second, a critical analysis of Australian copyright legislation was required to pinpoint the areas of concern and reflect how copyright is dealt with on a legislative basis and applied in practice.

Third, the research questions had to be investigated in practice, methods of obtaining the data had to be decided upon and the necessary structures put in place to obtain such data.

Purposive sampling through a combination of surveys and interviews allowed for a more goal-oriented investigation and for more introspection and reflection on the part of the researcher. The emphasis was not purely on data collection, but on the assimilation and critical analysis of research results, bearing in mind Brannen's cautionary remarks against the risks inherent in qualitative research:

For example, the current turn to reflexivity in qualitative research in respect of the focus upon the researcher risks neglecting research participants. By contrast ...there is the opposite risk whereby researchers attribute to their research participants a monopoly over meaning. There is a danger of downplaying the interpretive role of the researcher (Brannen, 2004, p. 313).

With these caveats in mind, care has been taken to identify and acknowledge the viewpoints of participants in the in-depth interviews where they were specific on certain issues. Furthermore, the online survey provided a means of utilising a larger sample group to obtain qualitative data against which the subjective interviewee comments and observations could be examined.

SCOPE OF THE RESEARCH

Two main groups of participants have been identified in the research - full time authors and part time authors. Only data obtained from published authors has been considered. In addition to the 156 published authors who responded to the online survey, all 17 in-depth interviewees were published authors. Furthermore, three publishers (two small and one large/mainstream) and a publishing contract consultant were interviewed to provide background information and a further perspective on the research questions.

In determining the scope of the research it was important to delineate the issues specifically, due to the wide scope of possibilities invited by the research topic. This was done by using an interview schedule for the in-depth interviews and designing survey questions to deal specifically with the research issues in the online survey. As stated by Bogdan and Biklen (2003, p. 51), the research should be 'reasonable in size and complexity so that it can be completed with the time and resources available.'

Certain sources, especially those regarded as 'elite interviews,' could provide valuable information on the research issues, such as in the case of Frank Moorhouse, who had played an instrumental part in copyright protection for Australian authors. Marshall and Rossman note some of the advantages of elite interviews as their possible familiarity with legal and organisational structures and their broad views on the development of policy fields; however, they also acknowledge the challenges in gaining access to these people due to their busy schedules and difficulties in contacting them (2010, pp. 155-156).

It was envisaged that the findings of the research would be strengthened by the inclusion of such high-profile or 'elite' participants with a high level of knowledge on the subject matter. These interviews were included as a purposeful sample providing the opportunity for more intensive study of their particular viewpoints, as proposed by Patton (2002, p. 46). Interviewees were asked whether they would consent to the use of their names in the research, with all but one of the 17 participants acceding to this request.

In respect of the online survey all responses were completely anonymous, with no identifying features other than broad demographic information, such as the respondent's state of residence, age, type of writing engaged in and income (optional response). The non-identifying approach was selected as the underlying basis for this strategy for the following reasons:

- It obviated ethical dilemmas arising from divulging personal information which might have impacted on the participant's contractual obligations and future relationships.
- It provided an increased ability on the part of participants to 'speak freely' without constraints.
- It provided a greater scope for objectivity on the part of the researcher.
- It facilitated a wider scope for data collection by using anonymous survey formats.
- It encouraged prospective respondents to participate in the survey due to the assurance of anonymity (Buchanan, 2004, p. 146).

The scope of the research therefore sought to include a number of different 'types' of authors, who could be classified as full time or part time writers, and also according to profession (for example, fiction writer, non fiction writer, academic writer, etc.)

THE TWO STAGES OF DATA COLLECTION

As explained above, the research process was executed in two stages, a **first stage** which consisted of limited open-ended face to face interviews with 17 authors, three publishers and a publishing contract consultant, followed by a second stage, which comprised an online survey which was distributed through the Australian Society of Authors, the professional association for Australia's literary creators, and various writers' centres nationally. This approach allowed for the collection of rich qualitative data through the in-depth interviews (Denzin & Lincoln, 2005, p. 12), together with a wider scope of data collection through the online survey.

Contact with authors was facilitated by a variety of means, such as telephone contact, email contact through Websites and written contact through agents. Once contact was established, an effort was made to interview the participants in person or telephonically. A total of 40 authors were approached, of whom 17 agreed to be interviewed. Interviews were conducted in the following locations: Brisbane, Gold Coast, Sydney, Northern New South Wales, and also by telephone and email contact.

A number of interviews were arranged through referrals or 'snowballing.' Patton describes 'snowballing' as the process whereby you ask a number of people 'who else to talk with' and then include those recommended sources where possible (2002, p. 237). Where referrals took place access was improved and interviews more readily agreed to.

As will be discussed below, this method had some limitations; however, the data obtained in this manner was rich, varied and informative. In designing the structure of the interview, the use of an 'interview guide' as proposed by Patton was favoured, which listed the questions or issues to be explored in the interview. In a few instances, where personal or telephone interviews were difficult to arrange, the participant was asked to respond to the questions in the interview guide and return it by email, with some follow-up email correspondence. A copy of the 'Interview Guide' is attached hereto as *Appendix 'A.'*

According to Patton the use of an interview guide leaves the interviewer 'free to explore, probe and ask questions that will elucidate and illuminate the particular subject.' He cites the following advantages of such a guide: 'It provides for better use of the limited time available for an interview; interviewing is more systemic and comprehensive and the issues to be explored are delineated in advance' (Patton, 2002, p. 343).

The open-ended structure of the interviews with this sample group provided the first valuable source of qualitative data and informed the second stage of the research by providing more insight into the copyright issues in question. Furthermore, the scope of the research questions evolved through the process of interviewing as key trends and changes in the industry became more evident. The publisher interviews provided information and comment on the economic burdens and risk placed on them as publishers, thereby providing some external insights into the research. In addition, the publishing contract consultant provided insight into contractual terms and royalty provisions, which was supplemented by information obtained from the ASA (Loukakis, 2010) as well as current author contracts.

In relation to 'elite' interviews, Marshall and Rossman discuss the problems associated with this category of interviewees and point out the following difficulties: 'Limited access to potential interviewees; the limited time the interviewees have available; their inclination to take control of or 'taking charge' of an interview' (2006, p. 114). The first two concerns were evident in interviews with high profile authors who were difficult to secure for interviews and required considerable notice. Once interviews were secured, they were provided with an interview schedule in the form of the Interview Guide and fully briefed on the nature and scope of the issues to be addressed, in advance of the interviews. They were also made aware that their responses to any questions were entirely voluntary. Issues such as these were addressed in the university Human Ethics Research clearance forms, approved by the University Ethics Committee, provided to each interviewee. This also addressed the need for tact and diplomacy required in the interview process, or, as Marshall and Rossman aptly point out, 'an awareness of the politics of organisations as well as a sensitivity to human interaction' (1999, p. 78).

The *second stage* allowed for a more focussed approach by utilising an online Web-based survey questionnaire, consisting of limited open-ended and multiple choice questions. The survey, which had also been approved by the University Ethics Committee prior to being conducted, was entirely anonymous and structured to take approximately ten to fifteen minutes to complete. Significantly, the online survey provided a national sample of data on the research issues, larger in scope than the face to face interviews. It was envisaged that the use of this additional instrument would increase the validity of the findings, as proposed by Marshall and Rossman (2006, pp. 79-111) and as favoured by Patton (2002, p. 306).

Web-based surveys have become more widely used in the last ten years and are regarded as inexpensive, with a short response time and able to achieve satisfying response rates compared to questionnaires delivered by 'classical' mail (Ganassali, 2008, p. 21). Web-based surveys are also regarded as having lower respondent errors and increasing the completeness of response (McDonald & Adam, 2003, p. 85).

Fontana and Frey recognise the fact that computer surveys are becoming more widely used as part of the data gathering process and state that developments in computer-assisted interviewing have called into question the division between traditional modes of interviewing such as the survey interview and the mail survey (2005, p. 703). They observe that

'today we are really looking at a continuum of data-collecting methods rather than clearly divided methods; in fact... many surveys today incorporate a variety of data-gathering methods driven by concerns such as time constraints, financial demands, and other practical elements' (Fontana & Frey, 2005, p. 703).

It was envisaged that an online survey promoted by the ASA would obtain responses from a wide geographic spectrum of authors, implemented by using a Web-based survey mechanism such as 'Survey Monkey,' which is a user-friendly research tool commonly used by academics. The ASA is a national organisation with approximately 3,000 members from all Australian States and Territories.

Through collecting the data in the first stage certain key themes such as authors' lack of knowledge about their digital copyright and concerns about the possible impact of parallel importing on their earning abilities were highlighted. Some of these issues, especially in relation to electronic publishing, were subsequently included in the online survey. It was envisaged that the results of the online survey would provide a national sample of qualitative data on the relationship between Australian authors and copyright, as well as their response to the changing nature of the publishing industry.

The online survey further enabled the collection of a substantial amount of demographic data on aspects such as authors' earnings from various sources. In addition to the ASA the following Writers' Centres were approached to distribute the survey: NSW; Queensland; South Australia; Western Australia; NT; ACT; Northern Rivers; Victoria and Tasmania. Of these organisations the only ones which were non-responsive were those in Victoria, Tasmania and South Australia. The process of obtaining data from a number of organisations in this way has been described as a 'trawling' exercise (Johnston, personal communication, 2010), whereby data is captured from a number of sources by casting a net as wide as possible to include as many participants as possible from the area under investigation (in this case members of the literary sphere). This approach proved to be successful in widening the scope of participants to include authors who were not members of the ASA.

The online survey commenced on 24 August 2010 and was scheduled to run until 30 September 2010; however, due to a low number of initial responses received, the period was extended to 31 October 2010 to allow for further exposure through the writers' centres.

The survey, titled *'Authors, Copyright and the Digital Evolution'* consisted of seven pages, two of which comprised an 'Introduction' and 'Thank you' page respectively. The other five pages were titled as follows:

1.   Demographic information.
2.   Your views on copyright.
3.   The existing copyright framework.
4.   The publishing industry.
5.   Publishing on the Internet.

The questions were presented in three formats, which included limited open-ended questions, allowing for a paragraph of comment per subject. The second format used was that of multiple questions, where the subject matter lent itself to such a format. The third type of question used was 'likert' scale choices, employed to scale participants' responses in relation to the questionnaire topics. The questions were structured to appear user friendly and unambiguous, to ensure a maximum number of responses. Apart from the initial demographic questions relating to age, occupation, place of residence, etc., none of the questions were peremptory and the participant could choose whether or not to answer the question. It was a concern of the researcher that peremptory questions would discourage the completion of the survey where respondents were unsure of an answer or objected to providing certain information (even though the survey was anonymous).

To access the survey respondents had to click on a link to Survey Monkey, an Internet based survey tool routinely used for research and training by businesses, academic institutions such as Bond University, and a variety of organisations, which provided a user friendly experience for respondents. A copy of the online survey is annexed marked *Appendix 'B.'* The survey instrument also allowed for *filtering,* which enabled the elimination of unpublished author responses to focus on results related to published authors. It further provided a function for cross tabulating results. This facility enabled *cross tabs* to compare the results of part time and full time authors, which provided some valuable insight into the research issues, as discussed in Chapters 8 and 9.

Limitations

There were certain inherent limitations in the techniques employed during the two stages, due to practical considerations associated with in-depth interviews and the procurement of online survey respondents.

The Interviews

The number of author interviews conducted (17 out of 40 requests) was reflective of the limitations of this method, such as unavailability, a reluctance to be interviewed, expense considerations and time factors. However, the purposive sample allowed for in-depth discussion and provided insight into authors' subjective viewpoints on the research issues as proposed by Patton (2002, p. 45).

The Online Survey

Whilst the online survey had the advantage of being cost effective and accessible to a large group of authors, there were limitations to a Web-based approach. The total number of responses obtained in the online survey (177) represented a relatively small group in view of the number of possible respondents. Possible respondents included members of the ASA (3,000) and an unknown number of members of the various Writers' Centres that provided links to the survey. These response figures were reflective of the limitations imposed by the online survey method.

One significant limitation was the fact that responses were limited to users of the Internet. This created a risk of non-response bias, which presented a threat to making inferences from the data obtained (Bech & Kristenson, 2009, p. 3). As a result the data was utilised as qualitative, rather than quantitative data, providing the researcher with insight into the research questions rather than the ability to draw generalisations.

Most of the Writers' Centres distributed weekly or monthly e-newsletters to their members, and were able to include the survey link in their newsletter. However, significantly, the ASA did not have an e-newsletter but placed the link in their published newsletter, which was sent to members by mail. This presented significant limitations, as members had to be sufficiently motivated to go to their computers, log onto the Internet and then type in the survey URL to complete the survey. The ASA did, however, provide a short abstract of the survey on their Website, with a link to the survey.

The period of the survey also had to be limited to a certain period of time due to time constraints in carrying out the research and allowing for the recording and analysis of the findings. Furthermore, participating organisations such as the ASA could only provide the link for a limited period of time due to valuable space on their Website, and writers' centres would typically only publish the link once in a newsletter or email bulletin.

Limitations on the part of respondents may include: a lack of online facilities (although it would be presumed that most authors would have access to the Internet), a lack of interest in the subject matter, apathy on the issue of copyright, a lack of understanding of the issues involved resulting in a reluctance to participate, a lack of motivation, a lack of time and a general reluctance to complete surveys. However, in the context of other similar surveys such as the national Queensland University of Technology survey on *Academic authorship, publishing agreements and open access* (Austin, Heffernan & David, 2008), where emails were sent directly to 27,385 academics, with a link to the survey, and only 509 responses were received, it appears that the level of interest displayed by authors in the present survey was not unusual.

However, whilst these limitations are acknowledged, based on the purposeful sampling strategy with the inherent purpose of 'in-depth understanding' as identified by Patton (2002, p. 230), the results of the survey provided sufficient data for meaningful analysis and discussion within the framework of this research.

Pre-Testing

The Interviews

A draft questionnaire was initially drawn up and presented informally to two senior academics, who were also published authors, for discussion. It was evident that the questionnaire was too lengthy and that it did not invite sufficient discussion on the salient issues. After some deliberation and further research, it was determined that the interviews would be based on the 'interview guide' or 'interview schedule' referred to above as proposed by Patton (2002, p. 343), and a list of closed-ended and open-ended questions were formulated to direct the interviewer. This schedule was presented to the same academics for comment and was favourably received.

The first test interview was undertaken through direct contact with a published part-time author known to the researcher, and carried out on an in-depth personal basis. By obtaining the author's feedback on the questions in the Interview Guide, the researcher was able to further consolidate and adapt the questions, in order to obtain effective responses which addressed the research questions in sufficient depth.

The Online Survey

The online survey was pre-tested by requesting the ASA to comment on the contents. It was also presented to four academics (two of whom were published authors) at Bond University for pre-testing. Favourable comments were made by two of the academics regarding the length and content of the survey, and all but one of the academics completed the survey successfully. Three changes were suggested which were duly implemented, before launching the survey on the ASA Website.

DATA ANALYSIS

It is useful here to highlight the difference in approach during the analysis process with regard to the two research stages. Although both sources of data were treated as 'purposive samples' obtained from the group of 'published authors,' the data differed in terms of focus and content. To expand further on this statement, it is evident in the following Chapters 8 and 9 that the in-depth interviews provided rich data regarding the participants' personal viewpoints. It was also significant that the interviews were 'open-ended in-terviews' conducted with an 'interview guide' of questions as proposed by Patton (2002, pp. 343-344), which facilitated in-depth discussion, examples of personal experiences and detailed information. The online survey, on the other hand, was more structured and restrictive by nature, allowing for limited description and elucidation in specific questions. Some participants noted that they were unable to answer the questions as fully as they would have liked to. In other instances, questions were skipped and left unanswered.

In the online survey, the comments of Markham are particularly relevant, where she states: 'A researcher's representation of others is inextricably bound up with the way data are collected and distinguished as meaningful versus meaningless. Methodologically, one must reflect carefully on what collected information is considered as 'data' (2005, p. 803). Although Markham is mainly concerned with interviewing subjects online (rather than surveying), her comments were borne in mind when analysing the data and only empirical (as opposed to inferential) data was included in the observations.

A significant strength of the two methodologies was that the data obtained from the survey could be used to amplify and support findings of the in-depth interviews. The survey data also provided further insight into the research questions through analysing the 'opportunities for comment' included in the online survey.

CONCLUSION

The purpose of this research, as with any qualitative research, was to provide insight into the research questions. Patton uses a number of metaphors to describe the transformation process of raw data into findings. One which resonates with, and reflects the 'bricoleur and quilt maker' approach referred to earlier, is the following observation: 'Findings emerge like an artistic mural created from collage-like pieces that make sense in new ways when seen and understood as part of a greater whole' (Patton, 2002, p. 432). By implementing this process and utilising these two 'purposeful samples' of published authors, this research aims to provide a window into the collective viewpoints of a group of Australian authors on various copyright issues, and to investigate how these viewpoints affected their creative practice.

REFERENCES

Austin, A., Heffernan, M., & David, N. (2008). *Academic authorship, publishing agreements and open access (Research Report)*. Brisbane, Australia: The OAK Law Project, Queensland University of Technology.

Bech, M., & Kristensen, M. B. (2009). Differential response rates in postal and web-based surveys among older respondents. *Survey research. Methods (San Diego, Calif.)*, *3*(1), 1–6.

Bogdan, R. C., & Biklen, S. K. (2003). *Qualitative research for education: An introduction to theory and methods*. Boston: Allyn & Bacon.

Brannen, J. (2004). Working qualitatively and quantitatively. In C. Seale, G. Gobo, J. F. Gubrium, & D. Silverman (Eds.), *Qualitative research practice* (pp. 312–325). London: Sage Publications. doi:10.4135/9781848608191.d25

Buchanan, E. A. (2004). *Readings in virtual research ethics*. Hershey, PA: Information Science Publishing.

Denzin, N. K., & Lincoln, Y. S. (Eds.). (2005). *Handbook of qualitative research* (3rd ed.). London: Sage Publications.

Fontana, A., & Frey, J. (2005). The interview: From neutral stance to political involvement. In N. K. Denzin, & Y. S. Lincoln (Eds.), *Handbook of qualitative research* (3rd ed., pp. 695–728). London: Sage Publications.

Ganassali, S. (2008). The influence of the design of web survey questionnaires on the quality of responses. *Survey Research Methods*, *2*(1), 21–32.

Gray, P. S., Williamson, J. B., Karp, D. A., & Dalphin, J. R. (2007). *The research imagination*. Cambridge, UK: Cambridge University Press. doi:10.1017/CBO9780511819391

Loukakis, A. (2010, July 10). E-books: Royalties and contracts. *Australian Society of Authors*. Retrieved from https://asauthors.org/files/pages/ebooks_royalties_and_contracts.pdf

Markham, A. N. (2005). The methods, politics, and ethics of representation in online ethnography. In N. K. Denzin, & Y. S. Lincoln (Eds.), *Handbook of qualitative research* (3rd ed., pp. 793–820). London: Sage Publications.

Marshall, C., & Rossman, G. B. (2006). *Designing qualitative research* (4th ed.). London: Sage Publications.

Marshall, C., & Rossman, G. B. (2010). *Designing qualitative research* (5th ed.). London: Sage Publications.

McDonald, H., & Adam, S. (2003). A comparison of online and postal data collection methods in marketing research. *Marketing Intelligence & Planning, 21,* 85–95. doi:10.1108/02634500310465399

Patton, M. Q. (2002). *Qualitative research evaluation methods* (3rd ed.). London: Sage Publications.

Stake, R. (2005). Qualitative case studies. In N. K. Denzin, & Y. S. Lincoln (Eds.), *Handbook of qualitative research* (3rd ed., pp. 443–446). London: Sage Publications.

Chapter 8
Research Findings:
Authors' Perceptions and the Copyright Framework

ABSTRACT

This chapter deals with the findings in relation to the first two research questions, namely: 1) How do Australian authors perceive copyright affecting them, and does it have any impact on how they practise? and 2) Do Australian authors believe that the existing copyright framework supports and encourages them in their creative efforts? Specifically, chapter 8 records the findings and preliminary observations in relation to authors' perceptions of copyright and the copyright framework, whereas chapter 9 looks at authors and publishers in a changing publishing industry. The chapter also includes a description of the demographics of the survey respondents and information on their incomes. Further issues discussed in chapter 8 are: whether authors see copyright as an incentive to create, how they view moral rights, their thoughts on existing copyright structures such as Copyright Agency Limited (CAL), perceived problem areas in the field of copyright and whether they regard authors as adequately protected by copyright legislation. Chapter 9 focuses on the relationship between authors and publishers, publishing contracts, ebooks, Google, and publishing options for authors in the digital world. Preliminary conclusions regarding authors' views on these issues lay the foundation for an in-depth discussion and analysis in chapter 10.

DOI: 10.4018/978-1-4666-5214-9.ch008

INTRODUCTION

The turmoil in copyright law in recent times might be compared to shifting tectonic plates. Consequently the research findings are viewed within the context of this changing landscape, and seek to capture some prevailing themes and viewpoints of Australian authors during this transitional period.

The findings in this chapter address the first two research questions, focussing firstly on authors' perception of copyright and how it affects them as creators and secondly, it examines whether they perceive the existing copyright framework as supportive and/or encouraging, and whether they have experienced any problems within this structure. On a broader level, these findings also provide a link with the philosophical concepts of copyright through history discussed in Chapter 3, by discussing the respondents' views on the meaning and significance of copyright to them as creators. Furthermore, it aims to enquire how the author functions in the subaltern sphere of the 'author group' in relation to the broader public sphere, within its ambits of socio-political and legislative change. The third research question, i.e. a discussion of authors' views on the changing nature of the publishing industry and how they have been affected by changes or advances in this area, will be discussed in the next chapter, traversing issues in the publishing industry as well as the emergence of new business and copyright models.

The results of the online survey are presented here in conjunction with the comments and responses of participants from the in-depth interviews, with comparative tables used to illustrate certain demographic variations.

Participants

As discussed in the last chapter, the participants consisted of 156 published authors who responded to a national online survey (September-October 2010), as well as a group of 17 authors, three publishers and a publishing contract consultant with whom in-depth, semi-structured interviews were conducted over a period of 16 months (July 2008 - November 2009). The author participants ranged from newly published to bestselling authors, including male and female respondents from a range of age groups, between 20 and 100+.

Presentation of Findings

The findings relate to the pivotal themes which emerged from the research questions plus further relevant issues that were identified during the course of the interviews and online survey. The diverse nature of the respondents produced a variety of responses on different issues, depending on how affected they were personally by the subject matter. For example, as expected, part time authors were in general less interested in copyright issues than their full time counterparts, who were financially dependent on their creative efforts. The findings in this chapter and the next allow for some preliminary observations, which will be more extensively discussed and analysed in Chapter 10.

Demographics

Of the 156 respondents in the survey group, 50 described themselves as full time authors and 106 as part time authors. A cross-tab function was employed in the survey as a tool to present the findings relating to the two groups, by distinguishing between them in respect of all survey questions. 51.3% of the respondents were members of the Australian Society of Authors (ASA).

The ages of respondents varied between 18 and 81 years of age, with one respondent in the 100+ category. Nearly 80% of respondents were over 40 years of age, with 14.8% in the 30-39 age group and only 5.7% under 30 years of age. The average age of full time authors was 50.8 years old, while the average part time author age was 45.3, indicating a higher level of interest in the subject matter on the part of more mature authors (over the age of 40). The majority of responses were from New South Wales (28.8%), with Queensland representing the second largest group at 25.6% *(See Figure 1, with the vertical bar indicating the number of authors).*

Although participants mostly described themselves as either a *'full time author'* or *'part time author,'* other ways in which they described themselves included: *'full time journalist,' 'freelance journalist,' 'poet,' 'playwright,' 'poet, editor, essayist, columnist,' 'lecturer in creative writing,' 'illustrator and author,' 'historian, educator and broadcaster,' 'academic and author,' 'writer,' 'freelance author/digital publisher,' 'freelance multimedia professional,' 'author, journalist, speaker and consultant,' 'freelance writer, book reviewer,' 'editor and writer,' 'a struggling writer,' 'recreational writer,' 'blogger, publisher, editor'* and *'cartoonist.'* Nearly 70% of the respondents described the type of writing they did as 'fiction,' 18.6% created 'non-fiction,' 7.1% 'academic' and 4.5% other writing.

Earnings from Writing

Only 132 of the 156 published authors responded to the question *'What is your approximate gross annual income from this source?'* regarding their income from their writing endeavours. It is acknowledged that the survey only

Figure 1.

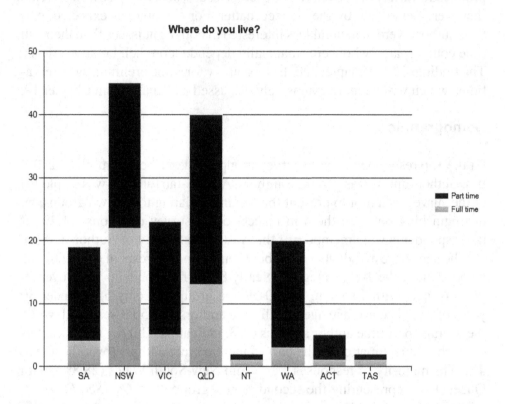

measured incomes of $1,000,00 upwards and it is possible that some of the non-responses may be due to this omission; however, the question was not peremptory. Two full time authors declared an income in excess of $150,000.00 per annum from their writing, with the lowest recorded incomes for 17.8% of full time authors falling in the '$1,000 - $2,000' category. The lowest income recorded for part time authors was 'nil' (as noted by two respondents), and the highest income declared from part time writing endeavours was 'between $90,000 - $95,000' (as recorded by one respondent).

Significantly, more than a third of all respondents to this question only earned 'between $1,000 - $2,000' per annum from their writing, which equated to 17.8% of the full time author group and 41.4% of the part time author contingent. In both groups this income bracket represented by far the largest number of respondents, with the second largest group (15.2%) falling in the '$5,000 - $10,000' bracket. *(See Figure 2, with the vertical bar indicating the number of authors).*

Figure 2.

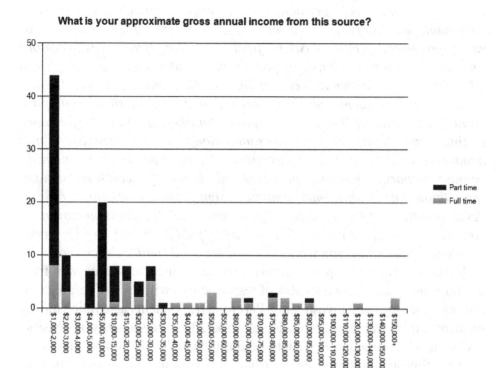

What is your approximate gross annual income from this source?

The top three earners (from writing endeavours) were all fiction writers, hailing from South Australia, Western Australia and Tasmania respectively. Whilst two of them claimed to spend a considerable amount of time on writing and writing related activities every week (65 and 86 hours per week respectively), one of them only spent 28 hours per week on writing and related activities. All three were receiving income from the Copyright Agency Limited (CAL), Educational Lending Rights (ELR) or Public Lending Rights (PLR), or a combination of these schemes, of between $12,000 -$17,000 per annum. Significantly, 61.7% of all respondents earned less than $10,000 per annum from writing and writing related activities.

Other Income

Approximately 57% of full time authors and 92% of part time authors disclosed another income source in addition to the writing income disclosed in the previous question. The professions and sources of income were varied and included the following descriptions: *'Disability pension,' 'librarian,' 'website designer,' 'government position,' 'theatre technician, actor, teacher,' 'casual teaching,' 'Centrelink,' 'pension' (several respondents cited this source), 'self-employed,' 'journalism,' 'investments,' 'part time job at Foodland,' 'university professor,' 'writing lessons,' 'freelance editor,' 'freelance illustrator,' 'business,' 'theatre director, actor, playwright,' 'waitressing,' 'teaching,' 'arts administration,' 'academic,' 'chairman,' 'public sector employee,' 'retail,' 'media work,' 'academic teaching and research,' 'partner/family support, grants,' 'casual tutor,' 'business consultant,' 'marketing manager,' 'freelance editing,' 'consultant solicitor,' 'superannuation,' 'IT content manager,' 'arts administration,' 'accounting,' 'instructor,' 'town planner,' 'bank interest,' 'spouse support,' 'parents,' 'part time cab driver,' 'research technician,' 'expedition staff on ship tours, graphic design,' 'share portfolio,' 'software development,' 'media training,' 'retail business,' 'business management consultant,' 'administration,' 'full time job,' 'public servant,' 'office work,' 'gardening, cleaning, care work,' 'consulting' and 'builder's labourer.'*

In the full time group the largest alternative income source was from teaching and academic work (36% of respondents), with 24% of respondents relying on savings and investments. Part time respondents also relied mostly on income from teaching and academic work (23%) and secondly on pension, savings and investments (21%). It therefore appeared that a notable number of both full time and part time author groups relied on these sources of income, in addition to their income from writing.

AUTHORS' PERCEPTION OF COPYRIGHT

The first research issue focussed on authors' perception of copyright and how it affected them as creators. The findings are presented here by investigating *first*, the authors' personal viewpoints on the meaning and value of copyright; *second*, whether they regarded copyright as an incentive to create; *third*, other considerations in the creative process and *fourth*, what moral rights meant to them as creators. During the interview process and online survey authors were given the opportunity to respond to questions dealing with the meaning and value of copyright to them as creators and the meaning and implications of the related concept of moral rights.

The Meaning and Value of Copyright

Authors' responses differed markedly in their perception of copyright and its effects on their practice as writers. Their viewpoints depended largely on their level of interest in copyright issues, awareness of the economic implications of copyright and financial reliance on their writing. Some authors placed a strong emphasis on the emergence of an Internet culture and the sharing and exchanging of creative work, contrasting new models such as the Creative Commons concept discussed in Chapter 5 with traditional publishing models. These authors were often of the view that copyright requirements have changed to such an extent that existing models no longer provided useful solutions for authors' needs. Others admitted to a lack of knowledge on the subject and expressed concerns about copyright protection of their work. In the following section the viewpoints of the interviewees are discussed and examined in relation to the results of the online survey.

During his interview Frank Moorhouse expressed the opinion that many authors did not want to know or did not particularly have an awareness of copyright. 'This has always been the case,' he said.

Authors who are essentially concerned with arts ethic tend to disregard commercial incentive, because the incentive there is self-expression and social communication and connections, readership, with essentially an arts ethic which has values other than commercial reward. So the attitude or posture of the literary writer tends to disregard those considerations and to go on with one's work.

He elaborated further and said:

But behind all that posture is ... a confidence that there'll be fairness and there's confidence that reward will come, and those writers who adopt that forget that a lot of other writers, including some of the great writers, fought very hard for copyright protection and for the Society of Authors in building up structures where they can exist and get rewarded and get compensation.

He felt this was, in some ways, a false and rather ignorant position for literary writers to adopt, though he acknowledged some literary writers had been quite fierce in their fight for copyright and protection of their rights over the years. In his view it was ultimately not only reward or compensation or commercialism; essentially the return on one's work was a way of funding or financing one's further work. Therefore it was in the interests of one's art to make sure one received as much as possible for one's work in the market and through other avenues.

Moorhouse recognised that some authors relied on a sense of fairness, an expectation that they would be rewarded for their work, without taking due measures to ensure that that happened. He further pointed out that copyright not only provided a reward for creative efforts, but practically enabled the author to produce further work by providing financial sustenance.

Kate Eltham, author and CEO of the Queensland Writers Centre remarked on authors' attitudes towards copyright as follows:

I think that it's perceived as a legal issue and not as a business issue, and yes, I think if more authors thought about copyright in relation to it being the essential asset of their business, they might have a different attitude to it, but I think they think of it as a legal thing and therefore a bit over their heads and not worth getting into.

This perception was also evident in authors' responses to questions on the copyright framework in Australia, which are discussed later in this chapter. One author (also a freelance journalist) stated candidly:

I suppose I'm aware of (it), but it's more along the lines of – do I know all my rights and where I stand with all that sort of stuff? That's where I start getting really kind of fuzzy, you know, as in the legal side of everything. If you're employed by somebody, you don't care as long as you get your pay cheque at the end of the day.

Nigel Krauth, author and academic made some salient observations about the intrinsic value of copyright to the author as owner of the work itself, and related the instance of a book he co-authored, of which the rights were sold overseas and which was translated into German. He said:

It's really interesting, that concept of a book of yours that's no longer yours. Nobody even tells me what happens to it. I can't feel the same link to it. It's a very weird feeling…this idea that without copyright the thing is not yours.

His comments acknowledged the emotional link that authors experienced with their work and the feeling of disconnection when they sold the copyright to that work, which indicated that copyright may have a deeper meaning to authors than a mere economic incentive.

He also showed insight into the commercial value of copyright and the need for writers to manage this asset, saying,

Writers, I know, are notoriously bad at managing their own career. One of the things I found when I was a full time writer, for nearly ten years, was that I suddenly saw myself as the self employed businessman. And that was a great insight into my own situation. The insight that I was actually a businessman managing my own products, managing my own career, managing my time.

'If I was a full time writer I'd be right on top of all of this,' he said, referring to current legislative issues and acknowledging that being employed, he was no longer as astute about legalities as he should have been.

Phillip Edmonds, author and publisher of literary magazine *Wet Ink*, agreed that authors needed to be more pro-active. Some interviewees viewed the concept in a simplistic manner. As one author said, giving voice to the 'author's proprietary right' premise proposed by Rose (1988, p. 53): 'Copyright to me is simply my right to say: this is mine.' The interviewee comments reflected an acknowledgement that many authors were slow to protect their own interests and that copyright had a commercial aspect which required proper management by authors. Copyright was seen by some authors as an 'after-the fact' issue, a given which automatically applied once one had created something.

In the discussion which follows, interviewees' perceptions are examined in relation to the incentive value that they ascribed to copyright, noting further which other elements were regarded as motivating factors by survey respondents.

Do Authors See Copyright as an Incentive to Create?

This question sought to determine whether Australian authors sufficiently appreciated the incentive value of copyright. If one accepts that the Australian system of copyright administration is essentially utilitarian, (as became evident in the discussion in Chapter 3) with a parallel tradition of 'author's rights' as proposed by Rose (1988, p. 53), it is necessary, in the context of this book, to determine how the Australian author views copyright in relation to creativity. Is it perceived as an economic incentive created in the interest of promoting creativity, a natural right in accordance with the Lockean viewpoint, or a moral right?

Frank Moorhouse referred to his essay 'The escape from 'eccentric penury': How should we pay literary authors? Policy visions for the Australian writing economy,' where he made the following observations about artistic motivation:

Paradoxically, the literary author is often characterised, at least in early career, by an indirect economic motivation. The young literary author (and even mature authors) at the time of setting out to write seriously make no attempt to calculate the return on the work and the book, say, is begun without much idea of how long it is going to take or how much it will 'cost' to create the work in monetary terms let alone in terms of life – of blood, sweat, and tears. Most young writers do not think much about how they will live and what the economics of their art form is. This is not wholly a romantic attitude. It is not possible for even an experienced publisher to clearly predict what a book will earn in the life of an author and least of all, in the life of the book. For the publisher it is a speculative venture. For the writer as well, it is, unconsciously, also a speculative investment (Moorhouse, 2008, p. 4).

These comments support the contention that most authors, at least initially, are not directly motivated by economic benefits, as this is often an unknown quantity in the creative process.

Respondents to the online survey had varying views on the incentive value of copyright in the creative process. Nearly 21% of full time and 21.4% of part time authors *strongly disagreed* with the statement *'I regard copyright as an incentive to create,'* with over 27% of full time and 32% of part time authors disagreeing with the proposal; thus, a total of nearly 52% of respondents disagreed to various degrees that they regarded copyright as an incentive to create.

In respect of the statement *'Copyright is a consideration for me when I create,'* 23.4% of full time and 18.4% of part time authors expressed strong agreement, with 38.3% and 41.7% respectively expressing agreement, thus a total of nearly 61% of respondents agreed that they considered copyright when writing creatively. It would thus appear that, whilst copyright was a consideration for most of the respondents in their creative efforts, they did not necessarily regard it as an incentive to create, as the responses to the previous question suggested.

The statement *'Copyright is a consideration for me when I publish my work'* evoked a strong response, with nearly 87% of all respondents agreeing with the statement. This demonstrated that more respondents regarded copyright as a consideration when it came to the publishing process than during the creative process.

Whilst these findings reflect the online responses, the issue was discussed in more detail during the in-depth interviews. Eleven of the interviewees expressed the view that they did not regard copyright as an incentive to create and perceived it as having minimal or no influence in their approach to their work, whereas five respondents said it was an important consideration in their practice. However, five of the negative respondents qualified their answers by adding that, although copyright did not motivate them to write, it was an important issue to be considered once they had created the work. These respondents were emphatic in their viewpoint that copyright afforded them no creative motivation, some authors even expressing surprise at the suggestion. However, they provided mixed responses at how it impacted at the publishing stage. Several interviewees indicated that they would write in any event, whether copyright existed or not, with some commenting as follows:

John Kelly - 'When I write I don't even think about copyright. When I'm at my most creative, copyright is the furthest thing from my mind. Once the book, novel or memoir is ready to be presented to the world…then copyright is important.'

Sally Breen - 'It's not something I actively think about when I'm creating a text. I don't feel that it's something that motivates me or that I'm overly concerned about.'

Michael Jacobson - 'I never gave copyright a second thought. You know, never ever.'

Abbas El Zein - 'It wouldn't stop me from writing if there were no copyright. On the other hand, it would make how I deal with the management aspects of writing-paperwork, communication etc. very different. It's not really a direct incentive for writing.'

Phil Edmonds - 'They just do it, the poor buggers.'

Daphne Taylor - 'No, I don't regard copyright as an incentive to write. I write because I must. I love to write. However, I believe copyright is most important and am always most careful in my publishing choices.'

Notably, none of the interviewees who responded in this manner were financially dependent on their writing, and all had careers or resources other than those of being full time authors. Two publishers had opposing views on the issue, one saying, 'In many cases I think authors are going to create no matter what;' whereas another mainstream publisher thought copyright was definitely an incentive to create as 'without copyright authors can't be assured of ownership and control over what they create, nor payment for their work.'

An insightful observation was made by Nigel Krauth, who stated:

I only gradually realised the importance of copyright. I never realised that copyright is the writer's bread and butter. My first superficial answer to the question is, well no, copyright isn't the incentive to create. Now, from a mature, hind-sighted viewpoint I would say that it is; because you have to have control over your copyright. There are some things you may not care about and there are some things that you may significantly care about. But these relate directly to your income, and it's the only thing you've got.

Those authors who regarded copyright as an incentive to create indicated that it was a consideration for them in how they practised their craft. However, all of them recognised that there was an element of passion or inspiration involved which fuelled the creative process. As aptly articulated by Robyn Sheahan-Bright:

Yes, the creation of writing, or any other art form, although obviously driven by a passion to create, is accorded value by the recognition that the product is the outcome of the creator's intellectual effort. Copyright is a recognition of that intellectual property.

One author stated paradoxically: 'Undoubtedly. Unless people can get some reward, they would not be nearly as creative…but some people will create anyway,' whilst Nick Earls considered copyright to be an incentive to create, but qualified his response by saying that the primary incentive to create was simply the act of making something itself.

Earls went on to explain:

When I'm sitting at home staring at the wall I'm thinking creatively and I'm making up stories. What I'm doing of course is generating intellectual property that I can then license around the world in order to earn an income. So copyright is a really important part of that and has been for three hundred years. But I'm very aware that when I make something I own it, and I want as many people to read it as possible. I'm very happy for people to read it in libraries and I don't have to make three dollars out of it every time someone reads it, but I am aware that I can then take to the marketplace and sell in a range of countries and to a range of media…That's what makes this a job rather than just a hobby.' He acknowledged that there would be differing viewpoints between full time and part time authors and between emerging and established authors.

He also recognised the longer term value of copyright, which he expressed as follows: 'Once you've sold your rights into a few different places and a few different media you've got a first hand example of the power of copyright and what it means to be the copyright owner.'

For example, the Perfect Skin film. There's a book that I wrote in 1999 in Australia that was published in 2000 in Australia, and filmed in Italy in 2008, years later, about the Italian edition of the novel. So the biggest single payday I've had in connection with that story came almost a decade after writing it when the film went into production. I think it's only fair that I should be paid for the right to turn that story into a film. It's when things like that happen to you that it reinforces what it really means to be the owner of copyright.

Another bestselling author, who writes as Anita Bell for non-fiction and AA Bell for her award winning fiction, distinguished between commercial works on the one hand and additional private self-expressive work not intended for commercial resale on the other. Regarding the former she said that copyright 'provides me with the reassurance that my work under any pseudonym cannot be stolen or sold, or given away without my consent' and in the latter instance it 'provides me with the assurance that others can't profit from my creations without my consent.' This distinction seems to reflect the notion that authors create for different purposes but that they nevertheless attach value to copyright, irrespective of whether there are commercial considerations attached to the work.

Other Considerations in the Creative Process

In addition to writing being described as a passionate pursuit or something that was done for the love of the creative act, the interviewees and published authors responding to the survey identified motivating factors other than copyright in the creative process. These factors included, to varying degrees, personal satisfaction, financial considerations and the prospect of achieving recognition for their work.

The online survey results focussed on whether any of these three factors were major motivational factors to the sample group. The analysis again distinguished between full time and part time authors and produced the following insights:

Both groups declared an overwhelming preference for the statement *'When I create I am mostly motivated by personal satisfaction,'* with nearly 90% of full time and more than 93% of part time authors agreeing with it. However, both groups, to a lesser degree of nearly 46%, also agreed with the statement *'When I create I am mostly motivated by achieving recognition,'* indicating that there was some overlap in their purpose, with some respondents being equally motivated by personal satisfaction and achieving recognition.

A more marked variation in the full time and part time group responses was however recorded in respect of the statement *'When I create I am mostly motivated by financial consideration.'* 83.4% of part time authors disagreed with the statement whilst only 5.8% agreed. While this response could be expected from a group who was pursuing writing as a part time activity, the majority of the group of full time authors also responded negatively, with nearly 67% disagreeing with the statement and 23% agreeing with it. It would thus appear that most members of the sample group (whether full time or part time authors) did not see financial reasons as their main motivation for writing. However, the higher percentage of full time writers who recognise financial considerations is noteworthy.

Once again the interviews provided some further depth to these broader findings. One author who was also a publisher regarded both personal satisfaction and the promise of financial gain to be motivating factors in the creative process, stating: 'It's something that gives me pleasure and I'm able to be commercially successful at it.' Another author and freelance journalist focussed on recognition and personal satisfaction as the two factors motivating her to create but commented that financial gain was important for self-worth. Both these interviewees expressed an appreciation for the economic value of their writing, but not as a primary objective.

An established author of three novels commented that he wrote because 'it is the only thing I can do, just about, apart from playing guitar. I've always just done it and some people, enough people, think I do it well enough that I'm motivated to keep going.' He continued in a candid fashion:

I was never ever kidding myself that I was going to be a millionaire from writing books. My first book, I did it purely for my family and was lucky enough that it was accepted by a publisher. The second book was written to fulfil a contract and the third book I'm still writing and that's five years later. Journalism is my occupation, whereas the novels are what I do with what time I have on the side. It's the one thing I can do and I like doing it.

His observations reflect the reality that an author may be motivated by several different considerations in relation to different projects at different times.

Moral Rights: Meaning and Value

As discussed in Chapter 2, the *Copyright Act 1968* (as amended by the *Copyright Amendment (Moral Rights) Act 2000*) defines a 'moral right' as *'a right of attribution of authorship; or a right not to have authorship falsely attributed; or a right of integrity of authorship'* (section 189). Part IX of the Act sets out the provisions dealing with authors' moral rights, providing statutory recognition of these rights. As an integral part of copyright the concept of moral rights merited an exploration of its constructive use and value to authors. The issue was approached on two levels in the context of the research: *First*, what do moral rights mean to the author as creator and *second*, do they feel that their moral rights are sufficiently protected under the current copyright structure.

In the online survey, 97.8% of full time and 92.9% of part time authors indicated that they viewed moral rights as *'important,'* with 62.2% and 64.3% of these respondents respectively stating that it was *'very important.'* Not a single respondent viewed moral rights as 'unimportant' or 'not important at all.' It would thus appear that most of the respondents were acutely aware of the importance of having moral rights in respect of their work.

On the question of whether they thought that their moral rights were sufficiently protected under the current copyright structure, the respondents appeared to be doubtful. Only 31.1% of full time and 27.5% of part time authors agreed with the proposition *'My moral rights are adequately protected under the current structure,'* with 40% and 65.3% respectively stating that they were undecided. Almost a third of the full time group and 7.1% of the part time group disagreed with the statement. This result reflected an uncertainty in the sample group regarding the adequacy of protection of their moral rights afforded by the current copyright legislation and Government structures. It also showed a greater concern on the part of full time authors, as opposed to the part time group, that their rights were not adequately protected. The findings here may however indicate that some authors are not yet familiar with the amendments brought about by the *Copyright Amendment (Moral Rights) Act 2000.*

Therefore, although the respondents expressed an overwhelming bias in favour of the importance of moral rights, there appeared to be a substantial lack of knowledge (with a total of nearly 60% being undecided) about the level of protection afforded to them by the current structure in respect of their moral rights. The responses by interviewees varied from indifference to strong appreciation, with some authors acknowledging the value of moral rights not only as a concept reflecting personality rights but rather as a specific right which results in an economic benefit. Although most of the interviewees were aware of the inclusion of moral rights in the legislation, one author admitted that he had no idea what moral rights were and another saw it as 'just another form of copyright.'

Most authors recognised that moral rights gave authors the right to be identified as the creator of the work and to be able to determine how their work should be treated. One author and publisher, Sally Collings, stated that it meant that 'creators' rights go beyond a fiscal matter and that they have a *genuine* say in how their work is treated.' Robyn Sheahan-Bright emphasised the importance of the right to be identified as the author, especially where writing had been commissioned for a flat fee and then made available online as a value-adding tool by the publisher, with no further payments (to the author) attached to the writing. This view was echoed by author Daphne Taylor who stated further: 'Moral rights mean a great deal to me. It is my right for my created works to be acknowledged as mine.'

A bestselling author commented as follows:

As a professional author, I require the moral right to assert or disclaim my authorship over a work, and to object to any editing changes which may undermine my reputation. In my experience, this also extends to the meta-documents and meta-processes which support the work, such as press releases, interview quotations, and even the types of third party companies which are permitted to use my books (or extracts there from) as promotional for their own products or services.

This viewpoint reflected the perception that moral rights not only entitled the author to assert his/her authorship rights, but also to determine how the material was treated by external parties. It further recognised the fact that without this right an author would lose the ability to control how his/her work was used.

Author Nick Earls regarded the value of moral rights as a tangible right to be asserted or alienated by the author at will. He described the meaning of moral rights to him as creator as follows:

It means that I can make some claims as to the integrity of the work, that people can't come along and change my work and have my name attached to it, and make it something that is drastically dissimilar to the book that I had written in the first place. In a way that changes its meaning or changes what I wanted to achieve by writing it. I think that it's good that there is some notion paid to the integrity of the work that honours the intention of the author who created it.

He went on to elucidate by again using the example of his book *Perfect Skin* where the Italian film rights were sold to an Italian filmmaker: 'When you sign off your film rights you have to sign away any moral rights over the film.'

… because in buying your film rights they reserve the right to do whatever they want with it in order to get it made. And they will change the characters and they will change the story and I'd much rather that was spelled out up front. I think they probably feel that in order to be able to make a film without that impediment, they need to know you're not going to take action against them saying, but that's not what my story was like.

Earls pointed out that, in this case, the producer not only changed the name of the characters and the name of the book to *Solo un padre (Only a father)*, but the setting was changed from Brisbane, Australia in mid-summer to mid-winter in Italy's north. He professed not to be unhappy with the changes as he had willingly parted with the moral rights in that instance, but observed: 'There were times when I was thinking, why did you even pay me at all? But I was happy to take it. I accept that and I think it's kind of good that contracts require that to be spelled out so that you know what you're up for,' he said. 'I've even signed contracts that have had specific clauses saying that I have no right to complain publicly if I don't like the end result.'

He explained that that was usually in the case of producers who had been 'burned' before by adapting the work of authors who had complained publicly and loudly. Other producers did not mind complaints by the author as it provided the film with attention and media exposure. 'So some producers are happy to have you hate what they do, other producers want you to hate it in silence,' he said. 'But very rarely does a producer make you happy. The one other adaptation I've had made was actually shot here in English and I was happy with that.'

His comments, based on his own experience, illustrated the practical value that authors may attach to their moral rights when contemplating the overseas sale of their copyright, especially film rights, and the consequences of the alienation of such rights. However, it is noted that Earls would be regarded as an 'elite interviewee,' more aware of and concerned with moral rights, due to the wide distribution of his work and his first-hand involvement with moral rights in his contracts.

CURRENT LEGISLATIVE FRAMEWORK

The second enquiry focussed on whether the current copyright framework, as discussed in Chapter 5, supported and encouraged creativity, and further examined how these structures, in the realms of the wider public sphere, impacted on the creative sphere within which authors function. Cognisance was taken of Australian copyright legislation as well as other supporting structures, such as collecting agencies created by Government to address copyright issues and royalty payments to authors. Authors were able to comment on the value and benefits of these bodies as well as the legislative structure in Australia. This section deals with authors' knowledge and perceptions of the Australian and international legislative copyright framework.

Current Legislation

Interviewees and online respondents were questioned about their level of knowledge of Australian copyright legislation and the contents and effect of the *Copyright Act,* as well as their understanding of international copyright structures and legislation. Interviewees were also asked to comment on the issue of parallel importation, which arose during the course of this research and will be discussed in the latter part of this section. Respondents varied substantially in their level of knowledge of Australian copyright legislation. However, it was generally regarded as a protective structure which was taken for granted by some authors, criticised by others and regarded as 'broadly adequate' by at least one mainstream publisher.

As discussed in the last section, many of the respondents appeared to regard themselves as well informed with regard to aspects of copyright, as reflected in their responses when asked to rate their knowledge of copyright, with a total of 75.2% perceiving themselves to be reasonably or well informed about copyright, evidencing a high level of confidence on the subject. However, the same confidence was not evident in their perceived knowledge of copyright legislation.

In response to the statement *'Australian authors are adequately protected by copyright laws,'* full time authors responded more positively than part time authors. However, a third of full time and nearly half of part time authors professed to be 'undecided' on the issue. A total of 48.9% of full time and 43.9% of part time authors agreed with the statement. Thus, although a substantial percentage of respondents perceived their copyright to be adequately protected, the percentage of respondents who were undecided (43.4% in total) demonstrated a measure of uncertainty about the effectiveness of copyright protection in Australian law.

Not surprisingly, the ability to probe more deeply in the in-depth interviews resulted in some further illumination on the issue, although the responses were far from cohesive among the author/publisher respondents.

'The infrastructure in Australia has changed in a number of ways over the past 25 years. In many ways the author's position has strengthened,' was the view of literary writer Frank Moorhouse, who continued by pointing out that the *Copyright Act* had been 'rewritten' in the late 70s, after the *University of NSW v. Moorhouse* (1975) case relating to photocopying, discussed in Chapter 2. Positive steps taken included the setting up of a Copyright Tribunal as well as the Copyright Agency Limited (CAL), which, to his knowledge, had distributed millions of dollars over the past 20 years. He also referred to the emergence of agencies such as the Association of Literary Agents and the Australian Society of Authors, which offer a contract advisory service to authors, as positive advances.

Moorhouse acknowledged that electronic rights had not yet been defined or policed by 1975 and that there were 'a whole new wave of problems emerging and challenges to copyright' which had to be confronted. He saw the 'Google issue' as something to be dealt with and recognised that Google's actions would have far-reaching ramifications for copyright, thereby acknowledging the influence of global developments on the Australian legislative structure. 'If copyright as we understand it, that is, obviously, the right to copy, is going to collapse in some sort of way or become porous, we have to look at other mechanisms for paying authors and musicians and other primary creators,' he said. He was of the view that the Australian infrastructure compared favourably to other countries and that the Australian copyright structure was more advanced than most of its European counterparts.

A different perspective was put forward by a mainstream publisher, who saw current copyright legislation only as 'broadly adequate' and voiced the concern that amendments have tended to be biased towards the interests of users, including those of libraries and educational institutions, to an extent not seen in other English speaking countries. 'This disadvantages content creators like authors and publishers,' she said. 'The Australian Copyright Act is far more generous towards users than a lot of its equivalent Acts overseas,' she observed, and blamed this partially on authors' and publishers' lack of diligence in lobbying Government on copyright issues.

In contrast, 'users such as libraries and educational institutions have had quite a degree of success in lobbying for "pro-use",' she remarked. Evidence of this was the current provisions in the Act relating to educational institutions and some of the aspects of digital reforms in 2001, which were 'fairly pro-user.' She ascribed this trend to the fact that Australia was a 'massive importer' of intellectual property, which provided the Australian Government and Attorney General's department with the justification for supporting pro-user changes to the *Copyright Act*.

With regard to their personal experiences within the copyright framework, most of the interviewees felt adequately protected. 'I feel pretty well protected,' said Nick Earls. 'People have tended to respect my copyright, and the occasions in which people have breached it have been innocent and generally harmless. You rarely have cases where people are accused of plagiarism, breaching someone else's copyright that way.' He stated further:

There's something inherently straightforward about the notion that when you create something, when you write something, it's yours and it's up to you to then sell it where you want, and when you want and how you want. And that other people can't just take it.

His viewpoint confirmed a perception that a Lockean natural rights approach (as discussed in Chapter 3) – more so than a utilitarian approach - had been applied to the legislative structure in a satisfactory manner, and that it was generally perceived by others in the same way. It is also interesting to note that Earls had, as discussed previously, experienced reasonably positive encounters with copyright and financial compensation for his work.

Other authors agreed that they felt protected by the current legislative framework and commented as follows: 'I just always thought that copyright laws were there to protect me so I was quite happy with that,' author and journalist Michael Jacobson stated; he added further that he assumed that his agent would 'take care of all of that.' Robyn Sheahan-Bright remarked: '[A]t present they [authors] are protected by the Act and the 30 day rule,' but acknowledged that 'increased access to digital sales has erased certainty in some regards.' Her comments reflected an awareness of the impact of global marketing trends on the existing copyright framework and were echoed by the views of Daphne Taylor, who said: 'I believe Australian authors of print works are adequately covered. I am not so sure about electronic or audio books.' Travel writer Claire Scobie, whilst admitting to not knowing the finer details of the legislation, felt that her work was adequately protected by the Australian copyright framework.

Another author differed from these interviewees as she did not feel that authors were adequately protected against copyright infringement under the current structure. She substantiated her viewpoint by referring to the fact that, on many occasions her 'content and unique concepts have been "borrowed" lawfully by other writers and business professionals,' who changed a few words, while maintaining her voice and style in the 'revised' work, in order to make their own work commercially saleable. She stated: 'In a perfect world, the copyright laws would be so simple and straightforward that no lawyers would be needed to defend them,' arguing that current legislation fell short in many respects.

In amplification of this statement she pointed out that, currently, if an Australian author's work was published in New York and breached digitally, an Australian law firm had to employ a New York firm to defend the creator's rights, which was financially untenable. She criticised the fact that, under the current structure, copyright thieves were able to get away with their crimes if it was not commercially viable to pursue them. She did not volunteer a solution as to how the issue could be addressed, but her comments took cognisance of the fact that the boundaries of copyright protection have expanded and may no longer be properly addressed by current legislative structures.

It was thus evident that, whilst most of the respondents in the online survey admitted to being reasonably to well informed about copyright, the same number did not express equal confidence when asked about the effectiveness of the protection afforded by the current copyright structure, with 33.3% of full time and 48% of part time authors professing to be 'undecided' on the issue. However, in the case of the interviewees most of them felt adequately protected within the current copyright framework, as evidenced by their responses (with a few exceptions), with knowledgeable commentators such as Moorhouse pointing out the advances that have been made in Australian copyright protection since the 1970s.

During the course of the research certain important developments took place with regard to Australian copyright legislation in respect of proposed changes to the *Copyright Act*. The most controversial and topical issue that emerged was the matter of parallel importation and the Productivity Commission's Report and recommendations, which were discussed, debated and finalised during 2008/2009. As indicated in Chapter 2, the Productivity Commission's recommendations were, after some debate, rejected by Government in its decision not to follow the Commission's proposals but to leave current legislative provisions intact. In view of the fact that the recommendations were made and the debate concluded in 2009, the topic was relevant during the interview phase of the research but was not included in the September 2010 online survey, due to its earlier finalisation.

The topic evoked a passionate response from the writing community, and some 563 submissions were submitted by authors, publishers and booksellers (Australian Government Productivity Commission, 2008). The issue was addressed in this research as it had been unresolved at the time of the in-depth interviews and its resolution could have had a dramatic impact on Australian authors' copyright. The perspectives and submissions of authors and publishers were instrumental in influencing the final decision in this matter.

A notable side effect of this controversial issue was to unite authors and publishers in their quest to retain the *status quo* on parallel import provisions, as was evident from the number and diversity of submissions made to the Productivity Commission. This landmark issue will be discussed in more depth in Chapter 10. The topic was important to these two groups for two reasons: first, it impressed on authors the significance and value of territorial copyright protection and second, it raised an awareness of the importance of preserving a viable publishing industry in Australia.

Whilst most authors and publishers argued fervently against the removal of parallel import restrictions, their supporting arguments relating principally to similar provisions in other English speaking countries, cultural values and the future of the Australian publishing industry, others expressed the view that these arguments were moot in view of the emergence of new globalised media structures and the diffusion of geographical borders in publishing. To this extent, and as a reflection of market considerations in Australia, the issue remains relevant even though the debate has been settled and parallel import provisions are to remain a part of the Copyright Act for the foreseeable future. Some interviewee perspectives on the topic follow below.

A mainstream publisher pointed out that the USA and Britain protected copyright holders in their own countries through parallel import restrictions, and warned against treating books as commodities similar to car parts or textiles. She reflected that books were also 'a public good' and 'cultural artefacts' and thus worthy of different considerations to general commodities. She further stressed the risk involved for publishers in printing, stocking, insuring and distributing books when there were no guarantees that the books were going to sell.

Australian book publishers publish hundreds of brand new and unique products every year, and thousands of new titles from international publishers are released into the Australian market annually. No other industry apart from the music industry turns out so many new products in one year. 'This puts us in a very dubious position,' she said.

Because each book is a risk, and only relatively few of these books sell well enough to do more than pay their way, and many fall by the wayside. A bookseller will only want to import those that become very successful, thereby cutting not only publisher and author income but also the capacity of local publishers to invest in future new local titles, as they need at least some older titles to be profitable to underpin the investment. A book is a one-off cultural product, not a regular commodity like most others. It is not like breakfast cereals, for which the market is relatively stable, and it is only a matter of whether your new marketing campaign or the new product you release this year might increase the market share for one product over another.

A flaw in the argument that parallel imports would allow for cheaper books to the consumer was that booksellers would be under no obligation to pass on any savings. As an example she referred to a book by Peter Carey, still on sale in Australia, being remaindered in the USA, which might be picked up by Dymocks as remaindered stock at a cheaper price. 'There's nothing to say Dymocks will pass on that cheaper price,' she observed, further commenting:

It's highly likely that they won't. They might drop the price by a couple of dollars but, chances are that they will drop the price by a little bit, enough to be what they perceive to be a competitive advantage. They might advertise it. But why are we suddenly expecting a retailer to pass on the cheaper price?

If parallel importing restrictions had been lifted, she foresaw that the Australian book publishing industry was unlikely to disappear, but would have become a much more risky enterprise, inevitably impacting negatively on the capacity of Australian based publishers to invest in Australian books.

Another problem that would have been exacerbated by the lifting of parallel importing restrictions, in her view, was the piracy of tertiary textbooks in Asia and the possibility that illegitimate editions of these books would then more easily have been bought in Asia and sold on the Australian market, undercutting the legitimate edition. This would have been to the detriment of campus booksellers and created great uncertainty for publishers and distributors, who were currently protected by the restrictions that made parallel imports illegal. If they had been forced to pull out of that market, due to competition from illegal operators, it would have meant that students may no longer have had ready access to the text books they needed on campus, but would have had to rely on the Internet or unreliable 'car boot retailers' for their books. It may be observed that, apart from publishers and distributors, authors would by implication also suffer a loss of their royalties as a consequence of these instances of piracy.

Publisher and publishing contract consultant, Alex Adsett, agreed that it was 'ridiculous to contemplate' getting rid of Australian parallel importing restrictions, as other English speaking countries such as the USA and Britain 'would never dream of getting rid of their territorial copyright, so why should Australia?' She said, 'I'm quite passionate on this, as is everyone in the trade.' In support of her viewpoint, she noted that 90% of Australian booksellers supported parallel import restrictions, the abolition of which would only benefit major booksellers such as Dymocks, Big W and Kmart. 'When the ABA, the Australian Booksellers Association, turned out their opinion on this, to come out against the restrictions being removed, I thought that was a very important and telling point that booksellers voted to keep the *status quo*,' she said.

Furthermore, if book prices in Australia compared unfavourably to those overseas, the price difference was often based on the Goods and Services Tax (GST). 'I think we're one of the only countries that put the GST on books. If the price difference is the government's problem then I think they should get rid of the GST, given we're the only ones that do it anyway,' she observed. This viewpoint was also expressed by author Sally Breen, who suggested the government remove GST from books if it wanted to lower book prices.

Frank Moorhouse supported the proposition that books were not mere commodities, having significant cultural value. He saw copyright zones as more than economic zones, rather as cultural zones that contribute to the development of cultural identity and protect cultural rights. He felt that the removal of these protective barriers would be detrimental to Australian authors and publishers, driving local publishers out of business 'because they know that their mature authors with overseas appeal will be lured away (by overseas publishers) and that new Australian writers with only local appeal will have no nurturing, commercial base.'

Moorhouse commented:

It is useful to remember that, legally and socially, books have a double nature. In all countries they are recognised both as commodities in commercial sense and are seen as social property - it is this character as social property which distinguishes them from refrigerators and TVs and cars.

He illustrated the special nature of books by referring to the fact that 70 years after the death of the author the work entered the public domain and was out of copyright:

They become the property of us all. And most dramatically, in our society, the work is made available to the community free of charge through the free-library system. No other product is treated this way in our society. They are given this special standing as social property - as property held in common and secured by copyright - because they are considered to be the building blocks, to a significant degree, of the other parts of our civilised life.

Other authors such as Katherine Howell, Robyn Sheahan-Bright and Nick Earls emphasised how the removal of the restrictions could have a detrimental effect on authors' livelihood. Howell echoed the sentiments of the mainstream publisher who remarked that Australian publishers would be loath to invest in emerging writers if the market were entirely unprotected, due to the possibility of UK or US copies flooding the market.

Sheahan-Bright pointed out that the Australian publishing and writing industry was challenged by the low level of government assistance offered to publishers, printers and distributors, whereas in other industries, larger subsidies and tariffs were offered in order to make Australian products more viable. It was also challenged by the online sales outlets, which were increasingly competing with retailers and wholesalers for that market share, she said. She saw the continued growth of the Australian book industry as a measure of its strength and expressed the view that the removal of importation restrictions would erode that strength and lead to a decline of the fortunes of local publishers. She was also concerned that these challenges might prove insurmountable for less established or emerging authors and create instances of increased 'dumping' of overseas-originated copies of their books here, which would seriously diminish their royalties.

Earls was equally concerned about these issues and predicted that authors would suffer greatly if the restrictions were lifted. Although Australians would, for a time, have that book available at a price that the Australian market could not currently match, he pointed out that it would not be cheaper for that long because eventually that stock would be exhausted and the local publisher would not print more books because of the threat of it being undermined. 'So that book would go out of print,' he concluded.

He referred to the effect these activities would have on the cultural value of books:

[P]articularly in the case of my American editions, they often change in hundreds of ways. Often in small ways, but hundreds none the less, from my Australian editions, which would spoil the reading experience in Australia. An Australian reading those books would notice things that didn't fit and it would take them out of the story and really affect the kind of reading experience they had.

As examples he referred to the use of the words 'sidewalk' as opposed to 'pavement,' the use of 'holiday' as opposed to 'vacation,' and the fact that American editions would refer to 'college' instead of 'uni' and in some instances even change the names of towns and seasons in a novel.

However, other interviewees disagreed with these views. In contrast with most of the 563 submissions to the Productivity Commission, which were markedly in favour of retaining the current structure and against the lifting of the restrictions, apart from a few dissenters, there were some interviewees who regarded the debate as limited and the issue as academic.

Sally Collings, author and publisher, expressed the view that the territorialism that had existed in publishing for decades would become a non-issue as digital books became more prevalent. This viewpoint was supported by author and self publisher John Kelly, who said that the possibility of self publication has effectively removed traditional territorial barriers. In his article *Publish and be damned* (2009), he stated that self publishers 'have access to a world-wide market by submitting their book to Google Books and Amazon and Lulu's Websites, all available for a start-up cost of less than $100.00.' On the issue of the deregulation of publishing and parallel importing, he commented: '…the bottom line is: I couldn't care less!' and continued:

The very nature of competition has been turned on its head and the once revered retail bookstore is staring its use-by date down the barrel just like the neighbourhood hardware store. But it isn't the threat of de-regulation that places it in this invidious position. The Internet already has! One can debate the positive and negative impacts of this development, but it has nothing to do with government regulation.

Kelly's observations were pertinent as he raised two issues, not only that of self-publication and the greater freedom it allowed, but also the fact that many books were bought online today across territorial copyright borders.

Former judge and author Ian Callinan noted that it would be difficult to resist 'the tide of American culturalism.' He referred to electronics as 'imperialism,' against which there was no suitable protection and suspected that no country had come to terms with the changes from a legislative perspective yet. He used the example of the *Gutnick* (2002) case to illustrate how copyright enforcement may be a problem in other territories. In that case an American publisher defamed an Australian citizen on the Internet and argued that the alleged defamation occurred at the place where the material had been uploaded onto the Internet. However, in that case the Court held that the defamation occurred where the material had been read. Considering the global reach of the Internet, this could cause litigation costs to soar and would render copyright protection ineffective against parties in other countries (should it be found that the breach occurred in that country). Furthermore, Callinan was of the opinion that the exponential increase in the use of English in countries such as China would exacerbate copyright protection problems in the relatively small Australian market.

This viewpoint indicated an awareness of the expansion of the public sphere within which copyright legislation has traditionally been utilised. It illustrated the fact that the 'global village' culture of communication has affected not only the social culture but in many instances the legislation as well. And to continue to be effective, it was necessary to adapt the legislation in keeping with new cultural trends, such as the increase in demand for English books in countries like China and the increased popularity of social media structures.

Kate Eltham commented that, although the issue of parallel importation had been resolved for the time being, there could well be further ramifications:

The position that Australian authors took on parallel imports, and those who are opposed to it, only really makes sense when you're talking about moving physical objects around between geographical markets, because of the objections that authors had about the arguments that were put forward on price, for example.

She further commented that a lot of the arguments put forward by publishers, some independent booksellers and authors were based on the costs that were added when you had to move heavy objects from geographic market to geographic market. Therefore, one of the reasons why books cost more in Australia was because exchange rates fluctuated, but also because shipping and distribution expenses were higher and taxation laws changed from country to country. Many factors would add to the cost for the intermediary in the supply chain and in the end they were reflected in the ultimate price the consumer paid.

Eltham compared these sobering realities to the digital goods market. 'A lot of those costs evaporate and you get de-centred mediation,' she explained, pointing out that middlemen were largely absent from the digital realm. 'I don't think it makes much sense to have restrictions on parallel importation of digital goods. It's an artificial limitation and there can be no real justification on economic grounds for that.' She saw it as a moral argument - whether Australian authors should be protected because it was the right thing to do, as opposed to whether there were sound business or economic reasons why that should be done.

Significantly, the parallel importing debate did not consider the reality of authors who publish in digital format, and remain unprotected against parallel importing, by virtue of section 112DA of the *Copyright Act*. It did, however, prompt a mention by the Government of the easy accessibility of books on the Internet, which they regarded as one of the reasons to reject the Productivity Commission's recommendation, on the basis that books were available to consumers over the Internet (in addition to bookshops) and therefore provided them with a greater diversity of choice and price. Despite the support for existing legislative structures shown by authors during the parallel importing debate, some of the interviewees illuminated issues such as the shift towards digital publishing, which will require issues such as territorial borders and import constraints to be revisited at some time in the future.

SUPPORTING GOVERNMENT STRUCTURES

Most interviewees and survey respondents appeared to have a significant appreciation of the governmental structures implemented to assist authors in obtaining a reward for their creative efforts. The CAL (Copyright Agency Limited) licensing programme was the most widely recognised by authors who received some financial benefit from their non-fiction work, whereas most interviewees with books in public and school libraries were aware of the PLR (Public Lending Rights) and ELR (Educational Lending Rights) payment schemes.

Other structures which were mentioned by authors included the Australia Council, recognised for their funding of authors, and the Australian Society of Authors (ASA), which provided authors with general advice, basic legal contract support and indicative fee structures. Arts Law was also perceived as a helpful support system, although authors such as Sally Breen lamented the demise of the Brisbane Arts Alliance, which previously assisted Queensland authors but had ceased operating due to a lack of Government funding. Her comments were echoed by Kate Eltham who pointed out that, in addition to the telephone assistance given by the Arts Law centre, the Australian Copyright Council provided email advice on general copyright issues and legislation, though not on specific legal issues.

Certain authors, such as Ian Callinan, expressed the view that government funding was misdirected and should be directed at assisting authors to get published by, for example, subsidising publishing and printing costs and the production of plays. He viewed writing grants to authors and the funding of seminars and writing classes as somewhat unproductive, stating that most great authors wrote better under pressure and that funding should be provided for the benefit of authors who had put in the hard work towards producing a deserving manuscript.

This viewpoint was not shared by authors such as Frank Moorhouse, who, in his essay *'The Escape from "Eccentric Penury": How should we pay literary authors? Policy visions for the Australian writing economy'* (2008, p. 4) proposed that the government should provide longer-term contracts (funding) for authors during mid-career through the Australia Council, as opposed to only funding emerging authors. He based his proposal on the fact that a book has many unpaid 'social uses' in addition to educational or commercial use:

A writer will have his or her books privately lent and borrowed, discussed privately and in public, studied, reviewed, used as the basis for scholarly critical works, used as "inspiration" for other works of art, used as the basis for journalism, quoted, researched, referred to, translated, set in examinations.

He added, 'In the absence of any adequate, direct, or simple financial mechanism to catch this form of use, governments could develop a cultural-economics policy which recognises the community use of the book described here together with a recognition of the longevity of the book in the life of the community.'

Moorhouse proposed further:

I argue that this 'social property' component of an author's work – ultimately illustrated by the fact that the intellectual property of the author is eventually returned to the public domain (copyright expires 70 years after the death of the author) – that is, authors go on working after they are dead - should be part of the calculation of the 'service' a living author provides in the economy.

He suggested the payment of a standard annual fee, similar to PLR, to all writers to compensate for this general social use and to cover fair use and quotation-use of their work in other books, newspapers, magazines, in film, and in radio, and also proposed a 'statutory licence.' This fee would be similar to the licensing fee currently paid by universities in respect of photocopying books in their libraries, and enable the copying of material for commercial or educational purposes for a single fee.

Moorhouse and several other authors commented on the roles of CAL, PLR and ELR and suggested ways in which these royalty systems could be improved and expanded, which principally included making payments to authors directly instead of via publishers and utilising more transparent accounting procedures.

In the online survey, authors were asked whether they were familiar with CAL's operations, how satisfied they were with CAL's administration and whether they derived a financial benefit from CAL (as well as other licensing schemes). They were also asked to respond to the statement: *'Australian copyright protections and licensing authorities (such as the Australian Copyright Act, CAL, etc.) support authors sufficiently in their creative efforts'* and to elaborate if they disagreed. Several interesting observations emerged from the results of these enquiries.

Familiarity and Satisfaction with CAL

Nearly 72% of full time authors stated that they were 'familiar with' the organisation and its operation, with 56.2% of part time authors acknowledging the same. A surprising 17.4% and 26.5% respectively admitted to being unfamiliar with the organisation's operations. In total, nearly two thirds of all respondents agreed that they were familiar with CAL and its operation.

When asked how satisfied they were with CAL's administration, the majority of respondents (60.7%) declared to be 'neither satisfied nor dissatisfied' with it. Although this would indicate some ambivalence on the part of respondents about whether or not CAL's administration was satisfactory, this high percentage could be explained by the fact that a reasonably large percentage of respondents did not appear to have any dealings or familiarity with CAL, as had been evident from the previous question. A very low level of 5.5% of all respondents expressed dissatisfaction with CAL. A total of nearly 34% of all respondents professed to be satisfied with CAL's administration,

Benefits Received from CAL, PLR, ELR and Government Grants

The respondents were further questioned on the financial benefits they derived from CAL and other Government mechanisms such as PLR, ELR and Government grants. Only 44.2% of authors responded to this question. Of these respondents only 37.7% received financial benefits from CAL, equating to 40% of full time and 35.9% of part time authors.

In contrast, the majority of respondents said they received financial benefits from PLR and ELR. This amounted to 82.6% of respondents in the case of PLR and 71% in the case of ELR. More than 23% of full time authors and 15.4% of part time authors derived a financial benefit from a Government grant or fellowship. Respondents were asked to indicate the approximate annual amounts received from each source and to specify which Government grants or fellowships they received. A total of 35.8% of the respondents provided further information in this regard, with almost 10% of respondents stating that they had not earned anything from these sources.

Incomes from these sources varied considerably and were, in many instances, not clearly identified by authors. The lowest earnings noted by *part time authors* from CAL, ELR and PLR sources was $50.00 per annum and the highest was $6,100.00, with four part time respondents receiving grants in addition to these payments. One part time author, who earned $10,000 - $15,000 from writing and $60,000.00 from part time employment, also received a $15,000.00 Australia Council grant. Two part time authors each received a $40,000.00 Australia Council grant and earned $1,000-$2,000 and $15,000 - $20,000 respectively from their writing (including CAL, ELR and PLR), whilst one part time author had received $22,000.00 in the form of a PhD stipend for creative writing and earned an additional $10,000 - 15,000 from teaching writing.

In the case of *full time authors,* the amounts were equally varied, with the lowest income from ELR, PLR and CAL sources stated to be $200.00 and the highest amount $50,000.00. The $50,000.00 earner also declared $65,000-$70,000 from fiction writing and $125,000.00 from employment as an academic. Approximately 9% of full time respondents earned $4,000.00 or less from ELR, PLR and CAL. At the other end of the spectrum, a fiction author who reported earnings of $30,000.00 from ELR and PLR sources, also earned $85,000-$90,000 from 'writing related activities.' Interestingly, a fiction writer who earned $17,500.00 from ELR and PLR declared the highest overall income from writing, between $120,000.00 and $130,000.00, as well as additional income 'from investments.'

Only two of the full time respondents disclosed particulars of their Government grants. One had received a Government grant of '$50,000+' for non-fiction writing in the preceding five years, but was anticipating it to end in 2011. This respondent earned $60,000-$65,000 in total from writing related activities. Another respondent received a $40,000.00 Australia Council grant, whilst earning an additional $1,000 - $2,000 from writing.

Do Australian Copyright Protections and Licensing Authorities Support Authors Sufficiently?

In the online survey, around half of respondents overall (50.7%) agreed that Australian copyright protections (such as the *Copyright Act*) and licensing authorities (such as CAL) supported authors sufficiently in their creative efforts. However, a large percentage of respondents (36.8%) were undecided. Significantly, 21.7% of full time and 9.2% of part time authors disagreed with the proposition, with 4.3% and 3.1% respectively expressing strong disagreement with the statement. Twenty-two respondents chose to elaborate on the reasons for their disagreement, voicing the following points of criticism:

- CAL's operation does not extend internationally and thus cannot protect authors against online piracy.
- Authors do not receive any payments from CAL despite work being copied in schools extensively.
- The lack of transparency in CAL payments.

At the time of the survey CAL was still in the process of upgrading its payment system to incorporate electronic payments. Whilst these changes would improve concerns expressed by authors, they did not address the issues of unauthorised online use of authors' work or the capturing techniques utilised by CAL to collect usage data, which only take into account the use of work in selected centres over any given time period. On its Website, CAL describes the current sampling system as 'a fair compromise of the interests of both copyright owners and licensees' <http://www.copyright.com.au>.

To further expand on the views of authors relating to the effectiveness of the CAL, PLR and ELR schemes, a summary of the in-depth interview findings follows below. It was apparent that most of the interviewees did not have intensive knowledge of the role and value of the CAL licensing scheme. The few authors who were more familiar with its operation, such as Frank Moorhouse, a founding member of CAL, were either involved with the organisation in some way or were non-fiction authors whose work was being used more frequently for commercial and educational purposes. However, the most common response was that the organisation served a useful purpose and provided authors with some measure (if limited) of financial reward for the use of their creations.

One bestselling author admitted to being curious about how much of the money collected by CAL was being passed on to the rights holders. He further observed that, as a novelist, he benefited more from ELR and PLR than from CAL payments. Another author of mainly non-fiction work criticised the CAL scheme and raised the following issues: Firstly, many publishers included a clause in publishing contracts which allowed them to collect and distribute CAL payments, which was not negotiable. She felt that payments should be made individually to each party instead.

This viewpoint was shared by Kate Eltham, who observed that CAL used to give the money to the publisher and then trusted that the publisher would pass on the author's portion to them. Now authors were able to register and the payments were split 50/50 between the publisher and the author. However, if there was nothing in the publishing agreement about splitting CAL fees, she did not see any justification for 50% being paid to the publisher, especially in the case of digital copies, where the publisher's input was minimal or non-existent. She believed that the split should be 80/20 in favour of the author, who would have done the most work in producing the individual 'units' (such as books, chapters or articles) upon which the payments were calculated. Another problem Eltham identified was that authors did not receive an account or notice whenever payments were made to the publisher and sometimes received notice of such payments only months or even years later. This information, she proposed, should be readily available to authors.

However, subsequent to Eltham's comments, the CAL payment system to members was overhauled, allowing for the use of electronic funds transfers (EFT) and electronic notifications, as well as a self-service portal. As discussed in Chapter 2, the system promised to address concerns raised by authors, who were previously onpaid from publishers, a structure which resulted in long waiting periods and a lack of timely reporting of payments (Nolan & Arcuili, 2010). Furthermore, during April 2011 CAL provided members with updated claims procedures whereby authors could complete claim forms electronically and receive payments four weeks later (Kluegel, personal email, April 6, 2011).

Despite her concerns, Eltham recognised the value of CAL's contribution insofar as it created 'blanket licences which it negotiates with Government, school sections, universities and so forth,' mainly in respect of non-fiction and educational material and academic writing. 'So for them it's great and

I much prefer a blanket license if it's a way of negotiating copyright with large numbers of people. It's so much better than trying to enforce copyright person by person...,' she observed.

Authors Moorhouse and Breen were appreciative of CAL's efforts. Moorhouse stated that although he had not been on the board of CAL for some time, he was aware that they were distributing substantial amount to authors and publishers and were also contributing about a million dollars per annum into cultural funding generally. 'I think it's been an amazing innovation and apart from the money it distributes to authors and publishers it also funds a number of programs.' Breen, having personally benefitted from CAL funding as Associate Editor of a publication, lauded CAL as 'funding some amazing things in the literary scene.' 'They're really putting a lot of money back into the Australian literary scene, which is fantastic,' she said and explained that CAL was funding festivals, editorial internships and other programs.

It was evident that CAL was perceived by some authors in a positive manner, whilst others were critical about certain issues, most of which were being addressed by the organisation. It appeared that CAL had positioned itself, however, not only as a licensing authority, but also as an organisation which provided support and funding for creative projects such as literary festivals. In general, as was the case with the CAL licensing scheme, the ELR and PLR schemes were viewed by the interviewees as useful systems, but with certain flaws that needed to be addressed. These structures were described by one author as follows: 'In theory, they're the greatest concepts since typesetting, but if any system was due for an overhaul with close scrutiny, it's this pair.' Several authors suggested that ELR and PLR should apply not only domestically but also internationally. Some proposed that international authors be included in these schemes and that provision should be made for an international fees structure to assist with funding, relieving the burden of educational institutions and local governments.

Eltham thought that most authors of the Queensland Writers Centre who had received payments through these schemes felt that they 'benefited immensely' from such structures, without which they would not be compensated for the use of their books in libraries and educational institutions. 'I think that Australia is one of only thirty or forty countries in the world that have a lending rights scheme, so we are very lucky,' she said. Based on the fact that the State Government funding for these schemes was limited to around $10 million per scheme, she was of the view that the current system was fair, whereby royalties to authors and publishers were calculated based on the number of books an author had in different institutions, rather on the number of times a book was borrowed.

Some authors had proposed that royalties should be calculated on borrowings, but as Eltham argued, this would favour bestselling authors over, for example, children's picture book authors, whose incomes were rather modest in comparison to other categories of publishing. In her view, the PLR and ELR schemes could be regarded as assisting authors such as children's and young adults' authors and providing them with an important source of income. One author, who was employed as a journalist, indicated that ELR and PLR payments did not add up to a large amount, but remarked that he serviced his car every year with the two cheques he received from lending rights.

According to Nick Earls, authors wanted their books to be available to people who are not in a position to buy books, and PLR and ELR was a great way to facilitate this usage. He pointed out that, although it only amounted to approximately $1.50 per book each year, it meant that people could read one's work in the libraries, thereby creating a word of mouth long-term benefit for the author. 'It's better to be read than not be read,' he observed.

Other authors leveled criticism at the manner in which ELR and PLR payments are calculated. At present, payments are based on a sample of public, school and university libraries each year. Comments referred to the fact that the sample was relatively small and thus unsatisfactory. Furthermore, it was suggested that the true figures based on actual stock levels were available 'at the press of a button' and that these figures should be used to calculate payments. This could be implemented through 'a set of secure Websites, which would be relatively cheap and easy to facilitate' and which would also decrease enquiries to administrative staff, as one author proposed.

A Resale Royalty Scheme for Books

Whilst no royalty payments are made to authors on secondhand book sales (either by law or in terms of Government support schemes), several authors, including Frank Moorhouse, saw merit in rewarding authors for the resale of their books. They referred to the Resale Royalty Scheme for artists, which came into operation under the *Resale Royalty Right for Visual Artists Act 2009* on 9 June 2010 and pointed out that there was no equivalent scheme for authors. There appeared to be a general belief that authors should benefit from the used book market in accordance with other royalty schemes such as PLR and ELR.

Moorhouse pointed out in his article that the Australian Bureau of Statistics calculated second-hand book sales in Australia at $131.1m (2003-2004) and that the re-cycling of books outside the royalty system had been vastly accelerated by the Internet where a 'second-hand' (or third-hand, fourth-hand

and on and on) copy of virtually any book could be simply found and ordered nationally or internationally. 'My estimate of household use and private lending (together with pass-on reading of both second-hand and remaindered books) multiply the original sales figure of a book by a conservative factor of 2,' he suggested. He further noted that second-hand books accounted for about 45 per cent of fiction found in household libraries, although he conceded that this figure would vary according to the affluence of the owner of the household library and a person's buying habits and that these figures were based on a small survey of a few household libraries (Moorhouse, 2008, p. 4).

He pointed out that, whilst second hand bookshops and Internet services received a payment for the use of a book from the buyer/user, the author did not receive anything. In view of these observations, Moorhouse favoured a small tax on the recycling of books, which could be directed to a fund for support of the writing community, or the use of statistical sampling to set up a mechanism similar to PLR, which would pay authors directly for the resale of their books. Such a scheme would resemble artists' rights under the Resale Royalty Scheme (Moorhouse, 2008, p. 4). However, Nick Earls regarded the current system of ELR and PLR payments as 'a really good trade-off' against the re-use of books by the public, acknowledging the advantages of word of mouth exposure and authors' intrinsic desire 'to be read.'

PROBLEMS WITHIN THE CURRENT FRAMEWORK

In addition to the limitations within existing structures already addressed by authors, some further copyright issues and complaints warrant consideration. One author noted the expense of obtaining advice on copyright as a problem, with another commenting that copyright benefited lawyers and entrepreneurs more than it did authors. Another pointed out that copyright benefited publishers rather than creators, whilst one respondent complained that his/her contributions and intellectual property had not been acknowledged in academic publications, yet stated 'I cannot bite the hand that feeds me by making enemies of those higher up the food chain.'

Another respondent was concerned about being 'ill-informed,' whilst two respondents admitted that their lack of knowledge of copyright caused them some concern. Two other authors cited 'a lack of knowledge on ebook rights' as a problem. One author was critical about 'anti-copyright activism' and stated: 'I think attempts to dilute copyright are dangerous and regressive.' Another respondent expressed concern about 'a lack of time, funds and knowledge' to pursue copyright breaches.

More than 76% of the comments related to theft of work on electronic media, 'online piracy' (a term favoured by a number of respondents), or reproduction of authors' work on the Internet without permission. Descriptions of concerns varied from 'a lack of fair use dealing in electronic documents' to concerns about 'identity, income and copyright protection.' Most of the respondents acknowledged that illegal online copying was a real concern for them, as the current copyright structure did not seem to address the problem adequately. Two respondents reported inaccuracies in respect of their work on Google Books.

Some comments reiterated concerns about moral rights (for example: 'My USA publisher changed the wording of one of my books without my permission') and royalty payments from CAL, ELR and PLR ('I have fewer than 50 books in libraries and am not receiving any payments'), whilst one respondent raised the issue of publishers' inclusion of CDROMs with text books without taking due precautions against illegal copying as a concern for rights holders.

One author complained: 'I discovered by chance that my work has been anthologized,' while another had a problem with 'my government employer who initially thought they had copyright on a reference book that I wrote in my own time.' Another fiction writer made mention of a story he/she had written in 1965 and then later saw 'a similar story' published by someone else in 1995. Despite the respondent's assertions that the story had been copied, he/she was unable to prove it, being only in possession of a handwritten copy.

A few respondents saw copyright as an impediment to their creativity. One non-fiction writer found the control by bureaucratic bodies 'irritating' when attempting to access and share information as a heritage researcher. Another criticised the use of Digital Rights Management ('DRM') by publishers online as 'creating barriers for readers.' Thus, although a number of additional concerns were expressed by respondents, the most prominent concerns related to the Internet and online publishing.

During the course of the interviews five authors and two publishers reported specific instances in which they had encountered copyright problems. A mainstream publisher explained the difficulties in enforcing copyright internationally as follows: 'The thing that is probably the most confusing here is the way that book rights are transacted internationally. You can have an originating publisher in one country with rights to sell in another country.' She saw this as a major problem in the Google book scanning issue, where the American edition of an Australian publication may have been scanned by Google, but the Australian metadata applied. This caused confusion about who the actual rights holder of such a book was and, consequently, made it difficult to enforce copyright. The Google Settlement will be discussed in more depth in the following section on findings relating to publishing; however, the problems caused by Google's unauthorised scanning of materials are inextricably linked to the operation and inadequacy of existing copyright structures.

Another publisher observed that, even though Australia applied parallel import restrictions, authors routinely experienced problems with illegal parallel importation of their books from countries such as China or India. Where illegal copies were being sold by reputable booksellers, the problem could be addressed by sending a letter requesting them to cease and desist from selling the book, but it was difficult to control offshore operators and Internet marketers. She explained that authors do not benefit financially from remainder deals that are sold at cost or below cost, as contracts generally provide that the author does not benefit once the book is sold by the publisher for less than the printing costs. This means that if a book by an Australian author is remaindered in the USA and sold into Australia at remainder cost, the author does not receive anything, even if the book is sold at full price in Australia.

Claire Scobie had experienced the problems of international publishing first hand. She explained that, if a book were published in both the UK and Australia, for example, royalty payments could become an issue because of territorial rights. These rights provided that British publishers get a significant percentage of the sale of a book in Commonwealth 'export countries' (Australia, New Zealand and South Africa). It was therefore possible that a UK publisher could export books to Australia and earn 'export royalties,' whereas if a separate deal was made with an Australian publishing house, the UK publisher would lose out. This meant that if an author were published in the UK, but resided in Australia, he or she would earn lower royalties despite it being his or her 'home territory.' Scobie said that for every copy of her book published in Australia, she only received around a third of the royalty payment, compared to if her book were sold in the UK. Essentially this meant that authors had to have a contract in each country in order to receive the same royalties or else be subjected to the publisher's manipulation of earnings. She cited an instance where an Australian author tried to negotiate separate deals with a UK and Australian publisher, and the deal was summarily stopped when the UK publisher became aware of this fact. This example served to illustrate, according to Scobie, that 'the author's back is against the wall,' and that authors had to accept that the power lay with the much bigger Commonwealth market and, therefore, with the British publisher.

Frank Moorhouse recognised further problems with regard to the collection of royalties internationally. 'It is difficult to police copyright zones in English speaking countries,' he said, referring to the problems of international collecting agencies. He ascribed this difficulty to the difference in the law and ethos of different English speaking countries, which was evidenced in the 'tricks, fraud and danger' inherent in protecting copyright internationally. These problems were less evident in compact cultural groups, such as the Danish, for example, who were confined to one country. For this reason, collecting agencies in Scandinavian countries were more successful than English speaking, European countries.

These comments accord with the concern voiced by a number of authors: that copyright measures and royalty schemes based in Australia do not sufficiently address the issue of loss of revenue from overseas sources, such as sales on the Internet and copyright infringements which occur overseas. This concern is being fuelled by a number of issues: the blurring of territorial copyright zones as a result of new media structures (and the expanding use of electronic devices) and actions by organisations such as Google, who actively defy traditional copyright expectations.

Two fiction authors described their specific copyright problems as follows:

Nigel Krauth and Matilda My Darling

A different copyright dilemma, experienced by author Nigel Krauth, related to the issue of the use of a poem that was still under copyright, the poet having died in 1941 and copyright having reverted to his estate for 70 years. The poem in question was 'Waltzing Matilda,' the work of Banjo Paterson, who was the subject of Krauth's 1983 novel *Matilda my darling*. The estate objected to the use of the poem in Krauth's novel, his granddaughters being of the view that the author's portrait of Paterson, based on his research, was flawed.

According to Krauth, the objection was based on the family's perception of Paterson. 'It's because there was an official version of the character profile of Banjo Paterson which never makes reference, for example, to the fact that he had a withered hand. It never makes reference to the fact that he was a cad in the situation he had with his fiancé, which is a historical event that I cover in this novel,' he explained. His research, said Krauth, showed that Paterson had been 'quite the wild young man in Sydney,' racing around Sydney with a horse drawn cart, much like the 'hoons' of today. The end result of the objection was that he could only quote 10 per cent of the song, which comprised of the first few words: 'Once a jolly swagman…'

However, paradoxically, the American copyright to 'Waltzing Matilda' had been obtained by an American publisher, Carl Fischer Inc. in 1936. This publisher agreed to the words of the song being printed in Krauth's book, creating the unusual situation that American editions of the book had the whole song printed, but Australian editions only had the first line. A further copyright issue arose in respect of the same poem when, at the 1996 Summer Olympics held in Atlanta, the Australian Government had to pay royalties to Carl Fischer Inc. to play 'Waltzing Matilda' at the ceremony. This example is a vivid illustration of the discrepancies that may arise where copyright is owned by different holders in different countries.

Nick Earls and ZigZag Street

Nick Earls discussed two separate issues that related to copyright problems. The first one related to one of his books, *ZigZag street* (1998). Earls discovered that copies of this novel were being sold on remainder tables outside newsagents in Australia, in breach of copyright provisions. In this instance, his UK publisher had overstocked and copies of the novel found their way to a remainder house in the UK, where they were bundled up and sent to Australia with other books, in breach of his territorial rights. He recognised, however, that it was difficult to prevent this from happening or to stop the newsagents from selling the books, as they had bought the books in good faith, thinking that they were legally entitled to sell them. In this case, Earls broached the issue with the UK publisher and reported that the problem had not recurred. He used this as an example to illustrate why parallel import provisions were important to protect authors. Had the restrictions been lifted, authors would have no remedy in such cases.

Secondly, he raised the issue of one of his novels being transformed into a comic strip without his consent. In this particular instance, the issue was resolved as the person approached him with the work and, being impressed with it, Earls agreed to the project. The adaptation included the acknowledgement 'words by Nick Earls,' with Earls having a share in the project and in any future proceeds.

SUMMARY AND CONCLUSION

These findings have highlighted some discrepancies in authors' perceptions and levels of knowledge in relation to copyright and the current copyright structures. Most of the participants in the online survey claimed to be reasonably to well informed about copyright (83.3% of full time and 71.1% of part time authors), as may be expected from this purposive sample group.

Further evidence showed, however, that the percentage expressing confidence in the protection afforded to them by existing copyright structures was considerably lower (45.5%). Even so, most participants (62.5%) expressed satisfaction under the current structures, whilst only approximately half of respondents agreed that Australian copyright protections (such as the *Copyright Act*) and licensing authorities (such as CAL) supported authors sufficiently in their creative efforts. Only 29.3% of authors agreed that their moral rights were adequately protected, with 57.3% being undecided. These discrepancies suggest that a large number of respondents had reservations about the level of copyright and (separate) moral rights protection and support provided by Government structures and copyright legislation.

In relation to the motivational value of copyright, authors in the online survey declared an overwhelming preference for the statement: *'When I create I am mostly motivated by personal satisfaction,'* with approximately 90%% of full time and 93% of part time authors agreeing with it. Copyright was regarded as an important consideration for authors when publishing, rather than during the process of creation, with nearly 87% rating it as a consideration when publishing, 60.7% regarding it as a consideration when writing and only 49.5% regarding it as an incentive to create.

In relation to copyright complaints and concerns, it was noted that most of the survey respondents were concerned about 'online pirating' and the protection of their work on the Internet, with 76.3% of complaints being in relation to this issue. These problems will be illuminated further in Chapter 9, in discussing the findings in respect of the publishing industry. Only a few incidences of complaints against the restrictive nature of copyright law were recorded, such as Krauth's problem with regard to the 'Waltzing Matilda' lyrics.

Finally, Australian authors (both part time and full time) in this sample were found to be somewhat heterogeneous in respect of their income from writing and supplementary income streams. Incomes from writing and payments from Government support structures varied considerably, varying from 'nothing' or 'between $1,000 and $2,000,' up to $150,000 plus per annum. It is instructive that the largest group of all respondents were in the $1,000 - $2,000 income bracket, with most relying on income from other sources, many completely unrelated to writing. A significant reliance on income from pensions, Centrelink, investments and spouses/partners was noted. However, many others drew income from academic positions plus upward of 50 different jobs or income streams.

REFERENCES

Australian Government Productivity Commission. (2008). *Copyright restrictions on the parallel importation of books: Submissions.* Retrieved from http://www.pc.gov.au/projects/study/books/submissions

Copyright Act 1968 (Cth) *Copyright Amendment (Digital Agenda) Act 2000* (Cth) *Copyright Amendment (Moral Rights) Act 2000* (Cth) *Resale Royalty Right for Visual Artists Act 2009* (Cth)

Copyright Agency Limited. (2009, March). *CAL's sampling and distribution: How do they work?* Retrieved September 16, 2010, from www.copyright.com.au/assets/documents/operations/Sampling and distribution.pdf

Dow Jones & Company Inc. v. Gutnick [2002] HCA 56 (Austl.)

Earls, N. (1998). *Zigzag street.* Sydney: Random House Australia.

Kelly, J. (2009, October 5). Publish and be damned. *The Drum.* Retrieved May 19, 2011, from http://www.abc.net.au/unleashed/28818.html

Moorhouse, F. (2008). The escape from 'eccentric penury': How should we pay literary authors? Policy visions for the Australian writing economy. *Copyright Reporter, 26,* 4.

Nolan, E., & Arcuili, R. (2010, May 25). *CAL today.* Brisbane, Australia: CAL Seminar.

Productivity Commission. (2009). *Restrictions on the parallel importation of books* (Research Report). Retrieved February 19, 2011, from http://www.pc.gov.au/projects/study/books/submissions.

Rose, M. (1988). The author as proprietor: Donaldson v Becket and the genealogy of modern authorship. *Representations (Berkeley, Calif.), 0*(23), 51–58.

University of NSW v. Moorhouse (1975) HCA 26; (1975) 133 CLR 1 (Austl.)

TABLE OF CASES

Dow Jones & Company Inc. v. Gutnick [2002] HCA 56 (Austl.)

University of NSW v. Moorhouse (1975) HCA 26; (1975) 133 CLR 1 (Austl.)

TABLE OF STATUTES

Copyright Act 1968 (Cth)

Copyright Amendment (Digital Agenda) Act 2000 (Cth)

Copyright Amendment (Moral Rights) Act 2000 (Cth)

Resale Royalty Right for Visual Artists Act 2009 (Cth)

Chapter 9
Research Findings:
Authors and Publishing–A Changing Industry

ABSTRACT

This chapter deals with the third question, namely: What are Australian authors' views on the changing nature of the publishing industry, and how have they been affected by changes/advances in this area? It focuses on the relationship between authors and publishers, publishing contracts, ebooks, Google, and publishing options for authors in the digital world. Preliminary conclusions regarding authors' views on these issues lay the foundation for an in-depth discussion and analysis in the next chapter.

INTRODUCTION

Nothing betrays the spirit of an age so precisely as the way it represents the future. - Geoffrey Nunberg

It has been shown in the previous chapter that the author sample group voiced a range of concerns in relation to their copyright. Of equal concern to authors, and in parallel with the operation of legislative structures discussed in the previous chapter, was the issue of the changing publishing industry and how it affected them. The third research issue posed the following questions: How did authors perceive the changing publishing industry? Furthermore, how did this perception affect their own work and their attitude toward digital publishing?

DOI: 10.4018/978-1-4666-5214-9.ch009

On the one hand, expanding opportunities in publishing and easier access were seen as advantageous by some authors, especially by self-published authors; conversely, most authors recognised that such advances were accompanied by new challenges in the field of copyright, which authors had to address in order to protect their intellectual property. This chapter examines the findings of the research in relation to the transforming publishing industry, publishing relationships and emerging business models and the evolution of copyright in this changing environment.

Unsurprisingly the in-depth interviews provided a range of perspectives, with some authors embracing new technology and the challenges it represented, others taking a more guarded wait-and-see approach, whilst another group accepted the changes reluctantly but resignedly and made an effort to keep up with the changing publishing industry. The online survey provided further insight into authors' relationships with publishers and their views on digital publishing. Of particular concern to authors were the actions of search engines/information providers (such as Google) in digitising books or parts of books without the authors' consent. These developments affected not only authors, but also publishers, and prompted many to re-think the use and value of copyright in cyber space publishing.

TRADITIONAL PUBLISHING AND PUBLISHING RELATIONSHIPS

The Author/Publisher Relationship

It has been shown that, historically, the greatest obstacle for authors, especially emerging authors, has been the challenge of finding a willing publisher. Publishers like Allen & Unwin state on their Website that they publish 250 titles a year out of approximately 1,000 submissions (2011), while others such as Scholastic refer to 'several thousand manuscripts' received in a year (2011). This difficulty has been exacerbated for authors without agents, as some publishers state that they will only deal with agents and do not accept unsolicited manuscripts. New authors have typically also found it challenging to engage a willing agent. During the research, authors were questioned on their relationships with agents and publishers.

Who Do Authors Deal With?

When asked who they generally dealt with in publishing matters, 62% of both full time and part time author groups stated that they dealt directly with publishers. Not surprisingly, more full time authors than part time authors used an agent: a third of full time and just over 10% of part time authors. Only a small number of the respondents dealt with a lawyer in relation to publishing and while only 4.8% of full time authors self-published, and 27.6% of part time authors said they generally published their own work. Thus, whilst approximately a third of the full time respondents generally used the services of an agent, the remaining two-thirds usually dealt directly with the publisher, save for a few self-publishers. In the part time group, the same percentage dealt with the publisher directly, but nearly a third self-published whilst only a small number dealt with an agent.

Having an Agent

In a separate question, 57.1% of full time and 64.4% of part time authors expressed the view that it was *'an advantage'* to have an agent, with 11.9% and 3.4% of full time and part time authors respectively regarding it as *'essential.'* These percentages, as opposed to the actual number of respondent authors with agents, would suggest that many respondents who did not have an agent recognised that having an agent was an advantage.

Relationship with Publisher

The majority of both groups had satisfactory relationships with their publishers. A total of 73.2% of full time and 53% of part time authors reported a *'satisfactory'* or *'very satisfactory'* relationship with their publishers. Only 10.2% and 11.8% of the respective groups regarded their relationships as *'unsatisfactory'* or *'very unsatisfactory,'* whilst 28.6% of all respondents opted for the *'neither unsatisfactory nor satisfactory'* option. Greater satisfaction was, therefore, recorded by full time authors, although many were ambivalent about the issue.

First Time Authors

Most respondents - 61.9% of full time and 64% of part time authors - agreed that first time authors in Australia generally found it *'very difficult to get published,'* with 26.2% and 27% respectively conceding that first time authors generally found it *'reasonably difficult to get published.'* Only 1.5% of respondents regarded it as *'easy to get published,'* whilst no one agreed with the suggestion that it was *'very easy to get published.'* From these results, it was apparent that over 90% of all respondents held the view that it was difficult to get published as a first time author in Australia. This viewpoint is in accord with the number of submissions reported by publishers such as Scholastic, mentioned above.

Many of these findings were borne out in the in-depth interviews. During the interviews, many authors admitted freely that being accepted for publication for the first time was so exciting that the issue of copyright did not enter their minds. Author and journalist Michael Jacobson said that he was so 'thrilled and shocked' to be published that he 'sort of let other things slide.' However, he explained that he had a good relationship with his publisher and that he also relied on his agent to negotiate a royalty deal for him on his first book, describing the role of his agent as 'absolutely imperative.' He recognised that well-known authors were more likely to receive favourable royalty deals. 'I didn't expect for one second to get the same publishing budget or deal as a Bryce Courtenay or Tim Winton or somebody,' he admitted. 'But I knew it would be a reasonable deal.' He described his publisher as 'extremely supportive' and was very happy with the relationship. He further said that, through his journalistic experience of interviewing approximately 500 authors for his book review column, he had never encountered an author who mentioned any problems with their publisher over royalty issues. 'The first time authors are so excited to be published - it's a great thrill for them,' he observed.

Abbas El Zein agreed that the role of an agent was very valuable: first, in getting the book published and second, in dealing with copyright questions. He would deal with his publisher first hand once the book was placed under contract. He described his publishing relationship as a very positive one. Whilst he also used the Arts Law service in negotiating his first publishing contract, he felt that he was in a better position to negotiate on his second book, having published the first. 'I can see how the relationship between authors and publishers could be unhealthy,' he admitted. 'There are a lot of factors that play out, there are personal factors, there's the extent to which the author depends on the book for income, the degree to which the author is aware of his rights.'

Another author who agreed that it was helpful to be represented by an agent was Katherine Howell. She credited her agent with looking after her best interests and helping her negotiate a contract on her first two books and another contract on the next two. In her case, the agent also assisted with the terms of the publishing contract and negotiations in this regard. 'Anything apart from the actual writing of the book goes through my agent,' she said. She acknowledged that some authors were less fortunate in their publishing experiences. 'I think people may feel so grateful they're being published that they don't want to rock the boat. You know, they don't have a lot of power,' she observed.

Author Daphne Taylor described her relationship with her publisher as 'most amicable.' However, she felt that the royalty paid to authors by publishers (traditionally 10% of recommended retail price) should be higher, considering the fact that the rest of the chain in the industry relied on the author, the primary producer, for the basic product.

Frank Moorhouse was of the view that the author's position had strengthened in relation to publishing relationships and described the ethos in publishing as 'very civilized.' In the event of disagreements between authors and publishers, there were forums for arbitration, such as the Society of Authors and lawyers who could facilitate arbitration. 'I don't think the authors or publishers or agents want to get into legal battles,' he commented. His viewpoint is borne out by the fact that there were no reported cases in the Australian Law Reports of such disputes between authors and publishers.

Nigel Krauth discussed his good working relationship with all his publishers. 'I've had a charmed run in terms of publishers,' he said, acknowledging that a number of his author friends had had problems and changed publishers as a result of disagreements. He himself had never had an agent and always worked directly with publishers, holding the view that an agent would not necessarily secure a better deal than the author himself.

Nick Earls declared himself to be 'happy overall.' He felt fortunate to be represented by an agent from a large agency that does a lot of business with publishers. To him it meant that publishers had to be 'straight' with the agent who would not be easily misled and could negotiate on his behalf. He voiced some criticism that publishers could take an author out to lunch and make promises if you signed with them, then fail to include those promises in the agreement and subsequently renege on them once the contract was signed. He conceded that most authors were inclined to 'just sign' a contract once they received it, assuming that everything that had been agreed upon was in the contract, such as promotional promises made by the publisher. Earls empathised with first time authors and relayed his own experience of being published for the first time. 'Even a small amount of money is exciting,' he said. 'And you're afraid to ask questions in case the whole dream will be over, and they'll go. And it's not like that, of course.'

Author and publisher Sally Collings described the traditional author/publisher relationship as a 'supplicant relationship' with the author begging for publication and the publisher offering them a slice of the action. 'I'd like to think we are making our way forward to a more collaborative style of working, where the author contributes expertise in their field and the publisher contributes expertise in book creation and marketing, and each facet is mutually respected.' She said that authors by and large earned 'a pittance' for the amount of time and energy they invested in a book writing project, but she saw the economic model of publishing as changing, with small publishing and self publishing becoming more widespread and viable. Her own small publishing house, Red Hill Publishing, was an example of a progressive publishing model, in Collings' view.

The advantages of dealing with a small press were echoed by author Ian Callinan, who reported a good working relationship with his publisher, a small press. Unable to secure the services of an agent, he dealt with the publisher himself but saw this as a positive experience. Kate Eltham pointed out that many Australian full time professional authors dealt with their publishers directly, as opposed to the USA where most professional authors had agents. In her view, the agent had the author's interest at heart more so than the publisher, as the agent was generally in a commission only relationship with the author and was only paid when the author was paid.

Sally Breen noted a number of problems in the author/publisher relationship, one stumbling block being many authors' inability to act professionally. On the other hand, she perceived a measure of arrogance towards writers by publishers and editors. Having been involved in aspects of publishing, Breen was aware of a resistance on the part of publishers to engage with new voices and an attitude that only those who had 'proven their stripes' deserved publication. She described first time authors as 'bunnies in the headlights,' momentarily blinded and willing to do anything to be published. Publishers, on the other hand, approached the buying of books as a commercial pursuit with commercial viability being the deciding factor. She observed that publishing was 'becoming like fashion rather than culture.' When Breen's memoir was selected for a Harper Collins prize and she was offered a book contract, the prizewinners were handed publishing agreements by the editors and asked to sign and hand them back. She explained: 'There was this expectation that you'd just sit there and sign it. Have a read, sign it....there are no traps here, just sign it.'

Alex Adsett, publishing contract consultant and publisher, also commented on first time authors' lack of confidence and unquestioning response to their first contract. She saw authors' power as related to their sales figures – the better the sales, the more room they had for negotiation. However, she regarded the relationship between authors and publishers as generally good and described it as a 'fair industry.' It had to be taken into account that the margins in publishing were quite tight and that the publisher had to ensure that the book was profitable to sustain its own business. She regarded the author/publisher relationship as a partnership, which could only work if it was balanced. A publisher had to take care of the author and act fairly to maintain a good future relationship. On the other hand, the book had to be commercially viable to succeed or both parties would lose.

Conversely, Claire Scobie was of the view that the author was always at a disadvantage in the publishing relationship as there were always more people wanting to get their books published than willing publishers. The economic downturn and small profit margins for publishers were also contributing factors to this power dynamic 'where the author has little power.' In her opinion there was a lack of respect and financial reward for authors generally, compared to other industries.

A different viewpoint was expressed by a mainstream publisher, who saw copyright as underlying the relationship between authors and publishers, and most of the focus being on the terms and conditions of such a relationship. Thus, from her point of view, the issue of copyright was regarded as an important aspect to be addressed between the parties.

Traditional Publishing Contracts

As part of the examination of the author/publisher relationship, the research also investigated the issue of publishing contracts and the way authors dealt with issues such as copyright and the related concept of royalties. As noted above, the online survey revealed that most respondents dealt with their publishers directly in contractual matters. However, most of them ensured that they understood the terms of the contract, as was evident from the question dealing with this issue.

Respondents were provided with several options in relation to the statement: *'In my publishing contracts I generally…'* and asked to tick the relevant boxes. To the suggestion *'I generally ensure that I understand the terms of the contract'* the overwhelming majority – more than 77% of full time and 84% of part time authors - responded in the affirmative. It is possible that the higher number of part time author responses to this question were a reflection of their greater initiatives to self-publish and their lack of agent representation (as evidenced from their responses). Surprisingly, 7.5% of full time and 7.3% of part time authors admitted that they were *'not concerned with the terms of the contract as it should be fair.'*

In interpreting the contract, only 5% of the full time and 7.3% of the part time group said that they relied on the publisher to explain the terms to them, whilst 15% of full time and only 2.4% of part time authors relied on their agent to explain the document. A small number (2.5% of full time and 4.9% of part time authors) made use of the services of a lawyer to explain the contract. These responses indicated a strong reliance by the respondents on their own understanding of the contract. It is suggested that this could be expected from this purposive sample, who might have a significant degree of motivation in respect of their copyright expectations as published authors.

The survey responses were generally supported in the interviews. A distinction was drawn by Alex Adsett between commercial publishers and 'vanity' publishers on the subject of publishing contracts. She stated that mainstream publishers generally used similar contracts that were essentially fair. However, many authors were not able to distinguish between 'genuine' publishers and 'vanity' publishers, whose sole aim was to make money and who did very little or nothing for the author. Many of these 'publishers' would do no more than print the book and fail to assist with any marketing, leaving an author with a large amount of books and nowhere to sell them. She cautioned that some of these 'publishers' mentioned royalties in their contracts, which were often not paid.

As far as mainstream publishers were concerned, Adsett was of the view that they were open to negotiation on certain issues, depending on the book. The standard wording of royalty clauses was usually not negotiable, but issues such as the base royalty percentage or the splitting of royalties on subsidiary rights could be negotiated, in her experience. Authors who had published multiple books and made many sales were in a better position to negotiate. In other examples, such as where the publisher had never in the past sold the French translation rights during a five-book publication history with an author, the author would be in a good position to withhold those rights from the publisher.

A different perspective was offered by Kate Eltham who, in contributing a chapter to a publication, had found that she received no contract from the editor, who had contracted directly with the publisher. This situation was potentially problematic, as the author in this instance had not agreed to the licensing terms, whilst the publisher would have an agreement with and certain expectations from the editor and contributors. The question then arose whether it was incumbent on a contributing author to obtain a copy of the agreement before submitting her work.

Sally Breen commented that the whole standardisation of contracts needed to be reconfigured to deal with issues such as digitisation. She was of the view that first time authors should have more options and that digital rights should be dealt with contractually. The standard contract, according to Breen, did not address the digital issue sufficiently. In her own experience, the publisher who awarded her with a contract for her first book had claimed a right of first refusal. As no time limit had been placed on the publisher, they could take as long as they wanted to exercise their option. She noted that, at the time of the interview, one of the other award recipients in her group had been waiting eight months for a response from the publisher. It would appear that these delays were even more extensive than the 14-16 week delays foreshadowed for responses to unsolicited submissions on the Allen & Unwin and Scholastic Websites.

Breen saw a large gap between the power of the emerging author and that of established Australian authors. One way of addressing that disparity, according to Breen, was for writers 'to be proactive in the literary landscape' by developing their own contacts and festivals. Such a culture would inform and empower younger writers and help them to emerge from such programs with a better understanding of the issues involved in getting published. The growing popularity of writers' festivals throughout Australia seem to support this viewpoint, considering the large numbers attracted to the Sydney, Melbourne, Brisbane and Northern Rivers Writers' Festivals each year, to name but a few.

Nick Earls, as an established Australian author, did not use the publishers' standard contracts but negotiated contractual terms with his agent and publisher on a book-by-book basis. Such negotiated contracts provided more room for give and take, according to Earls. He regarded the initial standard contract presented by a publisher as their 'opening offer' and emphasised the importance of authors considering closely the various aspects of a contract, such as film rights and merchandising rights. For example, if the contract provided that the publisher would get ten per cent of the proceeds from your film rights, it should be considered whether the publisher is also a filmmaker;

if not, why should they be given ten per cent of the film rights? In his view, unless the author has no other prospect of selling the film rights, this should be avoided. Similarly, if they claimed merchandising rights but were not planning to sell key rings and coffee mugs, for example, why should they get the merchandising rights?

Earls also pointed out that world rights to a book were usually included in the standard contract. He suggested that, if one did not have an agent and was prepared to let the Australian publisher try to sell the overseas rights, it might be sensible to give them world rights for a period of 12 months following the publication of the book, after which territories outside of Australia and New Zealand would revert to the author. This would give the publisher a year to sell overseas rights, a more reasonable option from the author's perspective.

An example of how world rights operate was provided by Katherine Howell, whose publisher bought the world rights to her novels and on sold them to foreign publishers. As the author, she received 80% of the royalties from such foreign sales. In her case, she was satisfied that her publisher had the experience and the contacts to sell the rights overseas and deal with the overseas publishing contracts.

Another bestselling author disagreed with this approach, commenting that authors would be better off securing contracts directly with international publishers to avoid paying a domestic publisher 'middleman costs,' which often included paying a foreign agent a part of the royalties. She pointed out that foreign income was usually calculated on the basis of net receipts and that these costs reduced the income to the author. In her experience, authors usually received 10% of the net receipts, whilst some received as little as 2%.

Travel writer and journalist Kim Wildman pointed out the difference in her copyright ownership depending on whether she worked for a company or freelanced. As a freelancer, she retained the copyright to her work and could sell the licensing rights to various concerns. She generally negotiated contracts with publications on a piece-by-piece basis and was able to contract with different publications and re-sell pieces of writing to more than one publication. However, she had found freelancing for *Lonely Planet* too limiting as they maintained ownership of her work and would not allow her to write for any other publisher on the same destination she had covered for them. Wildman conceded that authors might be prepared to accept lower payment for their work if they were receiving more exposure from being published by a major publisher.

EMERGING PUBLISHING MODELS
AND BUSINESS STRATEGIES

Discrepancies between the ASA recommended contract and the standard publisher contracts, discussed in Chapter 6, were a source of well-founded concern, especially for first time authors and where ebooks were concerned. It has been noted that ebook sales are constantly increasing (Loukakis, 2010, p. 1). and The sale of ebooks is further encouraged by the increased use of electronic devices such as the Kindle, Kobo and Sony Reader, pressing authors to familiarise themselves with ebook options and online marketing. Still, many authors are daunted by the technology involved and the move away from traditional copyright perceptions, as evidenced by Google's 'take now, ask later' approach in scanning books in US libraries. Whilst ebook publishers such as Smashwords and Lulu and online intermediaries such as Google are creating more options and greater opportunities for authors, these changed business models have left some authors very concerned about protecting their copyright and the income derived from copyright related royalties.

Ebooks and Other Online Publishing

Whilst ebooks are often protected by Digital Rights Management (DRM) software of some kind, online publication of articles and blogs are generally devoid of any copyright protection measures. In the majority of cases, it is as simple as copying and pasting content or downloading and saving content without any obstacles. This poses a problem for authors who expect to be remunerated and earn a living from their work. Many feel that they suffer financial detriment and infringement of their moral rights as a result of these occurrences.

Freelance writers are especially susceptible to a loss of control over their copyright, and some interviewees expressed concern over the online publishing of newspaper and magazine articles, which could be duplicated on other Websites without payment to the author. Previously, these authors may have been able to sell the article to more than one publication, but exposure on the Internet has made re-publishing an unattractive proposition for publications. Although this research deals specifically with authors' copyright, rather than the vast field of journalism and issues experienced by journalists with regard to their copyright on the Internet, it is instructive to note the comments of these freelance writers, who, in addition to authoring books, have dealt with online publication of articles.

Sales in Electronic/Digital Format

In the online survey, nearly two thirds of full time and one half of part time authors said that their work had been sold in digital/electronic format on the Internet as ebooks or articles. Only 17.4% of respondents sold their own work on the Internet, whilst more than 46% relied on their publishers to do so. It was apparent that full time authors appeared to have embraced the Internet market place but that most of them were relying on their publishers to sell their books on the Internet.

As noted in Chapter 6, ebooks are generally being sold at prices well below those of printed books on Amazon.com, generally between US$5 and US$15. The departure from traditional publishing models has allowed for a higher percentage of the sale price to be paid to the author; conversely, as the ebook sells at a lower price, the author is at risk of earning less income from the sale of an ebook than a traditional publication. Additionally, the option of publishing work through online publishers such as Smashwords has to be weighed up against the support and marketing provided by the traditional print publisher.

Electronic Rights and Royalties

As discussed in Chapter 6, the issue of electronic rights has become a matter of priority in authors' publishing contracts in view of the rapid increase in digital publishing. In the survey, over 44% of respondents stated that their contracts made separate provision for royalties on electronic work, while 23.4% said their contracts treated all royalties the same (electronic and print). Only 17.1% of respondents regarded their publishing contracts as 'satisfactory' in relation to electronic publishing.

A total of 40% of survey participants responded to a question regarding royalties received from electronic publications. Approximately 16% of these respondents were unpaid and received nothing for their publications, 10% received 5-6% of RRP, 20.6% received 10% of RRP, 10% received 100% (being self publishers) and the remaining respondents received varying amounts between 10% and 99% of RRP. One respondent reported receiving 'a flat rate from an education publisher for a specific title,' while another received 'a flat fee of $500.00 for a book to be included on an educational Website and others stated that payments varied depending on the publication. In additional comments, a few respondents used emotive language to indicate their dissatisfaction with their royalty payments. The highest reported royalties - except for self publishers - had been received by a full time fiction writer, who had received a 70% royalty from publishing ebooks online with Smashwords and 50% from publishing with www.regencyreads.com. Although the percentages fluctuated significantly, it was apparent that online publishers were paying up to 14 times the royalties paid by traditional publishers.

Most of the interviewees appreciated the need for keeping up with technology and electronic rights. Kate Eltham, a founding member of if:book Australia (a centre for research in digital publishing), expressed the view that publishing contracts needed updating and revision in order to properly incorporate digital rights. 'We are starting to see some standard royalty rates emerge for e-books and some of the trade publishers at around 25% of the retail price,' she commented and added that she felt there would be a lot of pressure for the royalty rate to rise in the near future. This did not appear to be the general norm for the survey respondents, who typically earned considerably less than 25%.

Eltham further mentioned cases emerging between authors and publishers as to who owned the digital rights in a work, such as the US *Random House Inc. v. Rosetta Books* (2002) case, where it was held that a licence to exploit a work in book form did not include ebook rights. She pointed out that many publishers who wanted to digitise their back lists had to go back to the authors and renegotiate an amendment to their contracts that would give them the license to digitise the book and sell it. She saw this as a very costly exercise for publishers, especially where they had to find paper copies of the old contracts and rewrite them after many years. This was especially onerous on mainstream publishers who had to incur huge costs in order to update agreements. These costs were usually reflected in the price of the digital book.

An important observation was made by Sally Collings regarding digital rights protection: 'We need to find ways of monetising content that reflect how consumers actually consume media via the Internet, not how we - the publishing industry - would ideally like the consumers to behave.' She saw DRM software as one way of restricting how an author's work could be used on the Internet and pointed out that digital copyright protection should enable the commercialisation of authors' work instead of restricting it. 'The DRM framework of "locks and keys" is broken, so to speak. New solutions need to be found,' she remarked.

Nick Earls stated that the existing notion of copyright was poorly prepared for how copyright should be handled in the digital domain and declared himself open to innovative ideas that could be applied to protect copyright on the Internet and compensate authors for the sale of their work, for example, in advertising revenue or a licensing fee. Another bestselling author was of the view that the Internet was threatening the territorial rights that had already been sub-licensed under publishing agreements from various countries. She saw it as 'grotesquely naïve and near-sighted' for any country to attempt territorial changes (such as the suggested lifting of parallel import restrictions), where publishing agreements were already being impacted by digital technologies and such changes would be moot. Conversely, other authors such as self publisher John Kelly had a relaxed attitude about digital copyright. 'If you are referring to the absence of international boundaries, I'm sure such matters will sort themselves out. There's nothing new under the sun.'

On the issue of territorial rights, Eltham saw no sense in dividing up territories geographically where digital rights were concerned, as consumers would expect to access digital contents anywhere in the world without being subject to different restrictions. However, some publishers still sold digital rights into different territories, which then precluded consumers accessing that material unless they were in the correct region. As an example, she mentioned an instance where she wanted to purchase a copy of a novel by an Australian author, Garth Nix, at the online bookstore Fictionwise. After selecting the book and proceeding to the payment point, the Website informed her that they did not have the licence to sell her the book as she lived in Australia. She established that the digital edition they were selling was supplied to them by a US publisher, who only had the right to sell the book to US customers. She said this system punished the customer unnecessarily and that, in the long term, customers would not accept it and reward those retailers and publishers who can provide them with 'whatever content they want, in the form that they want it, when they want it.'

Eltham recognised that many publishers had already come to the realisation that they needed to acquire worldwide digital rights when they purchased a book. Many publishers nowadays would only buy a book if they could secure the world digital rights. This limited the market for Australian authors who may have already sold a portion of their rights to a particular publisher, leaving them unable to sell the remaining rights elsewhere. She mentioned examples of some prominent international authors such as Ian McEwan, Stephen Covey and Terry Goodkind, who had taken their digital rights away from their publishers and given them exclusively to Amazon, due to receiving a much higher return than they would have through their publishers. This allowed Amazon to make these authors' titles available exclusively through Amazon and on their Kindle eReader. This trend had caused publishers to make a concerted effort to secure digital rights on their existing contracts.

The power wielded by Amazon as an ebook retailer was displayed in an incident at the end of January 2010, where an altercation took place between

Amazon and Macmillan publishers in the USA. The conflict arose because Macmillan wanted Amazon to deviate from their standard price of US$9.99 on Macmillan books and sell them according to prices determined by Macmillan. After failing to reach agreement on the issue, Amazon retaliated by taking the 'buy' button off all Macmillan titles in the store for 48 hours over the weekend, thereby preventing any customers from buying Macmillan books for that period. Eltham felt that this only served to punish the customer and the authors, who were at the mercy of these rights holders. This incident also served to illustrate the power and importance of digital rights.

if:book Australia advised authors to question publishers on their intentions with the world rights on their book to ascertain whether it would be worthwhile to sell them to a particular publisher. Eltham's approach was pragmatic regarding copyright protection on ebooks. 'There is nothing at all that a publisher or an author can afford to do that is going to prevent a determined person from ripping your content and then distributing it freely on line if they should want to do that.' She did not approve of DRM protection on ebooks as she felt it to be too inflexible and restrictive from the consumer's point of view.

Eltham suggested the following approach for authors producing digital content:

As a tool for entrepreneurs, you have to be a content producer. It should be flexible enough as a legal document to allow people to pursue their business in different ways, and that means that it has to be responsive to the kind of media and not kind of mired in a type of media that was the dominant thing 500 years ago and is not the dominant media now. But also, there is a balance that needs to be struck because authors benefit from audiences. They benefit from the public consuming their content. They can't make money by selling books if people aren't willing, as a mass audience, to consume them. So they should think about balancing the interest of that group against their own commercial interest.

Publisher Alex Adsett agreed that there were some problems with DRM and suggested that the model adopted by Canadian science fiction author Cory Doctorow of providing his material for free on the Internet might be a viable option for some authors as 'a way of free advertising.' She stated that many writers held the view that the more their work was disseminated on the Internet, the more printed copies they sold of their work and pointed out that Doctorow had achieved success through this approach, his attitude being that people who only read the online version were not going to buy his books anyway.

A mainstream publisher pointed out that the ebook was not a new phenomenon and that their company had been digitising books for years. The digitisation drive followed the *Copyright Amendment (Digital Agenda) Act 2000*, which regulated libraries' scanning of books that were commercially available. She was uncertain how well the legislation worked as many libraries continued to scan books illegally. The publisher stated further that digital technologies were generating major challenges to copyright at various levels for content creators, such as the perception and reality of copyright ownership, what constituted infringement and other formal legislative challenges. As publishers, they regularly experienced challenges with maintaining copyright online. Problems such as online piracy and instances of infringement in other works had to be addressed. This involved identifying what constituted use of a substantial portion of another work, identifying rights holders and paying permission fees to use third party work.

She noted that copyright was frequently a grey zone which could only be navigated with the help of judgment and experience. 'Legal advice, even when you can afford it, doesn't necessarily help resolve day to day practical issues,' she said. She further recognised that the book industry was experiencing great industrial change necessitating investment in new technology but felt that Australia did not have a very user friendly retail Website, causing a lot of Australian business to go to international retailers such as Amazon. Online retailers had an advantage in not having to run a 'bricks and mortar operation,' as purely an online offering. 'It's a bit like the weavers and stocking makers in the Industrial Revolution,' she observed. 'It was extremely hard for them to compete with the new big mills that were there. That's how it goes. It's often difficult to re-envisage your whole operation when it's starting to be under threat in that kind of way.'

Concerns about Electronic Copyright

It was evident from the online survey and the comments above that respondents showed a high level of concern about protection of their copyright online. Significantly, a total of 43.9% of all respondents professed to be concerned about protection of their electronic copyright, while a further 34.8% admitted that they were 'very concerned' about it, amounting to nearly 80% of all respondents showing concern about their digital copyright.

Two travel writers, Claire Scobie and Kim Wildman, cited problems with the copying of their work online. Scobie referred to several instances where her content had been reproduced on the Internet without her consent on other Websites or blogs. Where she wrote articles for newspapers such as those in the Fairfax group, she had no control over the online treatment of her material. In this regard, she saw freelance writers as being powerless to protect their copyright. Wildman reported similar problems, with some of her articles being reproduced by people on their own blogs or on another Website. She had previously dealt with this problem by sending the offender an email stating that they should remove the content from their site or be invoiced with an indication of the cost. Failing the removal of the material, she would send them an invoice, which would usually result in the material being removed. In other instances, such as where she was doing work for ninemsn, she involved their legal department to follow up on the infringement.

She saw it as a problem that if she sold an article to newspapers, they automatically put it onto the Internet, which effectively ruined her chance to sell the article anywhere else in the world. The newspaper's clause, providing for 'any of our publications,' allowed for publication on the Internet whilst the journalist did not receive any additional payment for publication on the Internet. On the other hand, Wildman saw publication on the Internet in a positive light from the perspective that it increased the author's exposure through social media or other opportunities. 'You've got to weigh everything up and try and work around it,' she said.

'I don't feel like there's much protection whatsoever,' she stated, mentioning an example of a woman who ran a newsletter and had her work stolen and wrote a 'cease and desist' letter to the offender. This resulted in the other party writing back, threatening to write negative things about her on the Internet, which would appear on a Google search. She did not press the issue any further, fearing that her reputation could be adversely affected if the threat was carried out. At the time of the interview, Wildman was in the process of writing a travel guide she was planning to make available online for purchase in the form of an ebook in PDF format. She was also writing a guide for an iPhone application, which required a different writing style due to the 150 word restriction and requirement that it be easily downloadable, which presented some new challenges for travel writers.

Protection of Copyright Online

When asked how they protected their copyright online, the respondents answered as follows: 16.5% reported using DRM for protection, nearly 9% used a Creative Commons licence, 35.7% posted a warning on their Websites or on the work and 13% used 'other means' such as relying on their publishers and daily Google alerts advising of illegal file sharing sites. Significantly, nearly half of respondents admitted to 'doing nothing' in order to protect their digital copyright, indicating what may be perceived as either a high level of apathy amongst respondents or, alternatively, a high level of trust towards Internet users. It may also be suggested that the respondents' lack of protective action could be a direct result of a strong reliance on their publishers. The level of concern about their online copyright (nearly 80% expressing concern) would indicate, however, that their concern is more likely caused by their lack of knowledge or a misplaced reliance on their publishers.

The non profit Creative Commons free licensing scheme, discussed in Chapter 6, has been gaining support from a number of Australian authors since its inception in 2001. However, surprisingly, 44.4% of respondents in the online survey indicated that they were not familiar with the Creative Commons concept, while 36.1% expressed support for the concept. A small number (4.5%) did not support the concept and 15% remained neutral. Eltham supported the Creative Commons model and had placed a Creative Commons licence on her Website, which encouraged people to use her material as long as they acknowledged the source.

Authors' Copyright and the Google Initiatives

As discussed in Chapter 6, Google has demonstrated the force of technological innovation through its digitisation programme with a disregard for traditional copyright values and a determined consumer focus. This research examines the extent of the erosion or the perception of erosion of authors' copyright. At the time of the online survey, the Court in *The Authors Guild et al v. Google, Inc* (2010) had not decided the matter of the Google Settlement. However, as noted, it has since rejected the Settlement and adjourned the matter to June 2012 for further negotiations between the parties. The issue remains relevant due to the unprecedented nature of the digital scanning project and especially in view of the further action instituted by the US Authors' Guild, The Australian Society of Authors and other complainants against US libraries and the HathiTrust. Furthermore, Google continues to make books and extracts from books available on its Google Books Website.

Authors and the Google Book Scanning Project

Authors were ambivalent in their responses to the Google initiatives. When asked whether they were familiar with *'the Google book scanning project (resulting in 'the Google Settlement'),'* at least 79% of full time authors said they were familiar with the project, just over half of part time authors expressed familiarity with the concept. A total of 47% of full time authors expressed a personal interest in the subject, whilst nearly 12% relied on their publisher to deal with the matter and 6% relied on their agent. In the case of part time authors, 31.4% left the matter to their publisher and nearly 6% to their agent, although more than 37% expressed a personal interest in the issue. Furthermore, a total of approximately 62% of respondents were *'uncertain'* about whether they would be prepared to license their work to Google, while only 27.5% of authors expressed a willingness to do so.

Whilst more than 20% of all respondents saw the Google library project as a negative step for authors' copyright control, 13.5% saw it as a positive step, with 12.5% being neutral and the rest failing to respond. One full time fiction writer commented: 'If you can't beat 'em join 'em,' while another said: '…not convinced. A while ago we were bombarded with all this stuff and had to opt in or out.' Respondents had diverse opinions on the issue, with one full time fiction writer stating that it did not apply unless you were published in America, and another complaining: 'I can't believe that Google has been allowed to rape the book sector in this way and am horrified that no government has bothered to deal with this.'

Most of the interviewees appeared to be positive about the Google book scanning project. Kate Eltham drew a distinction between the Google Book Settlement and the Google Publishing Partnership programme, explaining that the Google Settlement related to the Google Library Project, only covering books that were published until 1999. The books on the Google Book Search, on the other hand, were either in the public domain or subject to the Google Partnership programme, which entailed publishers signing up to the programme and deciding how much of the book would be available for preview. In this regard, the publisher negotiated with Google, and there was an assumption that the publisher had the right to make these determinations on behalf of the author. She further pointed out that the Google Book Search provided some useful free data to the publisher or account holder in relation to books included in the Google Publishing Partnership. Eltham's understanding was that publishers who joined the Google Partnership Programme generally made their whole list of books available, without necessarily auditing whether or not they had the right to do so. She suggested that if authors were dissatisfied with their books appearing on the Google Book Search, they should take the issue up with their publisher. It should be noted that Eltham's in-depth knowledge of these issues evidences her industry expertise and does not represent the perceptions of the majority of authors.

On a practical level, author and travel journalist Kim Wildman had seen her book, *Offbeat South Africa*, a travel guide, on Google Book Search and was disturbed by the amount of content displayed for viewing. She was concerned that, as so much of the book was available to be read online, there was less incentive for the browser to buy the book. She would have preferred that only a few excerpts of the book, the front and back cover, the Table of Contents and perhaps part of the first chapter be displayed, to enable people to decide whether or not they wanted to buy the book. At the time of the interview, 34 of the 149 pages as well as the front and back covers were on display. Although she did not profess to know much about the Google Book Settlement, Wildman regarded it as a positive step, 'as long as it's pay per view,' similar to charging for online news, which she saw as a protective measure for authors' work.

Alex Adsett compared the Google Settlement to the Australian CAL distribution system and saw it as a revenue stream that was not previously available to authors. However, she was critical of Google's behaviour and its attitude towards copyright and saw its actions as an attempt to 'reverse the core of copyright law.' Nevertheless, she said if Google succeeded in making the material available for the user whilst finding a way to remunerate the author, she saw it as being consistent with the original idea behind copyright law.

A mainstream publisher viewed Google's digitisation of books as a positive step, especially with regard to books that were out of copyright and out of print and books that were subject to copyright and out of print, as Google retrieved these books from obscurity and made them available online. This resulted in old works being 'brought back to life' by digital technology, even where the works were not commercially viable for publishers.

However, the publisher pointed out that Google was not alone in its quest to revive out of print books, as university presses such as Oxford and Cambridge had invested in digitisation of old titles which were in copyright and out of print and had made them available in ebook and print-on-demand format. Another publisher taking advantage of digital printing technology was Faber Finds, a UK literary publisher. Although she saw Google's actions as a blatant disregard for the basic principles of copyright, the question was whether the end justified the means: Should one accept this level of the breach of authors' rights for the sake of some genuine benefit? This publisher had decided to opt out of the Settlement and had signed a Publishing

Partnership Agreement with Google instead. She was concerned about the way Google reversed the normal work practices in relation to copyright and not only breached copyright, but also put the onus on the copyright owner to opt out. The ongoing commercial and cultural implications of the Google Settlement were still unknown and uncertain.

Author and publisher Sally Collings described the Google Settlement as 'incredibly complex,' noting that most authors were left in the dark as there was no unified industry position. The benefits to orphaned works were clear in her view, but Google's effective monopoly by virtue of its vast catalogue, was of some concern. Collings had taken her agent's advice and opted in to the Settlement. Nick Earls had also been advised by his agent to opt into the Settlement. Like many others, he had a 'wait and see' approach and was not sure how the system would work in practice as far as payments for transactions were concerned. In general, he approved of the increased access to books through Google initiatives. He said:

I think it would be great if new technologies improved access in the range of ways that they can, but not at the expense of the author, and in a way that acknowledges the author as the creator of that product. The author needs to receive some compensation for the use or sale of his work.

Sally Breen commented on the Google Book Scanning Project as follows:

I think what that does is open up for Australian writers a presence and a visual space in the world. We're quite isolated. I would think that if anything's in a library it's probably passed its shelf life in a bookstore, so therefore are you really losing that many sales from digitisation of library content? What is the difference between having it sit on a shelf of a library and having it sit on the Web? Where the full text is available in a library, but a portion of the text is available on the Web, and you've gone past the major sale period, I support it.

She conceded that the process was not what authors were used to, but thought that was 'the new digital way of doing things.' 'You can imagine how much longer it would have taken if they went around the world to ask permission before they did it? We would all be dead by the time everyone replied back,' she said.

They have to make it happen. People talk about books now lasting three weeks on a bookshelf in a bookstore, and then it's over. So if you have this other life, this other space where your work is circulating and can be read anywhere by anyone who can speak the language, I think that's really exciting.

John Kelly had signed on to the Google Partnership and as a self-publisher had no problem with the Google Settlement. Another author said she would 'reluctantly participate' in the Google Settlement, as digital technology had the potential to increase protection and sales for creators, producers and sellers, whilst minimising costs for consumers. She thought that Google should have approached it differently and asked creators and publishers to participate voluntarily. Although she was of the view that Google had to pay their 'lawful penalties' for breaching copyright laws, she saw great benefit in 'burying the proverbial hatchet after that and supporting Google's efforts.'

Another author who voiced a conflicted perspective of the Google Settlement was Nigel Krauth. On the one hand, he described Google's actions as 'a raid on copyright,' an imposition on writers and objected to the way in which Google went about digitising authors' work without their consent; on the other, he saw it as 'a terrific idea in itself.' Like most of the interviewees, Frank Moorhouse recognised the potential in Google's digitisation programme. Two American editions of his books had been digitised, and he intended to devote some time to an intensive study of the programme. 'If copyright as we know it is going to collapse in some way, or become porous, we have to look at other mechanisms for paying creators,' he commented.

Business Models and Marketing: The Copyright Effect

In addition to authors' views on copyright and copyright structures, this research has investigated how copyright is affected by the emergence of new publishing models, the most far-reaching being the publishing of books in electronic format and the increasing popularity of hand held reading devices. It has been shown that changes have already occurred in the way books are viewed and that further progress is underway. These findings further reflect authors' perceptions of how their copyright is being affected by the migration of the book from printed to digital concept and new publishing models.

In examining the evolving copyright models, it is also relevant to mention the emergence of alternative models of publishing in the form of small publishing houses, such as Red Hill Publishing, 'self publishing' models and initiatives such as the South Australian literary *Wet Ink* publication. Eltham, in particular, expressed the view that digital technology had changed the culture of writing and publishing and that electronic rights had become 'incredibly important,' which sparked a growth in the ereader industry. She stated that the Internet was allowing authors to take more control of how their copyright was managed. As an example, she mentioned Canadian author Corey Doctorow, who made his books available for free on the Internet and opposed the use of DRM and proprietary branded technology, arguing that the author's biggest enemy was not piracy but obscurity. She agreed with this philosophy and pointed out that Doctorow, despite publishing his books for free online, without DRM technology, was also a successful author in traditional book form.

Eltham saw the different treatments of copyright protection as being determined by the ethical viewpoints of authors such as Doctorow and, on the other hand, traditional publishers. She agreed with Doctorow that DRM technology punished the reader and still did not prevent the copying of the work. She also approved of the Creative Commons because of its focus on choice for the author, as it allowed authors to determine how they wanted people to interact with their content and choose the appropriate license. This system reflected the 'culture of the Internet,' which essentially provided that you could not engage with people effectively without 'openness and trust.'

She further voiced some concerns over ereader formats and the power of companies such as Amazon Kindle, to wield control over customers' purchases. She also referred to the American Kindle store's global distribution rights, which suggested the demise of territorial boundaries. Eltham felt strongly that she would not buy a Kindle as they used DRM on every title, meaning that content could not be moved between devices and was therefore too inflexible. She also mentioned an incident with George Orwell's *1984,* where the publisher questioned the Kindle store's right to sell the title and asked for it to be withdrawn. This resulted in Amazon removing the title from people's individual Kindle libraries.

Her concern was that people could lose their entire ebook libraries, if, for example, Kindle went out of business or decided to withdraw titles, as they demonstrated with Orwell's book. She regarded this as an important issue in copyright protection, as book lovers enjoyed a sense of ownership over their books and an emotional relationship with the books on their bookshelves. Her objection to DRM was that the digital market was trying to break the emotional bond readers had with their books by imposing DRM measures, telling the buyer they did not actually own it but were actually purchasing a right to use the material according to the licence attached to it. She saw this as a major departure from the traditional relationship book lovers had with books and foresaw a danger in breaking that emotional bond for the next generation of readers. Eltham cautioned that this would lead to increased copying and piracy because people would not have a sense of ownership and thus would more readily share the material.

Subsequent to the interview with Eltham an action was brought against Amazon by two Kindle owners, one of which was a student who had his copy of *1984*, together with his annotations, deleted from his Kindle by Amazon (*Gawronski & others v. Amazon Inc.* [2009]). Although the matter was settled in October 2009 and Amazon paid an amount of US$150,000 to the plaintiffs' lawyers, the court was not called upon to decide on the legality of Amazon's Kindle usage terms and the issue remains moot. As Seringhaus remarked:

It remains unclear which body of law governs Kindle e-book transactions, and whether Amazon's Kindle Terms will be upheld if they are challenged. If the Terms are upheld, ebook buyers will have virtually no meaningful rights in the content they have purchased. In addition to being unable to sell or transfer ebooks, users could lose access to purchased content at any time. If, on the other hand, Kindle ebook transactions are held to be sales, then the first sale doctrine and the 'essential step' exemption for necessary copies would apply (Seringhaus, 2010, p. 65).

Other interviewees also recognised the opportunities offered by digital publishing. John Kelly explained the benefits of self-publishing in his article 'Publish and be damned' (2009):

Since the introduction of print on demand technology...a self publisher can publish his/her work, develop some simple computer skills and design his/her own cover and enlist the assistance of a number of self-help Websites to have their work edited and reviewed free. They then have access to a world-wide market by submitting their book to Google Books and Amazon and Lulu's Websites, all available for a start-up cost of less than $100.00.

He pointed out that they could then join a plethora of author Websites offering assistance and encouragement to promote their work, some of which acted as a type of union with members buying each other's books.

Phillip Edmonds of the University of Adelaide also took a pro-active approach to exploring new models for publishing. In his article 'Interrogating Creative Writing Outcomes: Wet Ink as a new Model' (2007), he proposed the use of institutional resources to contribute to an intervention in the 'so-called literary marketplace.' He cautioned that:

...retreating from and lamenting our perceived publishing crisis could result in a depressive culture of inwardness and defensiveness in our institutional frameworks, and even a form of 'recreational grieving' as to the high-mindedness of our intentions.

He suggested that the university, and *Wet Ink* in particular, could be involved in 'interrogating a third space containing general readers,' rather than just other writing students or people trained in particular university discourses. Consequently, the magazine *Wet Ink* was self-funding, distributed nationally and involved people from within the university and outside. Whilst it had been challenging to build the magazine up as a viable business in a difficult and small publishing environment, he recognised the importance of developing a subscription base with constituencies such as reading groups and writers' centres in order to facilitate and expand their distribution base. Edmonds' insight reflected the willingness of many authors to embrace alternative publishing models.

Sally Collings noted that the whole economic model of publishing was changing, as small publishing houses and self publishing became more widespread and viable. She used her own small publishing house, Red Hill Publishing (Red Hill) at www.redhillpublishing.com as an example. Red Hill operated on a fee for service basis, where the author paid Red Hill a royalty on copies sold. As a result, authors kept nearly 90% of the revenues, retained their copyright and were able to license their work to other publishers. Collings was optimistic about the ability to sell books both in Australia and internationally.

In her blog of 18 June 2010 titled *Authorpreneur – The author as entrepreneur,* she described two options open to authors: the traditional publishing model where the author received a lump sum payment and thereafter a minority percentage of the profits (approximately 10%) and, on the other hand, the model whereby the author was supported by 'a business angel' (in this case Red Hill Publishing) who assisted the author to commercialise their business idea in exchange for 'a director's fee and a minority percentage of the profits (approximately 15%).' She suggested that the book should be regarded as a 'start-up business,' an asset that the writer could hold or sell, as they chose.

In relation to the marketing of ebooks, social media such as Twitter and Facebook were regarded by some interviewees as opportunities for authors to market their work on the Internet. However, others recognised difficulties in enforcing ownership of written content in the digital domain, using these marketing tools. Nick Earls mentioned the example of writing something on Twitter, which could then potentially be re-sent to thousands of other people. A loss of control occurred during this process, whereby the author essentially accepted that they were relinquishing their intellectual property in that tweet. He suggested that although people usually attributed tweets to the person who created it, it was possible that others could use that material or change it, without acknowledging the creator.

Sally Breen saw a great marketing opportunity for authors in Facebook and Twitter. She pointed out that, in promoting writers' festivals, they consistently created Facebook sites to promote awareness of the events, with good results. She regarded it as a 'fast, easy way to promote' and did not perceive any negatives in using these strategies.

Yaro Starak commented that new business models allowed creators to give away most of their content and still make a profit because of 'viral' distribution. To him, capturing the reader's attention was the main stumbling block on the Internet, and business models had to be tailored to the public response. He saw the marketplace changing into a 'longtail marketplace,' a longitudinal model where more people sold fewer copies of more books. This viewpoint accords with the instances where some books, that have not been viable propositions for publishers in the past, can now be electronically published at a very low cost by online publishers, as discussed in Chapter 6.

SUMMARY AND CONCLUSION

During this second part of the investigation, it became evident that copyright and copyright legislation were not viewed by the author participants as something localised, to be seen only in an Australian context, but rather in the wider context of global copyright. The reasons for this perception appeared to be two-fold: firstly, many of the interviewees and respondents had published books in other countries and had to contend with international copyright issues and regional considerations and secondly, with wider application, media platforms and structures such as the Internet and a variety of electronic devices provided increased forums for publication on an international level. These factors prompted authors to contemplate a departure from traditional copyright frameworks and, in many cases, to embrace alternative frameworks that allowed them to function creatively. These alternative structures, such as the Creative Commons and various forms of online publishing, as discussed more fully in Chapter 6, provide increasing options for authors and publishers.

Some of the writers expressed a preference for structures that were more flexible than traditional publishing models, with a more generous attitude towards copyright usage and a 'share culture' approach. This was particularly evident with writers who published online and used social media and forums such as blogging sites. Whilst some authors displayed a lack of knowledge on issues such as the Google Settlement and digital publishing, others were able to provide expert knowledge on these topics.

Once the enquiry shifted from traditional publishing models and their supporting legislative structures to the wider options offered by new technology, it also became clear that most interviewees and survey respondents felt that most preconceived ideas of copyright legislation would have to adjust in keeping with public expectations and the needs of copyright creators. These observations reflect the comments of Young where he refers to copyright laws as relating to 'a nineteenth-century mindset' and the industry as requiring a new copyright infrastructure (2007, pp. 158-159). As evidenced by both the interviews and the online survey results, many authors supported a need for change and were intent upon making technological innovations work for, rather than against them.

REFERENCES

Allen & Unwin. (2011). *About Allen & Unwin*. Retrieved June 5, 2011, from http://www.allenandunwin.com/default.aspx?page=432

Collings, S. (2010, June 18). *Authorpreneur – The author as entrepreneur*. Retrieved May 19, 2011, from http://sallycollings.com/2010/06/authorpreneur-%E2%80%93-the-author-as-entrepreneur/

Copyright Amendment (Digital Agenda) Act 2000 (Cth)

Edmonds, P. (2007). Interrogating creative writing outcomes: Wet ink as a new model. *TEXT, 11*(1). Retrieved May 19, 2011, from http://www.textjournal.com.au/april07/edmonds.htm

Gawronski & others v. Amazon Inc. [2009] (US) *Random House, Inc. v. Rosetta Books* LLC, 283 F.3d 490, 62 U.S.P.Q.2d (BNA) 1063 (2d Cir. 2002) (US)

Kelly, J. (2009, October 5). Publish and be damned. *The Drum.* Retrieved May 19, 2011, from http://www.abc.net.au/unleashed/28818.html

Scholastic. (2011). *Manuscript guidelines*. Retrieved June 5, 2011, from http://scholastic.com.au/corporate/manuscript.asp

Seringhaus, M. (2010). E-book transactions: Amazon 'kindles' the copy ownership debate (Paper 60). *Student Prize Papers*. Retrieved July 11, 2011, from http://digitalcommons.law.yale.edu/ylsspps_papers/60

The Authors Guild et al v. Google, Inc, (2009) US District Court, Southern District of New York, No. 05-08136 at 1 (US)

The Authors Guild, Inc. et al. v. HathiTrust et al, US District Court, Southern District of New York, filed 12 September 2011, 11 CIV 6351 (US)

Young, S. (2007). *The book is dead: Long live the book*. Sydney: University of New South Wales Press.

TABLE OF CASES

Gawronski & others v. Amazon Inc. [2009] (US)

Random House, Inc. v. Rosetta Books LLC, 283 F.3d 490, 62 U.S.P.Q.2d (BNA) 1063 (2d Cir. 2002) (US)

The Authors Guild et al v. Google, Inc, (2009) US District Court, Southern District of New York, No. 05-08136 at 1 (US)

The Authors Guild, Inc. et al. v. HathiTrust et al, US District Court, Southern District of New York, filed 12 September 2011, 11 CIV 6351 (US)

TABLE OF STATUTES

Copyright Amendment (Digital Agenda) Act 2000 (Cth)

Chapter 10
Discussion and Analysis

ABSTRACT

A discussion and analysis of the key aspects emerging during the course of the research comprise the basis of this chapter. It addresses, inter alia, the effect of the parallel importing debate on authors' rights, the issue of publishing contracts, the idea of a "heavenly library" and copyright protection on the Internet, including a discussion on how existing territorial copyright structures may be affected by electronic publishing. This chapter also considers the Google initiatives and possible new business models for authors. The emerging theme of resale royalties for authors is examined and compared with the Resale Royalty Right for Visual Artists Act 2009. In conclusion, observations are made on the role of the author in the changing publishing landscape, situating the author as member of the "author sphere" in the context of the public sphere.

INTRODUCTION

A number of central themes were revealed during the presentation of findings in Chapters 8 and 9. Significantly, it became apparent that authors find themselves on the cusp of a change from traditional book publishing to digital publishing. In this chapter, these findings are examined in more depth and discussed within the context of the literature review and philosophical theories relating to the concept of copyright, the notion of authorship and the author's role in the publishing industry. Further observations on the intersection of the subaltern sphere of the author group with other competing spheres illuminate the resulting tension between authors' interests, publishers' interests and

DOI: 10.4018/978-1-4666-5214-9.ch010

the public interest and how this impacts on the author's practice as creator. These observations will establish a foundation for the final conclusions and recommendations in Chapter 11, drawing into question how much authors as a group will be able to influence the future of copyright in Australia and examine whether authors are sufficiently interested in copyright to advance their own interests in the broader public sphere.

BROAD DEMOGRAPHICS

In evaluating the findings, it is necessary to consider the broad demographics of the purposive sample. As discussed, 177 responses were received in the online survey, of which 156 were published authors. Only the responses from published authors were used. Over 70% of the respondents were fiction writers and respondents had an average age of 45.3 years. Significantly, nearly 80% of them were over 40 and only 5.7% under 30 years of age. Approximately one third of the published authors were full time authors with the balance being part time. The sample group included several fields of creative writers, including fiction, non-fiction and academic authors, poets and playwrights. In addition, over 51% of these authors were members of the Australian Society of Authors (ASA).

AUTHORS' SOURCES OF INCOME

Notably, most authors reported additional means of income from a variety of sources. Given the low general income derived from their writing, it was not surprising that 92% of part time and 57% of full time surveyed authors reported a supplementary source of income. As noted, at least 66 different professions/sources of income were described in the survey, as diverse as 'waitressing,' 'town planner,' 'journalist,' 'university professor' and 'builder's labourer,' to name but a few examples. The interviewed authors described their occupations in a variety of ways, such as publisher, lecturer, marketer, legal practitioner, full time writer and in-retirement and wrote fiction, non-fiction, academic books, business books, memoirs and travel guides. This purposive sample group also included 'elite' interviews, by virtue of their expert knowledge of the writing industry. In both the full time and part time groups, the largest alternative income source was from teaching and academic work, with savings and investments the second most prevalent source. Several respondents also relied on Government grants to supplement their income.

It was evident that only 'bestselling' authors such as Earls relied purely on their writing to earn a living, whilst a number of interviewees derived income from teaching and journalism in addition to writing books. Even established and highly regarded authors such as Moorhouse recognised the economic difficulties faced by authors as evidenced by his earlier comments (2008, p. 4).

In the context of this research, the authors are earning even less than their counterparts (such as performing artists) in the arts industry (as reported by Cunningham & Higgs, 2010, p. 4), with authors reporting a higher incidence of multiple income sources. It is also evident from the list of job descriptions provided in Chapter 8 that many respondents are employed in capacities completely unrelated to writing and that many also rely on savings and investments. The largest group of respondents fell in the category of earning only $1,000 - $2,000 per annum from their writing, including nearly 18% of full time authors. Considering the fact that these were all 'published' authors, the findings show that financial motivation is not a primary concern for most writers, although a small percentage (2.3%) disclosed earnings in excess of $100,000 per annum.

These findings echo the observations of Cunningham and Higgs 'that arts employment is characterised by high levels of part-time work' (Cunningham & Higgs, 2010, p. 5). In addition, the Throsby and Zednik (2010) study established that 69% of writers had earned less than $10,000 per annum from their creative work, in the 2007/2008 financial year. The findings from this research confirm that this remains the case, with slightly fewer (61.7%) of the surveyed authors earning less than $10,000 per annum from writing and writing related activities. The findings therefore indicate a trend that writers consistently are unable to earn a living from their writing.

Author incomes and related issues are addressed in a recent Government commissioned report by the Book Industry Strategy Group (BISG), and a number of useful recommendations are put forward, including:

- Suggestions of tax relief measures for authors, such as legislation to exempt literary prizes, awards and Government grants and other tax concessions (2011, p. 84).
- A review of the Australia Council's Literature Board grants allocation process and criteria in order to provide additional funding directly to authors through, *inter alia*, more grants and fellowships (2011, p. 86).

- The establishment of a National Book Council to redress the 'current decline in the creation, production and reception of vital Australian cultural content in book form,' to include a Manuscript Fund to assist with the creation of new Australian works (2011, p. 88).

It is evident that these recommendations have been made largely as a result of the ASA Submission (Loukakis, 2011) made to the BISG, which addresses key issues confronting authors, *inter alia,* authors' rights and remuneration, and includes recommendations for authors to become involved in a review of the *Copyright Act* and ELR and PLR schemes, which would include payments for online access (2011, pp. 4-5). If implemented, these recommendations will be of great assistance to authors; however, their implementation will of necessity be subject to Government review processes (and legislative changes in some instances) and the availability of Government funding. Until such time, authors have to function in the existing structure.

On a philosophical level, it can be observed that the low earnings reported by authors suggest a lack of economic power exhibited by the author group as members of the literary sphere in the context of the broader public sphere as proposed by Habermas (1974, p. 49), confirming their place as a subaltern public which by definition is also either marginalised or weak. The absence of financial incentive and low reported incomes then begs the question: why do they do it?

AUTHORS AND MOTIVATION

The sentiments expressed by John Kelly in saying 'When I write I don't even think about copyright' embody the views of most of the participants. Authors' low earning profile suggested that most authors focussed on personal satisfaction or recognition rather than financial reward and copyright considerations, when creating. This was borne out by the findings, which show that a resounding 92% of survey respondents are mostly motivated by personal satisfaction. Additionally, approximately 46% indicated that they were also motivated by the prospect of achieving recognition.

Significantly, there was little difference between the views of part time and full time authors on these issues. Although there was a difference between the two groups when contemplating financial considerations, with approximately 83% of part time and 67% of full time authors indicating that they were not motivated by money, it was evident that authors - both full time and part time - were first and foremost motivated by personal satisfaction and, second, to a lesser degree, by achieving recognition and only remotely, by financial reward. Interviewees' observations reflect the reality that an author might be motivated by more than one consideration depending on the nature of the project and the circumstances and confirm that financial considerations are not paramount.

More than half of survey respondents said that they did not regard copyright as an incentive to create, while 65% of the in-depth interview group stated that copyright did not motivate them to create. Although both sample groups acknowledged the importance of copyright when publishing their work, copyright itself was not regarded as a significant consideration during the creative process. Publishers, however, had diverse views on the issue, one stating that many authors would create 'no matter what,' whereas another mainstream publisher strongly regarded copyright as an incentive to create as it assured authors of ownership and control over, and payment for their work.

It was suggested in Chapter 3 that Landes and Posner represented an academic rather than 'grass roots' viewpoint in discussing the incentive purpose of copyright to authors (1987, p. 265). The findings confirm that the Landes and Posner ideal of copyright serving its dual purpose – by providing not only a positive benefit to the copyright owner (as a result of the property right), but also an incentive for the author to create (1987, p. 265) - has not yet been achieved in practice.

EFFECT OF THE PARALLEL IMPORTING DEBATE

Another issue that emerged as a significant event for authors was the Productivity Commission investigation into parallel importing, discussed in Chapter 2, as it denoted the only ascertainable instance during the course of this research where authors became involved in a legislative issue as a group. The Government's rejection of the Productivity Commission's recommendations signified a victory for the literary sphere and Australian authors in particular, as the retention of parallel import restrictions on books allowed authors and publishers the continuing benefits of territorial copyright and associated royalty payments. Another such historical issue was the case of *Moorhouse v. University of New South Wales* (1975), where author support and funding by the ASA and Australian Book Publishers Association was instrumental in securing authors' rights in relation to copying.

The parallel importing issue afforded authors the opportunity to participate effectively in the legislative process by expressing their viewpoints on a proposed amendment to the legislation in respect of territorial copyright legislation. It also alerted many authors to the practical financial implications of the proposed changes to the legislation. Although the Productivity Commission Report was focussed on economic benefits to the public and the broader public interest, authors and affected organisations such as the ASA, through their submissions, highlighted the plight of authors and the importance of royalty income. Furthermore, authors emphasised the detrimental effect the proposed changes would have on the Australian literary culture (Keneally, 2008, p. 4). Some examples of authors' submissions were provided in Chapter 2, with further observations by interviewees providing deeper insight into the matter in Chapter 8. Significantly, a lawyer/publisher noted that the USA and Great Britain also had parallel import restrictions on books. By contrast, one interviewee said that it did not make much sense to have restrictions on parallel importation of digital goods, as it would be regarded as an unenforceable artificial limitation. It should be noted that, in view of the provisions of Section 44F of the *Copyright Act 1968,* which provide that there are no restrictions on importation of electronic literary works - except that it must be a 'non-infringing copy,' i.e. made lawfully in the country of origin - there are currently no parallel import restrictions on digital books. Because of this anomaly, sales of ebooks from overseas sources undermine the parallel import restrictions to a large extent where copyright owners are concerned.

The number of submissions received by the Productivity Commission from 268 Australian authors reflected a high level of interest in and concern about their copyright. The main consideration by authors, in addition to aspects such as cultural ramifications and the future of the Australian publishing industry, was the protection of their territorial copyright, and by implication, the royalties earned from the sale of their publications. The pro-active involvement of authors in this issue reflected an understanding that their livelihood would be directly affected by the proposed legislative changes. Despite economic and public interest pressures advanced by supporters of the Productivity Commission's proposal, authors - in addition to publishers and other interest groups - were able to successfully harness their persuasive powers as a group in the public arena. This outcome illustrates that authors, when united as a group within the broader public sphere, are capable of protecting their literary and creative interests.

Significantly, at the time of the parallel import investigation, most authors did not appreciate the inevitable inroads of digital publishing on the literary public sphere within which they create. In practice, parallel import restrictions effectively serve to protect their interests in relation to printed books but are inadequate to deal with online infringements, in view of the provisions of section 44F of the *Copyright Act.*

In the recent Book Industry Strategy Group report (2011), referred to above, it is averred that the 30/90 days parallel import provisions are ineffective in addressing online book sales and suggested that the timeframe for retention of territorial copyright be reduced to 14 days by industry agreement, rather than legislative change. This, according to the BISG, will enable Australian booksellers to compete more effectively in the digital marketplace (2011, p. 57). Whether this recommendation will find favour with authors and publishers remains to be seen. The findings show, however, that authors are gradually becoming aware of the difficulties associated with copyright protection in the digital environment, as discussed in the next chapter.

In addition, the BISG puts forward the merits of the removal of the Goods and Services Tax (GST) from books purchased in Australia (similar to the United Kingdom's approach) in order to compete with overseas booksellers (2011, p. 54). Notably the ASA, in its Submission to the BISG, pointed out the negative effect that GST on books has on Australian authors' remuneration (Loukakis, 2011, p. 14). These recommendations recognise that Australian booksellers have to compete in a competitive global marketplace and propose that the survival of a viable book industry is dependent upon a swift response by Government. However, it is apparent that there is little consistency in the implementation of parallel importing and GST (or other sales taxes) provisions globally, with countries varying substantially in their approaches (2011, p. 53). The outcome of the suggested GST abolition will have to be determined by Government discussions in future tax forums – until such time it is envisaged that GST on books will remain a drawback for Australian authors, publishers and booksellers.

AUTHORS, PUBLISHERS AND PUBLISHING CONTRACTS

Unfortunately, in the important area of publishing contracts, authors have not made any cohesive efforts to protect their publishing interests. The findings show that at least 62% of authors deal directly with their publishers and are generally not inclined to assert themselves, whereas only approximately 18% use an agent, which raise concerns in view of the possible difficulties associated with the example standard publishing contract discussed in Chapter 6.

As discussed, a number of discrepancies became apparent in comparing the standard mainstream publisher contract with the ASA recommended contract. Whilst it could be expected that both author and publisher groups would wish to include provisions favourable to themselves, these discrepancies are considerable. The standard publisher's contract is skewed significantly in favour of the publisher, and the ASA expectations remain a 'wish list' in many respects. As noted in Chapter 6, disparities exist in relation to provisions such as indemnity clauses, remainder clauses, title changes, the calculation of royalties ('net receipts' as opposed to 'recommended retail price' (RRP)) and royalties on ebooks, which are all in favour of the publisher.

These discrepancies may be due to authors not having an agent and a range of other factors, including inertia or a lack of interest on the part of authors. The fact that only approximately 17% of respondents stated that their publishing contracts were satisfactory suggests that authors tend to accept the terms of publishing agreements offered to them even though they might not be satisfactory. The findings also show that many of the survey respondents appear to rely heavily on their publishers in relation to issues such as the Google Settlement and do not necessarily make their own investigations. The findings therefore show a distinct need for author education on the issue of publishing contracts, especially in relation to digital rights, discussed below. Relevantly, approximately 51% of participants are ASA members, which entitle them to make use of the ASA contract assessment service at a very reasonable rate ($110.00), whilst nearly half of the respondents lack any professional reference point aside from their publishers.

These observations are consistent with the finding that many authors express either a timidity of publishers or an excitement at being published that cancels out any inclination to question standard contracts, or both. It was found that first time authors are generally perceived as having little or no negotiating power with a general disposition of gratitude at being published. This perception is borne out by the acknowledgment of 90% of respondents of the difficulties faced by first time authors in getting published.

Clearly the challenge of finding a willing publisher is a significant obstacle for authors, especially emerging authors. It was noted that publishers like Allen & Unwin only published 250 titles a year out of approximately 1,000 submissions whilst others such as Scholastic received 'several thousand manuscripts' in a year. This is reflected in the findings, which show that authors who secure contracts typically regarded themselves as fortunate and are loathe to jeopardise their good fortune by appearing too demanding when offered a contract.

It is further apparent from the findings that, although some authors regard the standard publishing contract as negotiable to a certain extent, the degree of negotiability will largely depend on the author's standing and proven sales figures. It was commonly acknowledged that high profile authors such as Tim

Winton or Bryce Courtenay would have substantially more negotiating power than a relatively unknown author. It was also noted that publishers' promises were sometimes reminiscent of election promises, before and after the signing of the contract. The important observation that film and merchandising rights should not automatically be part of the contract, unless the publisher could demonstrate the ability and intention to pursue such rights on behalf of the author, emerged from these findings.

With regard to overseas publications, some of the interviewees felt that it was more beneficial for authors to negotiate directly - or through their agents - with overseas publishers, rather than with local publishers. For example, a bestselling author commented that authors would be well-advised securing contracts directly with international publishers to avoid paying a domestic publisher 'middleman costs,' which often included paying a foreign agent a part of the royalties. A recent example of an Australian author who has done this successfully is crime author Peter Temple, who published his award winning book *The broken shore* with British publishing house Quercus in 2006 and sold close to 100,000 copies in paperback (Wilson, 2011, p. 32).

Significantly, the standard publisher's contract typically makes the widest provision for the publisher to be granted *the sole right and license* to publish and sell the author's work, including in ebook form, and to sublicense it *'for the legal period of copyright and throughout the World.'* In contrast, the contract proposed by the ASA suggests more limited publishing rights - a two-year licence to publish and sell the work in a specifically defined territory. The ASA proposal provides a more equitable approach, considering that the legal period of copyright is usually until the death of the author plus 70 years. This discrepancy is indicative of the imbalance in copyright expectations on the part of publishers and authors, and further denotes the tension between authors' private rights and public benefit considerations.

In relation to digital contracts, the findings show a distinct lack of any standard practice. Not only were large discrepancies noted between the standard mainstream publisher contract (where 10% of net receipts was stipulated) and the ASA recommended contract (which proposed 35% of RRP), but there also appeared to be no industry standard where ebook royalties were concerned. It was noted that online publisher Lulu pays authors approximately 56% in royalties, whilst online publishers such as Smashwords offer authors royalties of up to 85%. These percentages are considerably higher than the percentages offered by mainstream publishers for ebooks, however, it is conceded that, for the most part, these authors do not have the support and exposure provided by traditional print publishers.

In its submission to the BISG, the ASA suggests that:

A review of commercial contract law governing publishing agreements be undertaken to assist in the establishment of transparent, measurable and clear statements and expositions of rights responsibilities, obligations and practices under law (Loukakis, 2011, p. 5).

If this objective can be achieved it will result in greater certainty for authors and consequently a lesser reliance by them on publishers to explain complicated terminology (in what is potentially a conflict of interest situation).

In more recent copyright developments in Australia, the Australian Law Review Commission has released a Discussion Paper on *Copyright in the Digital Economy* (2013), calling for submissions from stakeholders. It considers several options for reform, set out in the Terms of Reference, one of which is the possible recognition of 'fair use' of copyright material in the *Copyright Act 1968* (as opposed to the current closed list of permitted purposes for 'fair dealing'), which will allow for expanded transformative use (2013, p. 24). Such an inclusion will align the Australian copyright approach with US provisions for 'fair use,' and will create a wider range of copyright exceptions, especially relevant on the Internet.

On a broader level, the current publishing situation is reflective of the limitations imposed on the author in the 'author sphere' within which he/she operates, vis-à-vis the financially more powerful 'publisher's sphere,' both of which are contained within the 'literary public sphere, which is part of the larger public sphere as envisaged by Habermas (1974, p. 49). It can be observed that the principle of supply and demand is manifested in this seemingly inequitable power balance, with writers clamouring for publication opportunities and publishers being able to dictate the terms of their offerings. Furthermore, authors have to adapt to changing copyright considerations as a result of a changed literary public sphere, which has been recast within the digital environment. In this regard, Vaidhayanathan's comments regarding the connection between copyright and the public sphere are relevant - 'copyright's subsequent transformations coincide with the general structural transformation of the public sphere' (Vaidhayanathan, 2001, p. 6). The findings suggest that, despite the promising indications of author autonomy in the digital domain, authors are neither sufficiently empowered to deal with existing copyright challenges posed by publishing contracts, nor are they able to successfully negotiate the changing demands of the digital sphere.

In addition to the competitive nature of the publishing industry, the solitary nature of the writing profession reinforces the writer's lack of power in the publication process. Furthermore, there is a distinct lack of involvement by agents or skilled middlemen to represent authors. The fact that authors often rely on the advice of their publishers to their own detriment (in respect of royalty calculations, for example) presents an anomaly in the structure of these two competing groups, serving only to weaken the author's position further.

However, commentators such as Mark Coker, founder of Smashwords, believe that the digital era heralds a new era for writers in the publishing world. In his article, 'Do authors still need publishers?' he predicted that the power center in publishing would shift from publisher to author, and the traditional line between the two would continue to blur, causing authors to become their own publishers and commercial publishers to become service providers (Coker, 2009). However, this study shows that this is not yet the case, with only approximately 17% of the online survey authors self-publishing online and 46% relying on their publishers to do so. Nevertheless, if one considers the wide range of publishing options on offer by online publishers such as Smashwords, Scribd and Lulu, it can be argued – in spite of the associated challenges - that the opportunities offered by digital publishing present the catalyst first time authors have been waiting for but have yet to fully realise.

THE IDEA OF A 'HEAVENLY' LIBRARY

The heavenly library could usher in an entirely new book ecosystem in which ideas are more important than objects. - Sherman Young

Falling squarely within the ambits of the third research question, which relates to authors' views on the changing publishing industry, the theme of the 'heavenly library' is relevant to the issue of digital publishing and merits some discussion here. Considering the finding that over 56% of the authors had sold work (either personally or through publishers) in digital format on the Internet, it appears that Young's concept of a 'heavenly library' is becoming a reality. The idea was previously framed as a 'heavenly jukebox' by Goldstein in his book *Copyright's highway: From Gutenberg to the Celestial Jukebox* (2003, p. 184), where he predicted 'a digital repository of books, movies and music available on demand' (2003, p. 246).

Young subsequently extended this idea of a 'heavenly jukebox' by relating music to books and imagined the 'heavenly library' 'as the world's collection of books available in an instant' (2007, p. 151). This concept, according to Young, had a number of advantages over printed books, including more flexibility and ease of publishing for publishers, greater accessibility for readers, environmental advantages, lower costs and portability. As early as 1993, Rawlins had enumerated the advantages of ebooks as being 'cheap, long lasting, easily copied, quickly acquired, easily searched and portable in bulk' (1993, p. 475).

The findings show that these advantages are recognised by many authors who see the digital market as a new way to connect with readers and transform the book supply chain. Full time authors in particular appreciate the growing significance of the Internet market place and the advantages of making their books available in digital form. During the course of this research, over a period of three to four years, ereading technology has also advanced rapidly and most of the interviewees and survey participants were conscious of the inroads made into traditional publishing by devices such as iPhones, iPads, Kindle, etc. New devices are constantly being introduced into the marketplace, and the concept of a digital environment where all books, music and films are available at the click of a button has become a reasonable expectation rather than a potential promise.

So what are the perceived disadvantages of a 'heavenly library'? Apart from considerations that book lovers may no longer have a library filled with printed books due to the smart economics of buying ebooks online, and that we may see a demise of the traditional book culture as a result, authors raised further concerns. Amongst these was the problem of digital copyright protection, which emerged as the main issue of concern raised in the findings, to be discussed in more depth below.

A further concern raised in relation to the 'digital library' was the power wielded by ebook retailers such as Amazon, who hold exclusive digital rights to certain books. In these instances titles are made available exclusively through Amazon and on their Kindle ereader, to the exclusion of many other reading devices. The incident between Amazon and Macmillan publishers in the USA illustrates how customers and authors are at the mercy of Internet rights holders. In that case, Macmillan wanted to determine the prices of their books for sale on Amazon (instead of Amazon's standard price of US$9.99). Failing to reach agreement on the issue, Amazon took the 'buy' button off all Macmillan titles in the store for 48 hours over the weekend, thus preventing any customers from buying Macmillan books. Another incident concerning Amazon's power to control readers' Internet purchases - where Amazon removed George Orwell's novel *1984* from individual Kindle libraries when problems arose with the publisher - was discussed in Chapter 9. Although a subsequent action against Amazon by two Kindle owners resulted in a settlement of the plaintiffs' legal costs (*Gawronski & others v. Amazon Inc.* [2009]), the Court did not decide on the legality of Amazon's Kindle usage terms, and purchasers remain subject to these terms. These issues are pertinent to the rights of consumers in the realm of a 'heavenly library' and will have to be addressed in the future, if readers are to have confidence in their online book purchases.

Young noted, as a further issue facing the digital library, readers' cultural attachment to the printed book. He acknowledged that the shift was 'not so much a technical shift as a cultural one, demanding a change in readers, writers and publishers' (Young, 2007, p. 156). This view was echoed by Eltham in her article 'Writing the digital future,' where she noted that digital technology had changed the culture of writing and publishing and that digital books signified a move away from traditional 'book culture' and did not confer the same benefits as the printed book (2009, p. 7).

Whether or not these concerns will prove to be well-founded in the future, it is evident that both authors and readers will have to make a cultural shift in embracing the idea of a 'heavenly library' and in dealing with the challenges associated with copyright and book ownership, especially in accepting the concept of licensing rather than physical ownership of a book. It can be expected that, whilst this concept has been integrated successfully into the world of music (as something that is *listened to* rather than *read*), as evidenced by the popularity of iPods and other devices, acceptance of a digital library may be hampered by a cultural attachment to the book and book culture. On the other hand, the findings show that a number of authors see the ebook as merely another incarnation of the book and express confidence in the parallel survival of the printed book. These views are echoed by Fisher's comments above regarding increased book sales (2010).

The findings are reflective of the range of conflicting opinions held by authors on the issue of print versus digital books and the inevitable transition to a digital library. On the one hand, there is the perception of a positive move towards electronic publishing and, on the other, a lack of confidence on the part of authors. There are indications that Young's commendable vision of a *heavenly library* 'as the world's collection of books available in an instant' (2007, p. 152) will not only require a cultural shift but will also need revised copyright models. However, the movement towards increasingly creative ways of publishing and licencing content, as discussed above, indicate that such a shift is imminent and that copyright models are already being reconsidered and modified.

DIGITAL COPYRIGHT PROTECTION

The findings show that nearly 80% of all respondents are concerned about their digital copyright. Most of the author comments relate to theft of work on electronic media or 'online piracy.' Some authors cite instances of copyright breaches on their Internet publications without any apparent solutions. It is significant that, although they acknowledge that illegal online copying is a real concern for them, as the current copyright structure does not seem to address the problem adequately, over 50% admit to doing nothing to protect their copyright online. Several survey respondents specifically cite a lack of knowledge on ebook copyright as a problem and voice concerns about a lack of time and funds to pursue copyright breaches on the Internet. Whilst these concerns are common amongst authors, equally prevalent is the lack of any action taken with regard to copyright breaches. In addition, publishers do not provide a shield for authors against online copyright infringement, with most authors and publishers accepting the inevitability of copyright infringements on the Internet.

Authors who take protective steps employ different measures to protect their online copyright. Significantly, only 16.5% of survey respondents use digital rights management (DRM) to prevent the copying of their work. Some express reservations about the use of DRM and describe it as 'a barrier' to readers buying their books. Whilst most respondents state that it is impossible to protect their copyright online, only a small number favour flexible licensing models such as the Creative Commons, which recognise the author's moral rights and provide licensing options pursuant to the provisions of section 189 of the *Copyright Act 1968*.

Although the Creative Commons has been in operation for 10 years, nearly half of survey respondents admit that they are not familiar with the concept, while approximately a third express support for the Creative Commons. Considering the purposive sampling method employed and the nature of the respondents – who are all published authors - one may have expected a greater awareness of the structure in this group. It is noted, however, that interviewees who support the Creative Commons are generally also bloggers, who have more Internet knowledge than others who have not previously published work online. It appears that this provides an opportunity for this concept to be better marketed to this group of professionals who would be a logical stakeholder group. However, a significant drawback of the Creative Commons licensing scheme is that it does not prescribe licensing fees or financial remuneration for participants due to its voluntary character.

As an alternative protective measure, nearly a third of the survey respondents state that they post warnings on their Websites or on the creative work itself, and 13% use 'other means' of copyright protection such as relying on their publishers and taking note of daily Google alerts advising of illegal file sharing sites. Loukakis advises authors to ensure that their digital rights are protected, noting that the ASA favours a cautionary approach and warning their members against piracy (Loukakis, 2011, p. 29). Significantly, as some authors point out, the problem with protecting online copyright is that it is usually not commercially viable to pursue offenders in the case of a breach. A mainstream publisher agrees that international copyright is a grey area and that legal advice will not necessarily help to resolve practical issues. The findings show that the prohibitive costs of protecting their copyright and litigating overseas is a stumbling block for most Australian authors, which is evidenced by the absence of Australian copyright litigation on books.

Most authors show an awareness of the challenges facing their profession in the expanding literary sphere in the digital domain but - perhaps not surprisingly - not many solutions are being offered. Publishers also regularly experience challenges with maintaining copyright online and face problems such as online piracy and other instances of infringement. Authors who are most optimistic about the future of online publishing acknowledge the limitations of DRM technology, yet there appears to be few other viable income producing copyright options available.

In their report, the BISG recognise the problems associated with protection of digital copyright and the necessity for reform. They suggest that the government should work with Internet industries to adopt a binding industry code on copyright infringement by Internet service providers to protect online copyright. These recommendations, based largely on the ASA Submission to the BISG (2011), are commendable, but would require not only a focussed intention by the Australian Law Review Commission (ALRC) and government to alleviate current digital copyright concerns, but also practical and enforceable measures, such as the punitive sanctions and anti-piracy copyright education campaign proposed by the ASA (Loukakis, 2011, p. 6). The final report of the ALRC in its consideration of *Copyright and the Digital Economy* (2013) will be a determining factor in whether the government's approach will be towards a relaxation of copyright control (by the introduction of 'fair use,' a wider defence than 'fair dealing' as is currently in use in Australia).

An issue of specific concern to authors is how the Internet impacts on their existing territorial copyright, the dilution of which seems inevitable. It was suggested that it would be short-sighted for countries to attempt territorial changes - such as the suggested lifting of parallel import restrictions - when publishing agreements were already being impacted by digital technologies. Others see no reason for dividing territories up geographically where digital rights are concerned, arguing that consumers would expect to have access to digital contents worldwide irrespective of where they live. The findings also show that the possibility of self-publication has effectively removed traditional territorial barriers for authors.

It is evident that most publishers have already come to the realisation that they need to acquire worldwide digital rights when they purchase a book and that authors and organisations such as the ASA are becoming acutely aware of the importance of world digital rights. This has further been demonstrated by the recent ASA involvement in the *Authors Guild* case against US libraries and the HathiTrust, referred to in Chapter 6, involving the scanning and distributing of books online. However, the US Court's application of the 'fair use' principle has resulted in a dilution of authors' and publishers' rights in this case.

Examples of existing problems relating to territorial copyright - such as those experienced by Nigel Krauth in the publication of his book *Matilda my darling* - illustrate the anomalies that might arise from territorial copyright provisions and present a strong argument in favour of those who support the removal of territorial copyright borders and uniformity in copyright laws. They also emphasise the inadequacies of the current copyright structure in the global environment and the need to provide creators with greater certainty, in order to maximise the utilitarian principles under which they operate.

Relevantly, these territorial copyright concerns lead to increased problems in collecting royalties internationally. A number of authors voiced the concern that copyright measures and royalty schemes based in Australia did not sufficiently address the issue of loss of revenue from overseas sources, such as sales on the Internet and copyright infringements which occurred outside Australia. New media structures and the expanding use of electronic devices further exacerbate these problems. It is evident that these issues can only increase as online publishing becomes more prevalent and territorial borders become less defined. However, despite the difficulties with digital transgression and copyright anomalies, there are no indications that territorial copyright will disappear in the foreseeable future.

Surprisingly, the findings reveal that many authors do not favour a hard-line enforcement of electronic copyright. There are those who see the Internet as a marketing opportunity and employ 'soft' licensing practices such as the Creative Commons and others who are happy to provide their creative work not only DRM free, but also free of charge. The findings also show an increased awareness of the necessity for changing business models and a need to embrace the digital market, as proprietary branded electronic readers become more widespread.

THE GOOGLE INITIATIVES: BEYOND COPYRIGHT

It has been shown that the Google initiatives have had a significant impact on how authors' copyright was perceived and applied on the Internet. The discussion highlighted specifically how authors' copyright had been infringed through Google's unauthorised copying of books in American libraries, thereby illustrating some of the difficulties in establishing the ideal of a 'heavenly library.' Although Google did not succeed in obtaining Court approval for its proposed Amended Google Settlement in the case *The Authors Guild et al v. Google, Inc* (2010), the lead-up to the case signified a major shift in the application of copyright law. As explained previously, this copyright dispute, which arose between authors and Google in 2009 with regard to the Google Library Project, resulted in a Google Settlement Agreement, which was subsequently rejected by Justice Chin on 23 March 2011 and is still under re-negotiation at the time of this research.

The significance of the Google Settlement is the unprecedented interference in rights holders' interests and the disregard shown by Google for existing copyright laws and conventions, by copying and publishing electronic copies of work in which they held no copyright interests. Considering the inroads such a settlement would have made on authors' copyright globally, it was surprising that 35% of the survey respondents were unfamiliar with the concept. Moreover, the findings show conflicting views amongst respondents on the impact of the Google initiatives. Some authors pointed out the advantages of being able to buy books that were previously out of print, while others criticised the way in which the 'opt out' provisions of the scheme. This pivotal point was also mentioned by Judge Chin who finally rejected the Settlement. The conflicting viewpoints in the findings are consistent with Strowel's observations that Google would have created opportunities for authors to benefit from previously out of print publications and his converse criticism that Google's actions were transgressing accepted copyright norms, due to the proposed opt-out provisions (2009, pp. 7, 18).

Strowel's further concern about the possibility of Google acquiring a highly dominant position for the future delivery of new digital books and exerting too much control over existing books (2009, p. 15) is also supported in the findings. More than 65% of respondents were uncertain about whether they would be prepared to license their work to Google in the future. These results show a distinct lack of understanding and/or trust on the part of authors in relation to the Google initiatives.

Aside from the Google Settlement, it was further noted that Google had already successfully implemented certain licensing agreements in relation to its Google Books store, where, pursuant to Partner Program Agreements with publishers, it was able to display portions of books online, varying in content depending on their agreement with publishers. The findings include instances in which these publisher agreements have been concluded with Google without the author's knowledge. For example, one author reported that she had seen her book on a Google Books search and had been disturbed by the amount of content displayed for viewing, without the publisher notifying or consulting with her. Such occurrences raise concerns about the consideration given to authors' interests by publishers in the online publishing process.

It is generally evident that, although most authors are aware of the highly publicised Google Settlement, they lack in-depth knowledge. Whilst some authors and publishers are of the view that 'the end justifies the means,' others are highly critical of Google's high-handed approach, whilst a third group has a 'wait and see' approach. On a broader level Google's actions can be criticised for deviating from the utilitarian principles articulated by Landes and Posner, which presuppose a balance between the public interest and reward to creators (1989, p. 325). Not only does it show a blatant disregard for authors' rights in favour of the public benefit, as well as Google's growing domination of this aspect of the publishing landscape, but its actions amount to an effective annexation of authors' copyright.

RESALE ROYALTIES ON BOOKS?

One possibility that emerged in the findings was the issue of royalties on second hand books. The proposition by Moorhouse that resale royalties should be payable on second hand books (as in the case of art, pursuant to the *Resale Royalty Right for Visual Artists Act 2009*) is a seductive one for authors. Such a system would continue to reward authors for their efforts and would be consistent with the electronic copyright approach of 'user pays.' This merits some discussion here in the context of the second research question dealing with existing copyright frameworks. This resale royalty argument is underpinned by copyright considerations, the cultural value of books in society as well as the current models being used for electronic books. Electronic book sales are generally predicated on the 'user pays' model, where each download incurs a fee, as the Internet system works much in the same way for books as it does for music or film downloads, where the user pays for a license to use the book rather than to 'buy' the book.

Moorhouse refers to the proposition as 'a payment for recycled use of the book' and argues that, whilst the second-hand bookshop owner or Internet seller receives a payment for the use of the book, the author does not. He suggests that a small tax on recycling of books could be directed to a fund for support of the writing community or that statistical sampling could be employed to set up a mechanism similar to PLR, which would pay authors directly for the resale of their books. He sees this as resembling the right that artists received for resale. Moorhouse considers the fact that book sales in Australia stood at over $131m during 2003-2004 (according to the latest available Australian Bureau of Statistics results). Furthermore, he suggests that second hand books account for about 45 per cent of fiction found in household libraries (Moorhouse, 2008, p. 4). These observations support the contention that a vibrant second hand book culture exists in Australia.

The flourishing of the second hand book industry globally gives credence to Moorhouse's contention. Occurring at the same time as the electronic print evolution, at the opposite end of the scale, has been the rise in popularity of second hand bookshops and book towns, where the sale of second hand books has become a significant part of print culture and the economy. For example, Clunes in Victoria hosts an annual event, Back to Booktown, which is described as 'the biggest collection of rare, out-of-print and second hand books in South East Asia' (*Back to Booktown*, 2011). During this event, around 60 booksellers from around Australia gather in the historic village in the tradition of a European style 'book town' in a celebration of the book.

The idea of a book town originated in Hay-on-Wye in Wales, UK in 1961, where approximately 40 second hand and rare bookshops line the streets of the small village. At the time of the research there were 20 locations worldwide describing themselves as Book Towns or Villages, promoting the culture of books and benefitting economically from a renewed interest in old books. This culture indicates that book enthusiasts continue to embrace the printed book despite the convenience and economics of ordering books online. In addition, there has been a rise in bookshops/cafes such as Berkelouws Books in Australia (with 13 stores countrywide), which buy and sell second hand books, rare books and new books, often incorporating a coffee shop or wine bar. It may be observed that the widespread usage of second hand books, together with the worldwide book town trend, augur well for the sustenance of the print book culture and economy alongside the digital dimension; however, in their current form they do not incorporate any reward system for authors.

Currently, sections 102 and 112A of the *Copyright Act* regulate the parallel importation of books but do not prohibit the resale of legitimately obtained second hand books. It promises to be a challenging enterprise if a resale royalty system for second hand book sales were to be considered in Australia. Firstly, booksellers would have to determine whether a book is under copyright and, if so, who held the copyright. This might be, for example, an author, the author's heir/s or a publisher, or a combination of these possibilities. Thereafter, the appropriate royalty would have to be calculated and charged at the sale of the book and payments made to the correct parties. Although this might arguably be done through licensing schemes like CAL, it is likely the administrative costs to the bookseller would be prohibitive. This might also mean an increase in second hand book prices to accommodate the additional cost to the bookseller. In view of such practical considerations, the argument that authors should receive ongoing financial benefits from the resale of their books may be a persuasive one in theory but perhaps too onerous in its execution.

It can also be noted that such a scheme cannot accurately be compared to the Artists' Resale Royalty Scheme. Works of art are generally singular creative works, as opposed to books, which may run into thousands of print copies. Moreover, the underlying principle of the Artists' Resale Royalty Scheme is that artists benefit from the increase in the value of their work between first and subsequent sales (Anderson, 2008). One author expressed the opinion that CAL, PLR and ELR payments provided a 'good trade-off' for authors against the perceived loss of revenue from second hand book sales. Additionally, there is an argument to be made that, although Australian legislation does not include a 'first sale doctrine' in respect of copyright in books (legislated in the US *Copyright Act*), this approach of an exhaustion of rights is in effect operational in the current marketplace.

NEW BUSINESS MODELS

While second hand bookshops or villages might be a growing 'cottage industry' - clearly the online environment is the expanding platform. Inevitably, authors' copyright has been affected by these technological advances, as evidenced by the need for new copyright models to sustain authors financially. The findings indicate that authors recognise the need for a change in their approach to writing and publishing as electronic publishing gains momentum. Along with the new opportunities presented by a global market, such as self-publishing and a plethora of online booksellers, authors have become aware of the need to revise traditional publishing expectations and embrace new marketing strategies.

This trend supports Eltham's observation that many authors now find that the more their work is disseminated on the Internet, the more printed copies they sell of that work. As discussed in Chapter 9, these changed perceptions have resulted in the emergence of new business models such as the 'honesty box' model utilised by international authors such as Doctorow, who argues that people who only read the free online versions are not going to buy his books anyway (2009). The concept of giving away 'free' content has been employed successfully by some authors, who feel that this gives the author a visibility that is difficult to obtain in the vast digital environment of the Internet. The findings show that this is regarded as a viable option for some authors, as a way of free advertising.

Social media such as Twitter and Facebook are seen as important marketing tools by several authors. Referred to as a 'fast, easy way to publish,' there is nevertheless a perceived danger of a loss of control over material sent via Twitter, for example, where others could use that material or change it without acknowledging the author. The possibility of these types of infringements is also admitted by Doctorow (2009); however, he continues to promote the idea of free access to his work and sees the relationship between author and reader as 'a social contract between creator and user' (2010).

The scope of publication possibilities continues to expand as digital technologies proliferate. For example, recent additions to the Apple iPad applications (apps) include a book app for T.S. Eliot's poem 'The Waste Land,' which is presented in electronic form with several inclusions, including two readings by the poet himself as well as Ted Hughes and other actors, an on screen text version as well as an annotated version of the poem, a facsimile of the original manuscript with handwritten edits and video commentaries by eminent writers and experts (Romei, 2011, p. 25). These advances illustrate how business models for authors and publishers will continue to evolve in order to meet readers' and users' requirements.

Furthermore, these evolving business models have impacted on the transformation of the concept of authorship and the definition of an 'author,' to incorporate bloggers, tweeters and Facebook contributors (Pelli & Bigelow, 2010). Thus, there appears to be a valid argument that the definition of authorship has been extended and is inextricably linked to the creative possibilities of new technology. Young has stated that in new media technology this meaning has been extended to include the 'electronic content creator' or 'digital writer' (2007, p. 71). To the literary author, this may present a competitive challenge as numerous 'authors' enter the literary sphere, especially for first time authors. Additionally, authors may be disadvantaged if they lack technological skills to make use of digital marketing tools. It was previously noted that there is merit in Alexander's argument that authors today are no more disadvantaged than their predecessors in the literary sphere (2010, p. 2). However, the findings show that the ever-expanding digital public sphere presents distinct challenges for authors – not only in relation to copyright, but also to the very fabric of their creative identity as authors.

We have seen that the current utilitarian system embraces the dual perspective of copyright, namely the positive benefit to the author as a result of the property right and the incentive purpose of the right which motivates the author to create (Landes & Posner, 1987, p. 265). This theory finds application in new business models which, in addition to public benefit considerations, also envisage a benefit to the author as an end result. Although the public benefit is served by making creative work freely available on the Internet, these models are underscored by the expectation of a 'social contract' between author and reader as seen by Doctorow (2010), that the author's moral rights will be respected and a confidence that the free dissemination of work will lead to book sales. These models thus also reflect Adeney's perception of authorship, by recognising notions of 'property' on the one hand and 'personality' or moral rights on the other (2002, p. 9).

CONCLUSION

Clearly the Internet has expanded the boundaries of copyright protection and it seems that current legislative structures may not offer authors the necessary protection. Several authors mentioned the need for new copyright solutions, although the findings showed divergent views on the subject. While some suggested that authors should be more proactive in their approach to copyright, others were of the view that the existing copyright structure is insufficiently suited to copyright use in the digital domain. The Internet has created a stronger focus on public benefit considerations by providing free access to information. This trend has, to an extent, eroded both authors' private creative rights and the utilitarian model. In order to remain competitive and gain acceptance in the marketplace, they have to be flexible in their copyright approach and embrace new business models. Conversely, in order to remain creative, they require reward. This dichotomy has resulted in some uncertainty in the author ranks about future copyright models, despite opportunities for new publishing and licencing opportunities.

REFERENCES

Adeney, E. (2002). Moral rights and substantiality. *Australian Intellectual Property Journal, 13*, 5.

Alexander, I. (2010, May). *All change for the digital economy: Copyright and business models in the early eighteenth century*. Paper presented at University of Cambridge. Sydney, Australia.

Anderson, P. (2008, March 11). *Resale royalties and new directions for the arts*. Retrieved July 5, 2011, from http://www.australiacouncil.gov.au/resources/reports_and_publications/subjects/marketing/sales/resale_royalties_and_new_directions_for_the_arts

Australian Law Review Commission. (2013). *Copyright and the digital economy* (Discussion Paper 79). Retrieved from http://www.alrc.gov.au/sites/default/files/pdfs/publications/dp79_whole_pdf_.pdf

Back to Booktown. (2011). Retrieved from http://www.booktown.clunes.org/program.htm

Coker, M. (2009, October 26). Do authors still need publishers? *Huffington Post*. Retrieved January 10, 2011, from http://www.huffingtonpost.com/mark-coker/do-authors-still-need-pub_b_334539.html

Cunningham, S., & Higgs, P. (2010). *What's your other job? A census analysis of arts employment in Australia (Research Report)*. Sydney: Australia Council for the Arts.

Doctorow, C. (2009). Download for free. *Makers*. Retrieved March 23, 2011, from http://craphound.com/makers/download/

Doctorow, C. (2010, September 2). *Copyright versus creativity*. Paper presented at Melbourne Writers Festival. Melbourne, Australia.

Eltham, K. (2009, November). Writing the digital future. *WQ, 190*, 6.

Fisher, J. (2010, September 27). Ebooks and the Australian publishing industry. *Meanjin, 69*(3). Retrieved March 23, 2011, from http://meanjin.com.au/blog/post/e-books-and-the-australian-publishing-industry/

Gawronski & others v. Amazon Inc. [2009] (US)

Goldstein, P. (2003). *Copyright's highway: From Gutenberg to the celestial jukebox*. Stanford, CA: Stanford University Press.

Habermas, J. (1974). The public sphere: An encyclopedia article (1964). *New German Critique,* (3), 49-55.

Jones, B. (2011). *Book industry strategy group report (Research Report).* Canberra, Australia: Government of Australia.

Keneally, T. (2008). *Submission to the productivity commission.*

Landes, W. M., & Posner, R. A. (1987). Trademark law: An economic perspective. *The Journal of Law & Economics, 30,* 265. doi:10.1086/467138

Landes, W. M., & Posner, R. A. (1989). An economic analysis of copyright law. *The Journal of Legal Studies, 18,* 325. doi:10.1086/468150

Loukakis, A. (2011, January). *Submission to the book industry strategy group.*

Loukakis, A. (2011). Giving contracts some clout. *Australian Author, 43*(1), 28–29.

Moorhouse, F. (2008). The escape from 'eccentric penury': How should we pay literary authors? Policy visions for the Australian writing economy. *Copyright Reporter, 26,* 4.

Pelli, D. G., & Bigelow, C. (2009, October 20). A writing revolution. *Seed Magazine.* Retrieved September 19, 2010, from http://seedmagazine.com/content/article/a_writing_revolution/

Rawlins, G. J. E. (1993). Publishing over the next decade. *Journal of the American Society for Information Science American Society for Information Science, 44*(8), 474–479. doi:10.1002/(SICI)1097-4571(199309)44:8<474::AID-ASI6>3.0.CO;2-3

Romei, S. (2011, June 25-26). A pair of ragged claws. *The Review,* 19.

Strowel, A. (2009, December). *The Google settlement: Towards a digital library or an inquisitive shopping mall?* Paper presented at Bond University. Gold Coast, Australia.

The Authors Guild et al v. Google, Inc, (2009) US District Court, Southern District of New York, No. 05-08136 at 1 (US)

The Authors Guild, Inc. et al. v. HathiTrust et al, US District Court, Southern District of New York, filed 12 September 2011, 11 CIV 6351 (US)

Throsby, D., & Zednik, A. (2010). *Do you really expect to get paid? An economic study of professional artists in Australia (Research Report).* Strawberry Hills, Australia: Australia Council for the Arts.

Discussion and Analysis

University of NSW v. Moorhouse (1975) HCA 26; (1975) 133 CLR 1 (Austl.)

Vaidhayanathan, S. (2001). *Copyrights & copywrongs: The rise of intellectual property and how it threatens creativity.* New York: NYU Press.

Wilson, P. (2011). The girl who saved the publisher. *The Deal*, 4(5), 30–32.

Young, S. (2007). *The book is dead: Long live the book.* Sydney: University of New South Wales Press.

TABLE OF CASES

Gawronski & others v. Amazon Inc. [2009] (US)

The Authors Guild et al v. Google, Inc, (2009) US District Court, Southern District of New York, No. 05-08136 at 1 (US)

The Authors Guild, Inc. et al. v. HathiTrust et al, US District Court, Southern District of New York, filed 12 September 2011, 11 CIV 6351 (US)

University of NSW v. Moorhouse (1975) HCA 26; (1975) 133 CLR 1 (Austl.)

TABLE OF STATUTES

Copyright Act 1968 (Cth)

Copyright Act 1790 (USA)

Resale Royalty Right for Visual Artists Act 2009 (Cth)

Chapter 11
Conclusion and Recommendations

ABSTRACT

This chapter deals with the research topics based on the discussion and analysis of the findings in chapter 10. It considers, first, what authors' views are on copyright and how these perceptions influence them in their creative work. Second, it examines the role of copyright support structures and the legislative framework in order to ascertain how they are perceived by authors. Third, it discusses how authors have been affected by changes in publishing and, more specifically, the impact of electronic publishing. This discussion includes observations on the author-publisher relationship, publishing contracts, and future business models for authors. Finally, the research questions are considered against the backdrop of philosophical theory with consideration of the author's place in the literary and public spheres. Factors such as developments in technology, parallel importing concerns, and changing trends in publishing and marketing are prompting authors to cultivate a greater awareness of issues that affect their livelihood. This chapter completes the discussion on the way in which authors are navigating their copyright in the expanded literary sphere and how they are dealing with digital technology in their creative work and publishing contracts. On a deeper level, it also reflects the author's role in the literary and the greater public sphere and the relationship between the competing groups in the publishing industry.

DOI: 10.4018/978-1-4666-5214-9.ch011

CONCLUSION

This book has examined the views of Australian authors in relation to various aspects of copyright, focusing on the position of authors in the current copyright framework and the relationship between authors and the publishing industry at a major historical juncture. The findings are considered within the ambits of global and Australian copyright legislation, which has its roots in philosophical theories such as utilitarianism and natural rights. Relevantly, the research timeframe has encompassed the Google digitisation, the parallel importing debate and a significant transition of publishing to the electronic media. In this context, it is evident that considerations relating to electronic copyright, specifically with regard to digital publishing contracts and copyright protection on the Internet, are of particular concern to authors. On a broader level, the expanded literary sphere within the digital environment, which links the issue of authorship to the transformation of this public sphere, provides a relevant framework for the discussion.

Specifically, the research has aimed to investigate Australian authors' views on copyright issues through the three primary questions. On a deeper, theoretical level, the research has investigated the underlying tensions and symbiotic relationships between different segments of the publishing industry, with authors as the main focal point. It also addressed the balance between the utilitarian interests of the public on the one hand, and creators on the other. The findings indicate that there are various factors causing authors to be in danger of being marginalised, which include a lack of negotiating power, knowledge and insight, and increased challenges to their copyright. Add to this the relative isolation in which authors work and the rise in the Internet as the growing, dominant and global environment for literary exchanges (as opposed to localised bookshops), and authors' power base is at risk of further erosion. Nevertheless, where they have been able to unite their efforts to challenge a perceived onslaught on their rights, they have proven to be a persuasive force.

The following conclusions are drawn with regard to the research topics:

How do Australian authors perceive copyright affecting them and does it have any impact on how they practise?

Writing is a compulsive, and delectable thing. Writing is its own reward. - Henry Miller

Authors' participation in the parallel import debate has indicated that authors are aware of the intrinsic value of copyright and territorial copyright protection. However, paradoxically, this sample shows that most do not regard copyright as an incentive to create (or a financial incentive) and are focussed instead on personal satisfaction and achieving recognition for their efforts. Most authors, and first time authors in particular, do not concern themselves with copyright during the creative process. Instead, they generally only become concerned about copyright at the publishing stage and see the value of writing resting in 'the doing of it' rather than financial reward. Thus, authors are not 'rational maximisers' in the economic sense but largely create for the love of writing. This viewpoint indicates a failure on the part of authors to fully appreciate and exploit the connection between their copyright and economic reward for their creative work. The fact that most authors are reliant on other sources of income and unable to sustain themselves on their writing income alone, support the contention that they are not adequately rewarded for their efforts. These findings explain, to a large degree, why authors continue creating despite low financial rewards.

Moreover, the concept of copyright is regarded by many authors as a complex legal notion, best left to agents or publishers, rather than an issue of personal concern. This perception causes an inordinate reliance on publishers, as only a small number of authors are represented by an agent, but we might need to consider that this is partly an economic choice, given the cost of paying an agent. However, the findings further indicate that most authors also regard copyright as a proprietary 'right' and take it for granted in the belief that it exists primarily for their benefit and protection. Significantly, they do not view it as an economic or creative incentive as envisaged by Government in the Ergas Report (2000). As one author said, giving voice to the 'author's proprietary right' premise [as proposed by Rose (1988, p. 53)], *'Copyright to me is simply my right to say: this is mine.'* This ambivalence in perception – between authors' perception and that of the Regulators' – also illustrates Goldstein's supposition of the two legal traditions protecting literary works, namely: copyright - with a utilitarian philosophical premise - and author's right (based on the philosophy of natural rights) (2001, p. 3).

Thus, authors pay little heed to utilitarian considerations but rather view copyright as something that exists mainly to protect their rights as a creator. This view only partly resonates with the Court's findings in the case of *Ice TV v. Nine Network* (2009), where 'authorship' was recognised as a fundamental principle underpinning copyright law (2009 HCA at 95 – 96), but the Court also considered a 'just reward for the creator' to be in the public interest (2009 HCA at 106). Authors thus chiefly regard their rights as being the natural rights of the creator in the Lockean tradition, as proposed by Macpherson (1962, p. 269).

In addition, authors are highly motivated by personal satisfaction and achieving recognition, indicating a strong reliance on personality or moral rights. Their dual belief in natural rights and moral rights is therefore more aligned with a philosophical viewpoint of seeing copyright as an instrument to indicate personal standing, self-expression and ownership rather than a financial tool. This ties in with Stokes' contention that natural rights should be regarded as part of the 'moral rights' theory, based on the idea of a 'just reward' for labour (2001, p. 12). It also resonates with Adeney's contention that the current system can be regarded as 'dualist', with the idea of property on the one hand and personality on the other (2002, p. 9) and her observation that the Australian copyright system is 'a hybrid system with authorial moral rights grafted onto a framework' that protects the economic interests of the copyright owner rather than the author (2002, p. 10).

However, only a small group of writers, who could be described as 'industry experts' by virtue of their extensive knowledge of publishing, sufficiently appreciate the scope of moral rights protection in Australia. They understand that moral rights not only entitle the author to assert his/her authorship rights, but also to determine how the material is treated by external parties. Furthermore, they acknowledge the fact that without this right an author would lose the ability to control how his/her work is used. On a philosophical level, their comments recognise Barthes' viewpoint (1977, p. 148), which suggests that an author only remains the author for the time he maintains control over the work. This recognition translates into concern where authors perceive a loss of control over their work on the Internet.

Although authors' moral rights are protected under section 189 of the *Copyright Act 1968*, the Internet has widened the scope for infringement of these rights (through unlawful transformation and appropriation), and authors seem unable to adequately deal with such violations. The Internet's strong user-focus presents a dilemma for authors in trying to address breaches of their moral rights and copyright generally. It is evident that these rights remain firmly subject to economic-utilitarian considerations and a general perception that electronic material should be freely accessible in 'the new public sphere', as referred to by Carpignano, Anderson, Aronowitz, and DiFazio (1993, p. 103). There may thus be a need for Government to revise the sometimes extreme user-focus in electronic copyright, which currently leans heavily in favour of the consumer, often to the detriment of the content creator.

In relation to digital copyright, the findings vary substantially. Discussed in more depth under the third research question below, it is clear that authors have quite disparate views on the value of copyright on the Internet and on how it should be enforced. The divergent viewpoints confirm the perception that the 'author group' is far from homogenous and can be divided into various categories of the subaltern author group or author sphere within the literary sphere, for example:

- Those authors who embrace the digital future of the industry and are informed about its possibilities.
- Those who write part time and are less concerned with copyright than with the act of creating.
- The 'trail-blazers', who recognise copyright challenges and take a pro-active role in resolving them.
- Those who are passive about copyright and authors' rights in general.
- The online publishers who shun traditional publishing.
- Those who have dealt mainly with print publishing in the past and are concerned about copyright protection in the digital publishing environment.

The findings thus confirm that, although many authors recognise the importance of copyright, this does not translate into an increased ability to manage and control their own copyright on the Internet. These observations also suggest an increasing tension between stakeholders in the current utilitarian structure, particularly in the digital domain. Unless these problems are addressed, there is a danger that a reversion to 16th century practices may occur, when authors' rights were practically non-existent (Armstrong, 1990, p. 21) and printers wielded their power at the expense of authors. The only difference appears to be that Internet search engines such as Google and Internet users may usurp authors' rights in the future; indeed, are already beginning to do so.

Do authors believe that the existing copyright framework supports and encourages them in their creative efforts?

A significant positive for authors has been the development of copyright structures established through the efforts of industry forerunners such as Moorhouse and the consequences of the *University of NSW v. Moorhouse* (1975) decision. Although those changes initially addressed copyright issues in relation to photocopying, and were gradually extended to include digital copying, current copyright structures do not adequately address authors' concerns in the changed environment of electronic publishing.

The findings indicate that authors are ambivalent about the level of support afforded to them by existing government support structures and have a limited awareness of support structures such as the Copyright Agency Limited (CAL), Public Lending Rights (PLR) and Educational Lending Rights (ELR).

Only approximately half of the sample groups felt that Australian copyright protections (such as the *Copyright Act*) and licensing authorities (such as CAL) supported authors sufficiently in their creative efforts. Significantly, the vast majority of respondents received financial benefits from PLR and ELR, but only a third received earnings from CAL. This could be ascribed to the fact that CAL payments are generally made in respect of licensing of non-fiction work, whereas PLR and ELR payments cover the entire spectrum of publications.

The finding that annual amounts earned from these combined sources vary significantly, indicates substantial scope for authors to supplement their income from these sources. The use of government grants or fellowships by some authors also suggests that alternative significant support structures are in place for authors, if they choose to pursue them.

On a practical level, some authors expressed concerns about CAL's administration, with over 60% expressing doubts about CAL's efficiency. One point of criticism was that CAL's operation did not extend internationally and thus could not effectively protect authors against online piracy. Other complaints included authors not receiving any payments from CAL despite authors' work being copied in schools and a lack of transparency in CAL payments. Whilst it was acknowledged that recent electronic changes effected by CAL could alleviate some of these concerns, issues such as the unauthorised online use of authors' work and CAL's data capturing techniques had not been addressed. However, CAL is still a relatively young organisation that has evolved quite quickly to its present state - it would seem prudent that it should be allowed to continue to grow to accommodate the changes and demands of the various publishing spaces it services.

Authors do recognise the significance of organisations such as the Australia Council, Arts Law, The Australian Copyright Council and the Australian Society of Authors (ASA) but there is room for improvement. Although approximately half of the respondents believe they are adequately supported by Australian copyright protections and licensing authorities, nearly 37% are undecided. This uncertainty may be the result of a lack of knowledge, a lack of interest, or both. Authors' ambivalence about their copyright protection within the existing framework thus also extends to Australian copyright laws. Fewer than half of respondents were of the view that they are adequately protected under the law. This relatively low percentage demonstrates a significant measure of uncertainty about the effectiveness of copyright protection under Australian law, especially in relation to copyright infringements on the Internet.

These concerns are justified when one considers the legislative trend towards 'pro-user' legislation, reflected in the Productivity Commission's 'pro-user' recommendations in the parallel importing investigation. In that instance, Government objectives were defeated by strong author/publisher lobbying groups and submissions, demonstrating the potential for creators to influence legislative trends. However, the findings demonstrate that, at this critical juncture in publishing and migration of printed work to the digital media, authors lack cohesion as a group and do not actively promote their own interests. Not only does the disparate nature of their issues and concerns make unity a significant problem, but authors are also engage in a variety of unrelated professions and fields of writing. Additionally, the solitary nature of the writing profession adds to their isolation.

On a philosophical level, it has been suggested that authors belong to a subaltern 'author sphere' within the literary sphere, which is itself subordinate to the wider public sphere. However, Habermas' description of the literary sphere 'as a means of fostering a process of "self-clarification" (such as novel writing) which enables a community of private individuals to recognise themselves as a public' (1989, pp. 28-29, 49-50) falls short of its objective if authors fail to adhere to common goals. Furthermore, it is apparent that authors in the author sphere typically fail to initiate change within the literary sphere, which is largely dominated by the publisher sphere. Authors can thus be seen to be *undergoing* rather than *governing* change in the public sphere.

The fragmentation within the author group also contributes to this general lack of economic and political power as a group. Although authors generally earn very little from writing and are reliant on additional sources of income - including Government grants, CAL, ELR and PLR - very little lobbying (apart from ASA initiatives) is being done to address copyright concerns mentioned by authors or to improve income streams. Furthermore, despite authors' access to organisations such as the ASA and writers' centres for guidance and support, it is evident that much uncertainty prevails regarding formal copyright support structures and that many of these organisations are not pro-active in pursuing authors' copyright and economic interests.

A notable exception is the ASA, which provides publishing guidelines and contract assistance for authors who are members of the organisation. The legal action undertaken by the ASA and a number of Australian authors, in joining the USA *Authors' Guild* case against US libraries and the HathiTrust for the scanning and distributing of books online, was a positive step in protecting Australian authors' rights [*The Authors Guild, Inc. et al. v. HathiTrust et al* (2011)]. However, as the scanning occurred outside of Australia, the US Court was able to apply the 'fair use' doctrine to find in favour of the HathiTrust, and at present it remains to be seen what the outcome of the appeal will be. It was envisaged that this would be a landmark case in the preservation of authors' copyright in the digital environment, much as the *Moorhouse* case resulted in protective measures for authors in relation to unauthorised copying of their printed work. However, it may well serve to illustrate the inability of Australian authors to protect their copyright in other jurisdictions.

Additionally, the attempts by Apple to collude with five large publishers to increase the price of e-books, illustrate the power wielded by large online publishers to control ebook prices and ebook libraries of readers, thereby impacting on authors' royalties. Although Apple was convicted for anti-trust collusion [*United States of America et al v. Apple Inc et al* (2013)], at the time of writing Apple had lodged an appeal. As noted, this is not an issue confined to the United States. In 2012, Apple settled a separate ebook price-fixing case with the European Commission, without admitting wrongdoing (Flood, 2012).

Apart from the ASA's consistent efforts to advance authors' rights through the publication of relevant industry papers (Loukakis, 2010) and submissions to Government appointed committees (2011), the absence of focused lobbying with Government for authors' rights reflects an underestimation by authors of their value and the vital impact they have had on the public sphere and more specifically, Australian culture. Unlike journalists, who have union protection under the Media and Arts Alliance, authors are largely left to fend for themselves. In 1994, the Copyright Law Review Committee released a comprehensive *Report on Journalists' Copyright*, yet there has been no similar examination of authors' copyright by Government. At this critical juncture in publishing, it is imperative that authors' copyright concerns be afforded the same scrutiny. The current review by the ALRC addresses digital copyright reforms, but it envisages the introduction of public interest benefits (such as the extension of 'fair dealing' to 'fair use' exceptions) (ALRC, 2013, 24), rather than protective measures for creators. In this, it falls short of dealing with these vital concerns facing authors in the digital sphere.

Arguably, media issues engender a greater sense of interest in the political arena, due to privacy, arguments of their role within democracy and other considerations. However, authors' cultural, political and economic influence over the centuries provides ample evidence of their important role in society. If the writing industry is to endure and make a healthy transition into the digital arena, authors need to be heard and increased Government support is essential. The glaring implications of ignoring these pertinent issues are that authors' literary creativity becomes substantially reduced and that creative outputs are, in time, reduced at worst to blogs and tweets whilst authors labour in unrelated professions to make ends meet.

What are authors' views on the changing nature of the publishing industry and how have they been affected by changes/advances in this area?

In the digital age, the book has been liberated from its print container. This is the biggest shift that writers, readers, and publishers must make. - Kate Eltham

Authors are becoming increasingly aware of the opportunities offered by new media technology and the simultaneous challenges posed to their copyright. Significantly, more than 80% of respondents express concern about protecting their copyright electronically, and nearly half of these are 'very concerned'. The majority of complaints relate to online publishing, with 'online pirating' being a major concern. The accessibility of information on the Internet is perceived to increase the risk of unauthorised copying of work, and digital rights management systems and other protective measures are not necessarily effective enough at this point in time.

This expanded publishing arena has also precipitated the rise of new and online publishing models such as Smashwords and Lulu, which make self-publishing a viable option. Authors can now self publish, publish with a mainstream publisher, a small publisher or an online publisher. They can decide on their own copyright licensing scheme and the degree of copyright protection they wish to apply to their work. They can decide on a marketing strategy and support their marketing through online blogs, Twitter and Facebook. Thus, a paradox exists within the new digital publishing landscape. Although the author has obtained new publishing opportunities in the decentralised literary public sphere of the Internet and thus an increased power, copyright enforcement has become more onerous as a result. Furthermore, self publishing options must be weighed up against the support and marketing provided by the traditional publisher, causing many authors to choose earning a smaller percentage on a larger number of book sales, as opposed to a larger percentage of fewer sales, due to a lack of marketing skills on their part.

In this regard, electronic publishing contracts can be a major issue of concern for authors. Less than half of respondents indicate that their contracts provide for separate electronic rights, with royalties varying significantly between authors and between different publishers. Only a small percentage have ever sold their own work on the Internet. This trend suggests that authors continue to look to their publishers for guidance in the digital domain, thereby exhibiting a lack of power as a stakeholder group within the public sphere Moreover, the increased opportunities for anyone to assert 'authorship' on the Internet has made it more difficult for an author to be noticed, although an 'honesty box' strategy of giving away free books could reap significant rewards in the long run. However, implementing such strategies authors would require a significant level of technical and marketing knowledge.

The research also shows that, in addition to copyright law, the perception of 'authorship' has been evolving and that the definition of 'author' is an ever expanding concept, influenced by a changing literary public sphere brought about primarily by technological advances. This can be attributed to the effects of hypertext, reader participation and increased collaboration and reliance within the digital arena. Just as the invention of the printing press signalled an irrevocable change in the status and recognition of authorship, so has digital technology precipitated a different perspective on the subject of authorship. Not only are authors in the twenty-first century presented with a variety of publishing options (and related copyright challenges), but the Internet can also be credited with further re-defining the concept of what an author is. The increasing capabilities of reading devices have also changed readers' expectations, who now have more reading options (such as the ability to manipulate print size) and possibilities of interaction with the text. These technological changes, together with the expanded publishing arena, continue to challenge authors in the twenty-first century, requiring them to be resilient and innovative in their creative work.

The changing relationship between authors and publishers is also reflective of the transformation of the publishing industry, not only in the context of Australian publishing, but also with regard to the global opportunities offered by digital publishing. Ebooks are being sold at prices well below those of printed books, with the departure from traditional publishing models allowing for different royalty calculations and a perception by authors that a higher percentage of the sale price should be paid to the author, due to the publisher's reduced production costs. In reality, however, standard publishing agreements still favour the publisher, and royalties are usually paid on 'net receipts' rather than on the recommended retail price, as favoured by the ASA.

Paradoxically, authors continue to rely heavily on their publishers, despite the fact that there are many areas of disparity between the standard publisher's agreement and the 'ideal' contract suggested by the ASA. The findings indicate that authors regard publishers as their 'default mode' and rely on the publisher when in doubt, especially in respect of online copyright protection and the Google issues. It seems incongruous that authors would negotiate contract terms unfavourable to themselves, yet on closer examination, it is apparent that authors severely lack negotiating power in the publishing process. The survey results show that, more important to authors than money, is the stamp of approval, acknowledgement and recognition that a publishing contract affords a writer. Clearly there are difficulties in getting published, and very few authors have the advantage of having an agent to explain the terms of their publishing contracts. In the absence of agents, there is considerable scope for improving the terms of publishing contracts to create a more equitable balance between authors and publishers, especially with regard to digital publishing contracts.

Not surprisingly, authors generally recognise the disempowerment of the 'author group' as opposed to the 'publishers' group', especially in the case of marginalised emerging authors who do not have a voice in the literary sphere. Established authors, as expected, usually have more bargaining power than unknown authors, and in some instances, have the support of agents and/or support groups such as the ASA. This is undoubtedly compounded by the competitive nature of the industry - as evidenced by the publishing statistics – as authors tend to focus on their own endeavours rather than industry considerations. This isolation, in turn, can undermine the collective voice of the author group.

Nevertheless, some authors embrace the 'culture of sharing' facilitated by the Internet and favoured giving away their work for free, thereby providing readers with the option of paying for material or using licensing options such as the Creative Commons. Whilst these authors are of the view that 'obscurity, not piracy, is the writer's greatest enemy', others disagree and complain about the erosion of their copyright online. Yet, it is apparent that authors are generally not in favour of a hard line copyright enforcement approach because of the limiting nature of some copyright protection systems, such as DRM protection, which restricts readers unnecessarily. Despite the differences in their viewpoints, authors by and large recognise the necessity of a utilitarian strategy as proposed by Landes and Posner (1989, p. 325), whereby some balance between the consumer's right of access and the creator's right is achieved.

Significantly for Australian authors - as in the case of the UK and USA - territorial rights remain in existence. Although the ASA has cautioned authors to ensure that these rights remain protected in the digital domain (Loukakis, 2010, p. 9), it is clear that authors will find this advice more and more difficult to implement, considering the global reach of the online book market, which has made it unlikely for any publisher to accept a book without securing the world rights. This trend points to a dilution of the value of territorial rights, which supports Young's contention that the industry requires a new copyright infrastructure (2007, pp. 158-159), and also the more recent recommendations of the ASA (Loukakis, 2011, p. 4). A proposal by one author, that world rights should be limited to 12 months from publication, provides one option, though not necessarily a feasible one for unestablished authors who are at the bottom of the subaltern group and have little or no negotiating power with publishers. In addition, court decisions - such as *Kirtsaeng* - dealing with the application of the 'first sale doctrine' in the cross-border sale of books, will continue to affect the enforcement of territorial copyright by authors and publishers in the USA and beyond. Territorial copyright borders have become blurred, difficult to enforce, and are ineffective in preserving authors' copyright. Clearly new copyright solutions are required, demanding that authors embrace digital technology, improve their knowledge of online publishing and apply creative publishing models to their advantage.

These observations show a strong indication that there is a need to address the tension exhibited between the utilitarian approach characteristic of Australian copyright law, and the natural rights views of authors, to create a sustainable balance. Authors' views should inform copyright structures, and additional processes should be considered whereby authors are adequately rewarded for their creative efforts in recognition of their cultural and literary contributions.

Another issue of consideration for authors in the future, is the extent of Google's innovations on the Internet. Google's unauthorised scanning of books constituted a breach of existing copyright law, as shown in *The Authors Guild et al v. Google, Inc* (2009), yet nevertheless some authors see merit in their actions. Despite expressing unequivocal criticism for Google's disregard for traditional copyright considerations and the proposed 'opt out' model, the possibility of making previously out of print works available online is a significant benefit for authors and readers. It is evident however, that the proposed model will have to be revised if it is to gain acceptance by the Court. Judge Chin condemned Google's actions as being in breach of existing copyright laws, being predicated upon an 'opt out' instead of 'opt in' model (*The Authors Guild et al v. Google, Inc.*, 2009, p. 49). Additionally, the related *Author's Guild* case against USA libraries and the HathiTrust for the unlawful scanning and digitising of library databases (*Authors Guild, Inc. et al. v. HathiTrust et al* (2011), pp. 4, 22-23) has now provided a further dimension in the book scanning dispute. The central role played by the ASA as a plaintiff in this case will ensure that Australian authors are heard on these issues.

Copyright has historically had a reactive, rather than proactive, function towards changing technology. Moreover, copyright laws have traditionally adapted to changing technology to meet the needs of copyright users. That was the purpose when the English Crown started to regulate Caxton's revolutionary printing press technology (Goldstein, 2001, p. 5), and it remains the focus of copyright legislation today. Recently, it has become apparent that licensing terms and conditions are becoming paramount in the digital milieu, especially in relation to ebooks, such as Kindle sales. This trend reflects the observations of John and Reid (2011, p. 2), that owners' and users' copying rights are now being determined more by individual licenses and less by provisions in copyright law than in the past. It supports Young's contention (2007, pp. 158-159) that copyright requires a re-assessment in the digital environment. At the very least, Australian publishers and authors must apply close scrutiny to the terms and conditions of international electronic licensing agreements such as Google and Kindle agreements, but the power of the individual –both author and localised publisher—is sliding backward as global publishing giants advance forward.

Alexander has relevantly warned against a 'looking backwards attitude' in the copyright industry, and has said, 'Copyright law has always been as much… about struggles between competing economic interests, or clashes of business models, as it is about public interest and encouraging creativity' (2010, p. 20). Keeping these considerations in mind, it is imperative that copyright law continues to evolve to meet the demands of new business models and protect the rights of creators in the digital domain.

Undertaken at a critical time of transition, this investigation shows an urgent need for authors to strengthen their position in the literary sphere, not only with regard to their copyright protection but also in relation to publishing relationships. The various developments – Google initiatives, parallel import issues and electronic rights – represent crucial issues for authors to stay abreast of. The dynamic, even chaotic nature of copyright in the contemporary environment is confusing for authors, rendering them paralysed in the face of irreparable change. Clearly, the 'author group' requires a stronger and more assertive presence to benefit individual authors and the creative writing community as a whole. As the parallel importing debate showed, when authors act collectively as a group they are able to achieve meaningful political and legislative objectives, but a common objective is needed. Notably the Book Industry Strategy Group (BISG) Report (2011) has taken cognisance of a number of issues raised by the ASA in its comprehensive Submission Paper (2011) referred to in Chapter 10, but their recommendations require a practical application.

RECOMMENDATIONS

While this research shows that there have been significant steps by the ASA to create an awareness of prominent issues, such as the provision of precedent model contracts and informative articles on ebook royalties, further initiatives are necessary to educate authors on their rights. Inevitably, the difficulties in getting published have a weakening effect on authors' bargaining powers in relation to publishing agreements. However, measures should be implemented to ensure that authors are not disadvantaged in the publishing process. To create an environment in which authors can remain creatively active, it is essential that they be financially rewarded for their efforts, through appropriate royalty, licensing contracts and schemes. It is further necessary that they are provided with sufficient information about possible streams of remuneration and available grants. This will require the involvement of authors on a national level in educational programs, such as the copyright education suggested by Loukakis (2011, p. 6). Such educational initiatives can be implemented through the ASA and writers' centres nationally but will require funding to be provided by Government bodies such as the Australia Council. It is suggested that it would be appropriate for the ASA, in its capacity as Australian authors' representative body, to undertake an in-depth investigation into possible educational programs for authors and to make further recommendations in relation to standard publishing contract terms, especially in view of authors' general inability to negotiate with publishers.

In addition, it is recommended to investigate if and how copyright and the rights of authors are included in university education. The Australasian Association of Writing Programs list 50 tertiary institutions in Australia and New Zealand offering Creative Writing courses (2011). Furthermore, in a 2009 *TEXT* journal article, 30 Australian universities were identified as offering postgraduate Creative Writing degrees (Boyd, 2009). It would be worthwhile follow-up research to investigate how the issues discussed in this book –notably copyright and the rights of authors in the digital age – are addressed in existing tertiary courses and whether creative writing students have the benefit of Media Law/Copyright or equivalent subjects, which are generally provided to journalism students. The substantial lack of knowledge exhibited by many authors indicate the need to educate Creative Writing students with concrete, clear information on issues such as publishing contract terms, royalty calculations (especially in relation to ebooks) and electronic copyright protection.

Based on this research, it would serve the writing industry to consider a range of recommendations to navigate a way forward which balances the rights of authors with the changing and somewhat overwhelming digital publishing landscape.

First, in relation to institutional concerns such as the Australian Law Reform Commission (ALRC), Australian Copyright Council (ACC), TAFE, Copyright Law Review committee (CLRC) and Copyright Agency Limited (CAL):

- Transparency in existing structures such as CAL could be improved, and additional measures might be put in place to better reward authors for digital copying.
- Where territorial copyright applies to authors' work, it should be enforceable – this will require greater cooperation and enforcement by international agencies such as the International Federation of Reproduction Rights Organisations and Australian representative bodies such as CAL.
- The ACC, which makes submissions on copyright issues to Government based on its own research, should further address the plight of authors, copyright income structures and ways of extending the scope of earning mechanisms for authors, in amplification of the BISG report (2011), taking into account the ASA Submission to the BISG (2011) and Loukakis' recent observations regarding authors' incomes in his paper 'The author as producer, the author as business' (2011).
- In view of the limited focus of the ALRC investigation into digital copyright, the CLRC should, as a matter of priority, draft a *Report on Authors' Copyright* – in a similar vein to the 1994 Journalists' Copyright enquiry – addressing all pertinent copyright issues and electronic copyright issues in particular.
- This report should include a review of the user-focus in electronic copyright, to adequately address the rights of the author.
- A practical course component that includes information on copyright, authors' rights and industry support structures for authors should be considered as a Core Subject inclusion in tertiary Creative Writing courses at TAFEs and universities.

A second set of recommendations which relate to authors include:

- Common legislative objectives should be identified by authors to achieve meaningful political and legislative change, i.e. authors need to work together to establish a potential lobby presence.
- Commercial objectives should be identified by authors, i.e. how might authors better exploit their copyright for financial benefit, especially on the Internet.
- A proactive, rather than reactive approach by authors is called for to address the challenges posed by the digital environment. In this regard, the following issues should be addressed:
    - ○ A requirement for better consultation procedures between authors and publishers when negotiating with online providers such as

Google Books publishers and greater transparency towards authors in deciding how much of an author's work should be made available on the Internet.

◦ More involvement by authors in representative associations such as the ASA, to enable effective consultation between these organisations and Government committees and bodies (such as Australian Law Reform Commission and Copyright Law Review Committee).

◦ Raising author awareness of mechanisms to identify and deal with copyright infringements of their work on the Internet.

◦ Requiring minimum accepted standards of royalty percentages on ebooks for authors.

◦ A thorough revision of existing publishing contracts to address authors' electronic copyright concerns (based on the ASA recommendations).

◦ Creating greater awareness of and familiarity with authors' moral rights.

◦ Lobbying for government funded workshops/tutorials for authors on dealing with the challenges associated with electronic publishing and publishing options, including self publishing and online copyright protection.

◦ Requiring that online publishers/distributors such as Amazon and Google provide information on copyright licensing structures to authors in advance of publication and/or distribution of ebooks.

These recommendations reflect an examination of the views, opinions and impressions of authors with regard to copyright, copyright structures and the changing publishing industry at a critical moment in history. They suggest changes that will invigorate and empower the often marginalised subaltern sphere of authors who are caught at the cross-roads of change in the publishing industry. This investigation has focussed squarely on copyright perceptions of Australian authors in this literary sphere which are subject, not only to current legislative provisions but also encompassed by the expanding digital sphere within the broader public sphere envisaged by Habermas. In considering these findings on both a functional and philosophical level, against the backdrop of existing legislation, policy and theory, it has been shown that authors will have to equip themselves to deal with the challenges of new media technology to ensure that they are adequately rewarded for their creative efforts. This will require an increased familiarity with electronic licensing agreements and copyright protection measures, knowledge of publishing options and a stronger awareness of royalty provisions. It will also require authors to assert their rights as creators and to be consistently proactive in addressing future copyright challenges.

REFERENCES

Alexander, I. (2010, May). *All change for the digital economy: Copyright and business models in the early eighteenth century*. Paper presented at University of Cambridge. Sydney, Australia.

Armstrong, E. (1990). *Before copyright – The French book-privilege system 1498-1526*. Cambridge, UK: Cambridge University Press.

Australasian Association of Writing Programs. (2011). *Writing courses*. Retrieved December 3, 2011, from http://www.aawp.org.au/courses?title=&tid=18&tid_1=All

Barthes, R. (1977). *Image music text* (S. Heath, Trans.). New York: The Noonday Press.

Boyd, N. (2009). Describing the creative thesis: a census of creative writing doctorates, 1993-2008. *Text, 3*(1).

Carpignano, P., Anderson, R., Aronowitz, S., & DiFazio, W. (1993). Chatter in the age of electronic reproduction: Talk, television and the 'public mind. In B. Robbins (Ed.), *The phantom public sphere*. Minneapolis, MN: University of Minnesota Press.

Ergas, H. (2000). *Review of intellectual property legislation under the competition principles agreement (Final Report)*. Canberra, Australia: Intellectual Property and Competition Review Committee.

Flood, A. (2012). European Commission and Apple reach settlement over ebook price-fixing. *The Guardian*. Retrieved November 10, 2013, from http://www.theguardian.com/books/2012/dec/14/european-commission-apple-ebook

Goldstein, P. (2001). *International copyright: Principles, law and practice*. Oxford, UK: Oxford University Press.

Habermas, J. (1989). *The structural transformation of the public sphere*. Cambridge, MA: MIT Press.

John, J., & Reid, M. A. (2011, April 28). Making content pay online. *Australian Copyright Council*. Retrieved 29 April 2011, from http://www.copyright.org.au/news-and-policy/details/id/1945/

Jones, B. (2011). *Book industry strategy group report (Research Report)*. Canberra, Australia: Government of Australia.

Landes, W. M., & Posner, R. A. (1989). An economic analysis of copyright law. *The Journal of Legal Studies, 18*, 325. doi:10.1086/468150

Loukakis, A. (2010, July 10). E-books: Royalties and contracts. *Australian Society of Authors*. Retrieved from https://asauthors.org/files/pages/ebooks_royalties_and_contracts.pdf

Loukakis, A. (2011, January). *Submission to the book industry strategy group*.

Macpherson, C. B. (1962). *The political theory of possessive individualism*. Oxford, UK: Oxford University Press.

Rose, M. (1988). The author as proprietor: Donaldson v Becket and the genealogy of modern authorship. *Representations (Berkeley, Calif.), 0*(23), 51–58. doi:10.2307/2928566

Stokes, S. (2001). *Art and copyright*. Oxford, UK: Hart Publishing.

Young, S. (2007). *The book is dead: Long live the book*. Sydney: University of New South Wales Press.

TABLE OF CASES

IceTV Pty Limited v. Nine Network Australia Pty Limited [2009] HCA 14 and [2009] 239 CLR (Austl.)

Kirtsaeng v. John Wiley & Sons 568 U.S. WL 1104736 (U.S. Mar. 19, 2013)

The Authors Guild et al v. Google, Inc, (2009) US District Court, Southern District of New York, No. 05-08136 at 1 (US)

The Authors Guild, Inc. et al. v. HathiTrust et al, US District Court, Southern District of New York, filed 12 September 2011, 11 CIV 6351 (US)

United States of America et al v. Apple Inc et al, US District Court for the Southern District of New York, 10 July 2013 (US)

University of NSW v. Moorhouse (1975) HCA 26; (1975) 133 CLR 1 (Austl.)

List of Abbreviations

- **ACC:** Australian Copyright Council
- **APRA:** Australian Performing Rights Association
- **ASA:** Australian Society of Authors
- **Berne Convention:** Berne Convention for the Protection of Literary and Artistic Works
- **BIEM:** Bureau International des Sociétés Gérant les Droits D'Enregistrement et de Reproduction Mecanique
- **BISG:** Book Industry Strategy Group
- **CAL:** Copyright Agency Limited
- **CISAC:** International Confederation of Societies of Authors and Composers
- **CMS:** Copyright Management System
- **DRM:** Digital Rights Management
- **Droit Moral:** Moral Rights
- **ECL:** Extended Collective Licensing
- **ECR:** Ergas Committee Report
- **ELR:** Educational Lending Rights
- **EU:** European Union
- **IFFRO:** International Federation of Reproduction Rights Organisations
- **PIR:** Parallel Import Restriction
- **PLR:** Public Lending Rights
- **RRO:** Reproduction Rights Organisations
- **TRIPS Agreement:** Trade Related Aspects of Intellectual Property
- **UCC:** Universal Copyright Convention
- **WCT:** WIPO Copyright Treaty
- **WIPO:** World Intellectual Property Organization
- **WTO:** World Trade Organisation

Compilation of References

Adeney, E. (2002). Moral rights and substantiality. *Australian Intellectual Property Journal, 13*, 5.

Alexander, I. (2010, May). *All change for the digital economy: Copyright and business models in the early eighteenth century.* Paper presented at University of Cambridge. Sydney, Australia.

Allen & Unwin. (2011). *About Allen & Unwin.* Retrieved June 5, 2011, from http://www.allenandunwin.com/default. aspx?page=432

Allen Consulting Group. (2003). *Economic perspectives on copyright law.* Strawberry Hills, Australia: The Centre for Copyright Studies Limited.

Anderson, P. (2008, March 11). *Resale royalties and new directions for the arts.* Retrieved July 5, 2011, from http://www.australiacouncil.gov.au/resources/reports_and_publications/subjects/marketing/sales/resale_royalties_and_new_directions_for_the_arts

Armstrong, E. (1990). *Before copyright – The French book-privilege system 1498-1526.* Cambridge, UK: Cambridge University Press.

Associated Press. (2009, September 17). One million copies of Dan Brown's The Lost Symbol sold in one day. *Sydney Morning Herald.* Retrieved October 2, 2009, from http://www.smh.com.au/news/entertainment/books/1m-readers-find-lost-symbol/2009/09/17/1252780384841. html

Austin, A., Heffernan, M., & David, N. (2008). *Academic authorship, publishing agreements and open access (Research Report).* Brisbane, Australia: The OAK Law Project, Queensland University of Technology.

Australasian Association of Writing Programs. (2011). *Writing courses.* Retrieved December 3, 2011, from http://www.aawp.org.au/courses?title=&tid=18&tid_1=All

Australasian performing Rights Association Ltd v. Commonwealth Bank of Australia (1992) 25 IPR 157 (Austl.)

Australia Council for the Arts. (2013). *About.* Retrieved from http://www.australiacouncil.gov.au/about

Australian Copyright Council. (2011). *About us.* Retrieved from http://www.copyright.org.au/about-us/

Australian Copyright Council. (2011, May 23). *Digital opportunity – The Hargreaves report.* Retrieved May 24, 2011, from http://www.copyright.org.au/news-and-policy/details/id/1958/

Australian Government Productivity Commission. (2008). *Copyright restrictions on the parallel importation of books: Submissions.* Retrieved from http://www.pc.gov.au/projects/study/books/submissions

Australian Law Review Commission. (2013). *Copyright and the digital economy* (Discussion Paper 79). Retrieved from http://www.alrc.gov.au/sites/default/files/pdfs/publications/dp79_whole_pdf_.pdf

Australian Society of Authors. (2011). [from https://asauthors.org/history]. *History (Historical Association (Great Britain)),* (January): 10. Retrieved December 10, 2010

Australian Society of Authors. (2011). *Our partners.* Retrieved December 10, 2010 & January 10, 2011, from https://asauthors.org/our-partners

Australian Society of Authors. (2011). *Types of publishers.* Retrieved December 10, 2010 & January 10, 2011, from https://asauthors.org/types-of-publishers

Babauta, L. (2010). Uncopyright. *Zenhabits.* Retrieved March 23, 2011, from http://zenhabits.net/uncopyright/

Back to Booktown. (2011). Retrieved from http://www.booktown.clunes.org/program.htm

Barlow, J. P. (1992). *The economy of ideas: Selling wine without bottles on the global net.* Retrieved January 15, 2011, from https://projects.eff.org/~barlow/EconomyOfIdeas.html

Barnhart, C. L., & Barnhart, R. K. (Eds.). (1981). *The world book dictionary.* Chicago: Doubleday & Company.

Barthes, R. (1977). *Image music text* (S. Heath, Trans.). New York: The Noonday Press.

Bazin, P. (1996). Towards metareading. In G. Nunberg (Ed.), *The future of the book* (pp. 153–168). Los Angeles, CA: University of California Press.

Bech, M., & Kristensen, M. B. (2009). Differential response rates in postal and web-based surveys among older respondents. *Survey research. Methods (San Diego, Calif.), 3*(1), 1–6.

Belsey, C. (2006). Structuralism and semiotics. In S. Malpas, & P. Wake (Eds.), *The Routledge companion to critical theory* (pp. 43–54). Oxford, UK: Routledge.

Bogdan, R. C., & Biklen, S. K. (2003). *Qualitative research for education: An introduction to theory and methods.* Boston: Allyn & Bacon.

Bolter, J. D. (1996). Ekphrasis, virtual reality, and the future of writing. In G. Nunberg (Ed.), *The future of the book* (pp. 253–271). Los Angeles, CA: University of California Press.

Boyd, N. (2009). Describing the creative thesis: a census of creative writing doctorates, 1993-2008. *Text, 3*(1).

Boyle, J. (2002). Fencing off ideas: Enclosure and the disappearance of the public domain. *Daedalus, 131*(2), 13.

Boymal, J., & Davidson, S. (2004). Extending copyright duration in Australia. *Agenda (Durban, South Africa), 11*(3), 23–246.

Brannen, J. (2004). Working qualitatively and quantitatively. In C. Seale, G. Gobo, J. F. Gubrium, & D. Silverman (Eds.), *Qualitative research practice* (pp. 312–325). London: Sage Publications. doi:10.4135/9781848608191.d25

Brennan, D., De Zwart, M., Fraser, M., Lindsay, D., & Ricketson, S. (2011). *Directions in copyright reform in Australia (Report)*. Canberra, Australia: Copyright Council Expert Group.

Buchanan, E. A. (2004). *Readings in virtual research ethics*. Hershey, PA: Information Science Publishing.

Burke, S. (1992). *The death and return of the author*. Edinburgh, UK: Edinburgh University Press.

Butler, B. C. (2002). *Postmodernism: A very short introduction*. Oxford, UK: Oxford University Press.

Carpignano, P., Anderson, R., Aronowitz, S., & DiFazio, W. (1993). Chatter in the age of electronic reproduction: Talk, television and the 'public mind. In B. Robbins (Ed.), *The phantom public sphere*. Minneapolis, MN: University of Minnesota Press.

Carr, B. (2011, February 19-20). It's the lunacy of protectionism writ large. *The Weekend Australian*, p. 3.

Caslon Analytics. (2003, June). *Caslon analytics collecting societies*. Retrieved July 12, 2008 and October 9, 2010 from www.caslon.com.au/ipguide3.htm

Cellan-Jones, R. (2010, December 7). *Who's afraid of Google's book store?* Retrieved January 9, 2011, from http://www.bbc.co.uk/blogs/thereporters/rorycellanjones/2010/12/whos_afraid_of_googles_book_st.html

Clickbank. (2013). *Clickbank DIY*. Retrieved from http://www.clickbank.com/clickbankdiy/

Coker, M. (2009, October 26). Do authors still need publishers? *Huffington Post*. Retrieved January 10, 2011, from http://www.huffingtonpost.com/mark-coker/do-authors-still-need-pub_b_334539.html

Collings, S. (2010, June 18). *Authorpreneur – The author as entrepreneur*. Retrieved May 19, 2011, from http://sallycollings.com/2010/06/authorpreneur-%E2%80%93-the-author-as-entrepreneur/

Computer Associations International, Inc. v. Altai, Inc. 1241, 23 IPR 385 (2d Cir 1992) (US)

Coogi Australia Pty Ltd v. Hysport International Pty Ltd & Others (1998) 157 FCA 1059 (Austl.)

Cooney, S. (2010, May). New publishing models: A shifting of power. *Writing Queensland, 196*, 10.

Compilation of References

Copyright Act 1968 (Cth) *Copyright Amendment (Digital Agenda) Act 2000* (Cth) *Copyright Amendment (Moral Rights) Act 2000* (Cth) *Resale Royalty Right for Visual Artists Act 2009* (Cth)

Copyright Agency Limited. (2009, March). *CAL's sampling and distribution: How do they work?* Retrieved September 16, 2010, from www.copyright.com.au/assets/documents/operations/Sampling and distribution.pdf

Copyright Agency Limited. (2010). *International copyright: Treaties and organisations.* Retrieved September 16, 2010, from http://www.copyright.com.au/get-information/about-copyright/international-copyright-treaties-and-organisations

Copyright Agency Ltd v. Queensland Department of Education & Others (2002) 54 IPR 19 (Austl.)

Copyright Amendment (Digital Agenda) Act 2000 (Cth)

Copyright Law Review Committee. (1994). *Report on journalists' copyright.* Canberra, Australia: Author.

Cornish, W. R. (1999). *Intellectual property.* London: Sweet & Maxwell.

Cunningham, S. (2013, October 15). BOOKish. *Meanjin.* Retrieved from http://meanjin.com.au/blog/post/bookish/

Cunningham, S., & Higgs, P. (2010). *What's your other job? A census analysis of arts employment in Australia (Research Report).* Sydney: Australia Council for the Arts.

Debray, R. (1996). The book as symbolic object. In G. Nunberg (Ed.), *The future of the book* (pp. 139–152). Berkeley, CA: University of California Press.

Dempster, L. (2010, May). Creative commonsense. *Writing Queensland, 196,* 12.

Denzin, N. K., & Lincoln, Y. S. (Eds.). (2005). *Handbook of qualitative research* (3rd ed.). London: Sage Publications.

Doctorow, C. (2009). Download for free. *Makers.* Retrieved March 23, 2011, from http://craphound.com/makers/download/

Doctorow, C. (2010, September 2). *Copyright versus creativity.* Paper presented at Melbourne Writers Festival. Melbourne, Australia.

Dow Jones & Company Inc. v. Gutnick [2002] HCA 56 (Austl.)

Earls, N. (2008). *Submission to the productivity commission.*

Earls, N. (1998). *Zigzag street.* Sydney: Random House Australia.

Eco, U. (1979). *The role of the reader: Explorations in the semiotics of texts.* London: Hutchinson.

Eco, U. (1989). *The open work.* Boston: Harvard University Press.

Edmonds, P. (2007). Interrogating creative writing outcomes: Wet ink as a new model. *TEXT, 11*(1). Retrieved May 19, 2011, from http://www.textjournal.com.au/april07/edmonds.htm

Eisenstein, E. L. (1979). *The printing press as an agent of change: Communications and cultural transformations in early-modern Europe* (Vol. 1). Cambridge, UK: Cambridge University Press.

Eley, G. (1994). Nations, publics, and political cultures: Placing Habermas in the nineteenth century. In N. B. Dirks, G. Eley, & S. B. Otner (Eds.), *Culture/power/history*. Princeton, NJ: Princeton University Press.

Eltham, K. (2009, November). Writing the digital future. *WQ, 190, 6*.

Eltham, K. (2009, October 28). What do authors need? *Electric Alphabet: Writing and Publishing in the Digital Near-Future*. Retrieved January 10, 2011, from http://www.electricalphabet. net/2009/10/28/what-do-authors-need/

Epstein, R. A. (2004). Liberty versus property? Cracks in the foundations of copyright law. *IPCentral Review, 1*, 1.

Ergas, H. (2000). *Review of intellectual property legislation under the competition principles agreement (Final Report)*. Canberra, Australia: Intellectual Property and Competition Review Committee.

Fisher, J. (2010, September 27). Ebooks and the Australian publishing industry. *Meanjin, 69*(3). Retrieved March 23, 2011, from http://meanjin.com.au/blog/post/e-books-and-the-australian-publishing-industry/

Fisher, W., & Hughes, J. (2009, May 5-15). Copyright and wrongs. *The Economist*. Retrieved May 17, 2009, from http://www.economist.com/debate/overview/144

Fisher, W. (2000). Theories of intellectual property. In S. Munzer (Ed.), *New essays in the legal and political theory of property*. Cambridge, UK: Cambridge University Press.

Flood, A. (2012). European Commission and Apple reach settlement over ebook price-fixing. *The Guardian*. Retrieved November 10, 2013, from http://www. theguardian.com/books/2012/dec/14/european-commission-apple-ebook

Fontana, A., & Frey, J. (2005). The interview: From neutral stance to political involvement. In N. K. Denzin, & Y. S. Lincoln (Eds.), *Handbook of qualitative research* (3rd ed., pp. 695–728). London: Sage Publications.

Foucault, M. (1997). What is an author? In D. F. Bouchard, & S. Simons (Eds.), *Language, counter-memory, practice*. New York: Cornell University Press.

Fox Film Corp v. Doyal (1932) 286 US 123, 127 (US)

Franki, R. (1976). *Report of the copyright law committee on reprographic reproduction (Research Report)*. Canberra, Australia: Government of Australia.

Fraser, N. (1992). Rethinking the public sphere: A contribution to the critique of actually existing democracy. In C. Calhoun (Ed.), *Habermas and the public sphere*. Cambridge, MA: MIT Press.

Ganassali, S. (2008). The influence of the design of web survey questionnaires on the quality of responses. *Survey Research Methods, 2*(1), 21–32.

Gawronski & others v. Amazon Inc . [2009] (US)

Gawronski & others v. Amazon Inc. [2009] (US) *Random House, Inc. v. Rosetta Books* LLC, 283 F.3d 490, 62 U.S.P.Q.2d (BNA) 1063 (2d Cir. 2002) (US)

Gerhards, J., & Schafer, M. S. (2009). Is the internet a better public sphere? Comparing old and new media in the US and Germany. *New Media & Society*, 1–18. Retrieved from http://nms.sagepub.com

Godwin, M. (2001). Book keeping. *American Lawyer Media*. Retrieved from http://global.factiva.com

Goldstein, P. (2001). *International copyright: Principles, law and practice*. Oxford, UK: Oxford University Press.

Goldstein, P. (2003). *Copyright's highway: From Gutenberg to the celestial jukebox*. Stanford, CA: Stanford University Press.

Google. (2013). *Removing content from Google*. Retrieved from https://support.google.com/legal/troubleshooter/1114905?rd=2

Gray, P. S., Williamson, J. B., Karp, D. A., & Dalphin, J. R. (2007). *The research imagination*. Cambridge, UK: Cambridge University Press. doi:10.1017/CBO9780511819391

Groth, S. (2011, March). Cloud atlas. *Writing Queensland, 205*, 17. iiNet. (2013). *Illegal content*. Retrieved from http://www.iinet.net.au/about/legal/illegal-content.html

Habermas, J. (1974). The public sphere: An encyclopedia article (1964). *New German Critique, (3)*, 49-55.

Habermas, J. (1984). *The theory of communicative action*. Boston: Beacon Press.

Habermas, J. (1989). *The structural transformation of the public sphere*. Cambridge, MA: MIT Press.

Hamm v. Middleton (1999) 44 IPR 656 (Austl.)

Hansen, H. (1996). International copyright: An unorthodox analysis. *Vanderbilt Journal of Transnational Law, 29*, 579.

Hargreaves, I. (2011). *Digital opportunity: A review of intellectual property and growth (Research Report)*. London: Government of UK.

Hitchens, C. (2003). *Unacknowledged legislation: Writers in the public sphere*. Washington, DC: Verso.

Hohendahl, P. (1974). Jurgen Habermas: The public sphere (1964). *New German Critique, (3)*, 45-48.

Hughes, J. (1988). The philosophy of intellectual property. *The Georgetown Law Journal, 77*, 330–350.

IceTV Pty Limited v. Nine Network Australia Pty Limited [2009] HCA 14 and [2009] 239 CLR (Austl.) *Kirtsaeng v. John Wiley & Sons* 568 U.S. WL 1104736 (U.S. Mar. 19, 2013)

International Confederation of Societies of Authors and Composers (CISAC). (2010). *About CISAC*. Retrieved October 9, 2010, from http://www.cisac.org/CisacPortal/page.do?name=rubrique.1.1

International Federation of Reproductive Rights Organisations (IFFRO). (2010). *Homepage*. Retrieved October 9, 2010, from http://www.ifrro.org

Jassin, L. J. (2010, May 24). The publishing story behind Mark Twain's unpublished autobiography. *Copylaw*. Retrieved December 30, 2010, from http://www.copylaw.org/2010/05/mark-twains-unpublished-autobiography.html

John, J., & James, F. (2011, March 28). Copyrighting Google. *Australian Copyright Council*. Retrieved March 28, 2011, from http://www.copyright.org.au/news-and-policy/details/id/1907/

John, J., & Reid, M. A. (2011, April 28). Making content pay online. *Australian Copyright Council*. Retrieved 29 April 2011, from http://www.copyright.org.au/news-and-policy/details/id/1945/

Johnson, P. (2008). Dedicating copyright to the public domain. *The Modern Law Review, 71*(4), 587. doi:10.1111/j.1468-2230.2008.00707.x

Jones, B. (2011). *Book industry strategy group report (Research Report)*. Canberra, Australia: Government of Australia.

Kant, I. (1907). Metaphysische anfangsgrunde der rechtslehre (The metaphysical elements of justice, 1797), Kants werke, vol.6. Berlin: Druck und verlag von Georg Reimer.

Kelly, J. (2009, October 5). Publish and be damned. *The Drum*. Retrieved May 19, 2011, from http://www.abc.net.au/unleashed/28818.html

Keneally, T. (2008). *Submission to the productivity commission*.

Kirtsaeng v. John Wiley & Sons 568 U.S. WL 1104736 (U.S. Mar. 19, 2013)

Knapp, S., & Michaels, W. B. (1985). *Against theory: Literary studies and the new pragmatism* (pp. 19, 101, 104). Chicago: University of Chicago Press.

Knorr, E., & Gruman, G. (2010). What cloud computing really means. *InfoWorld*. Retrieved March 16, 2011, from http://www.infoworld.com/d/cloud-computing/what-cloud-computing-really-means-031?page=0,0

Landes, W. M., & Posner, R. A. (1987). Trademark Law: An economic perspective. *The Journal of Law & Economics, 30*, 265. doi:10.1086/467138

Landes, W. M., & Posner, R. A. (1989). An economic analysis of copyright law. *The Journal of Legal Studies, 18*, 325. doi:10.1086/468150

Landes, W. M., & Posner, R. A. (2003). *The economic structure of intellectual property law*. Cambridge, MA: Harvard University Press.

Landow, G. P. (1992). *Hypertext: The convergence of contemporary critical theory and technology*. Baltimore, MD: John Hopkins University Press. doi:10.1145/168466.168515

Landow, G. P. (1996). Twenty minutes into the future. In G. Nunberg (Ed.), *The future of the book* (pp. 209–238). Los Angeles, CA: University of California Press.

Lange, D. M. (2003, Winter/Spring). Reimagining the public domain. *Law and Contemporary Problems*, 463.

Lee, J. (2010). *Digital technologies in Australia's book industry* (Book Industry Strategy Group Research Report). Retrieved April 29, 2010, from http://www.innovation.gov.au

Lessig, L. (2010, January 26). For the love of culture: Google, copyright and our future. *The New Republic.* Retrieved March 19, 2011, from http://www.newrepublic.com/article/the-love-culture

Locke, J. (1689). *Of civil government: Second treatise*, ch. IX, par. 123, ch. V, par. 26, 31.

Loukakis, A. (2010, July 10). E-books: Royalties and contracts. *Australian Society of Authors*. Retrieved from https://asauthors.org/files/pages/ebooks_royalties_and_contracts.pdf

Loukakis, A. (2010, November 22). Warning: More ebook loopholes. *Australian Society of Authors*. Retrieved December 10, 2010, from https://asauthors.org/news/warning-more-ebook-loopholes

Loukakis, A. (2011, January). *Submission to the book industry strategy group.*

Loukakis, A. (2011). Giving contracts some clout. *Australian Author*, *43*(1), 28–29.

Loukakis, A. (2011, June). ASA advocacy – 2011 and beyond. *ASA Newsletter*, 4.

Loukakis, A. (2011b). *The author as producer, the author as business*. Canberra, Australia: Australian Society of Authors.

Lulu. (2013). *eBook publishing*. Retrieved from http://www.lulu.com/publish/ebooks/free

Macpherson, C. B. (1962). *The political theory of possessive individualism*. Oxford, UK: Oxford University Press.

Macquarie Dictionary. (2003). *Macquarie: Australia's national dictionary.* Sydney: The Macquarie Library Publishers.

Malik, S. (2012, August 6). Kindle ebook sales have overtaken Amazon print sales, says book seller. *The Guardian.* Retrieved from http://www.guardian.co.uk/books/2012/aug/06/amazon-kindle-ebook-sales-overtake-print

Malpas, S., & Wake, P. (Eds.). (2006). *The Routledge companion to critical theory*. Oxford, UK: Routledge.

Markham, A. N. (2005). The methods, politics, and ethics of representation in online ethnography. In N. K. Denzin, & Y. S. Lincoln (Eds.), *Handbook of qualitative research* (3rd ed., pp. 793–820). London: Sage Publications.

Marshall, C., & Rossman, G. B. (2006). *Designing qualitative research* (4th ed.). London: Sage Publications.

Max, D. T. (2006, June 19). The injustice collector: Is James Joyce's grandson suppressing scholarship? *The New Yorker.* Retrieved from www.newyorker.com/archive/2006

McCutcheon, J. (2008). The new defence of parody or satire under Australian copyright law. *Intellectual Property Quarterly*, 2, 163.

McDonald, H., & Adam, S. (2003). A comparison of online and postal data collection methods in marketing research. *Marketing Intelligence & Planning, 21,* 85–95. doi:10.1108/02634500310465399

McDonald, I. (1999). *Copyright in the new communications environment: Balancing protection and access (Research Report).* Redfern, Australia: The Australian Copyright Council for The Centre for Copyright Studies Limited.

McLean, K., Poland, L., & Van den Berg, J. (2010). *A case for literature: The effectiveness of subsidies to Australian publishers 1995-2005.* Sydney, Australia: Australia Council for the Arts.

Milton, J. (1644). *Areopagitica: A speech of Mr. John Milton for the Liberty of Unlicenc'd Printing, to the Parliament of England.* London, UK: Government of UK.

Ministry for the Arts, Australian Government Attorney-General's Department. (2011). *Lending rights.* Retrieved June 5, 2011, from http://arts.gov.au/literature/lending-rights/guidelines

Moorhouse, F. (2007, June 3). From quill to keyboard. *Age.*

Moorhouse, F. (2008). The escape from 'eccentric penury': How should we pay literary authors? Policy visions for the Australian writing economy. *Copyright Reporter, 26,* 4.

Needleman, R. (2010, January 22). Amazon adds optional DRM for Kindle publishers. *CNET News.* Retrieved March 16, 2011, from http://news.cnet.com/8301-19882_3-10439335-250.html

Netanel, N. (1996). Copyright and a democratic civil society. *The Yale Law Journal, 106,* 283. doi:10.2307/797212

NewsCore. (2011, May 20). Kindle sales overtake paper books. *News Limited.* Retrieved June 5, 2011, from http://www.news.com.au/business/e-book-sales-overtake-paper-books/story-fn7mjon9-1226059335499

Nix, G. (2008). *Submission to the productivity commission.*

Nolan, E., & Arcuili, R. (2010, May 25). *CAL today.* Brisbane, Australia: CAL Seminar.

Nunberg, G. (1996). Farewell to the information age. In G. Nunberg (Ed.), *The future of the book* (pp. 103–138). Los Angeles, CA: University of California Press.

Nygh, P., & Butt, P. (Eds.). (1997). *Butterworths concise Australian legal dictionary.* Sydney: Butterworths.

Orr, W. (2008). *Submission to the productivity commission.*

Pacific Film Laboratories Pty Ltd v. FCT (1976) 121 CLR 154 at 167 (Austl.)

Paltry, W. (2009). *Moral panics and the copyright wars.* Oxford, UK: Oxford University Press.

Patton, M. Q. (2002). *Qualitative research evaluation methods* (3rd ed.). London: Sage Publications.

Pelli, D. G., & Bigelow, C. (2009, October 20). A writing revolution. *Seed Magazine.* Retrieved September 19, 2010, from http://seedmagazine.com/content/article/a_writing_revolution/

Potts, J. (2010). Book doomsday: The march of progress and the fate of the book. *Meanjin, 69*(3). Retrieved March 23, 2011, from http://meanjin.com.au/Ed.s/volume-69-number-3-2010/article/book-doomsday-the-march-of-progress-and-the-fate-of-the-book1/

Productivity Commission. (2009). *Restrictions on the parallel importation of books* (Research Report). Retrieved February 19, 2011, from http://www.pc.gov.au/projects/study/books/submissions.

Quain, J. R. (2013). *Apple loses e-book pricing lawsuit, but are consumers the real losers?* Retrieved November 13, 2013, from http://www.foxnews.com/tech/2013/07/11/

Rawlins, G. J. E. (1993). Publishing over the next decade. *Journal of the American Society for Information Science American Society for Information Science, 44*(8), 474–479. doi:10.1002/(SICI)1097-4571(199309)44:8<474::AID-ASI6>3.0.CO;2-3

Reid, M. A. (2011). Authors create a new sub-plot in the quest to digitise the world's books. *Australian Copyright Council.* Retrieved from http://copyright.org.au

Ricketson, S. (1987). *The Berne convention for the protection of literary and artistic works: 1886.* London: Kluwer.

Romei, S. (2011, June 25-26). A pair of ragged claws. *The Review,* 19.

Rose, M. (1988). The author as proprietor: Donaldson v Becket and the genealogy of modern authorship. *Representations (Berkeley, Calif.), 0*(23), 51–58. doi:10.2307/2928566

Rose, M. (1993). *Authors and owners.* Cambridge, MA: Harvard University Press.

Rose, M. (2003, Winter/Spring). Nine-tenths of the law: The English copyright debates and the rhetoric of the public domain. *Law and Contemporary Problems,* 75.

Rushdie, S. (1989). *The Satanic verses.* New York: Penguin.

Samuelson, P. (2011). Legislative alternatives to the Google book settlement (UC Berkeley Public Law Research Paper No. 1818126). *Columbia Journal of Law & the Arts, 34,* 697.

Samuelson, P. (2010). Google book search and the future of books in cyberspace (UC Berkeley Public Law Research Paper No. 1535067). *Minnesota Law Review, 94,* 1308.

Saunders, D. (1992). *Authorship and copyright.* London: Routledge.

Schmitter, E. (1995, September). Boycott Lufthansa: Literature and publicity today – A few ruminations and a suggestion. *TriQuarterly,* 155.

Scholastic. (2011). *Manuscript guidelines.* Retrieved June 5, 2011, from http://scholastic.com.au/corporate/manuscript.asp

Scribd. (2013). *About.* Retrieved from http://www.scribd.com/about

Seddon, N. C., & Ellinghaus, M. P. (2002). *Chesire and Fifoot's law of contract.* Sydney: LexisNexis Butterworths.

Seringhaus, M. (2010). E-book transactions: Amazon 'kindles' the copy ownership debate (Paper 60). *Student Prize Papers*. Retrieved July 11, 2011, from http://digitalcommons.law.yale.edu/ylsspps_papers/60

Sexton, C. (2007). In conversation with Frank Moorhouse. *IPSANZ IP Forum*, *68*, 6.

Simone, R. (1996). The body of the text. In G. Nunberg (Ed.), *The future of the book* (pp. 239–252). Los Angeles, CA: University of California Press.

Simpson, S. (1995). *Review of Australian collection societies report*. Canberra, Australia: Government of Australia.

Smashwords. (2013). *How to create, publish, and distribute ebooks with Smashwords*. Retrieved from http://www.smashwords.com/about/how_to_publish_on_smashwords

Sony Corporation of America v. Universal City Studios Inc. (1984) 2 IPR 225 (US)

Spicer, J. (1959). *Report of the copyright law review committee (Research Report)*. Canberra, Australia: Government of Australia.

Stake, R. (2005). Qualitative case studies. In N. K. Denzin, & Y. S. Lincoln (Eds.), *Handbook of qualitative research* (3rd ed., pp. 443–446). London: Sage Publications.

Stokes, S. (2001). *Art and copyright*. Oxford, UK: Hart Publishing.

Strowel, A. (2009, December). *The Google settlement: Towards a digital library or an inquisitive shopping mall?* Paper presented at Bond University. Gold Coast, Australia.

Suzor, N. (2006). *Transformative use of copyright material*. (Thesis). Queensland University of Technology, Brisbane, Australia.

The Authors Guild et al v. Google, Inc, (2009) US District Court, Southern District of New York, No. 05-08136 at 1 (US)

The Authors Guild, Inc. et al. v. HathiTrust et al, US District Court, Southern District of New York, filed 12 September 2011, 11 CIV 6351 (US)

Thomas, D. (1968). *Copyright and the creative artist*. London: Institute of Economic Affairs.

Thompson, L. (2009, October). Australian book publishing in 2008: Thriving in uncertain times. *Australian Bookseller & Publisher*, 12–13.

Throsby, D., & Zednik, A. (2010). *Do you really expect to get paid? An economic study of professional artists in Australia (Research Report)*. Strawberry Hills, Australia: Australia Council for the Arts.

Toschi, L. (1996). Hypertext and authorship. In G. Nunberg (Ed.), *The future of the book* (pp. 169–208). Los Angeles, CA: University of California Press.

United States of America et al v. Apple Inc et al, US District Court for the Southern District of New York, 10 July 2013 (US) [1] As one of the parallel arenas within the public sphere as proposed by Fraser (1992, p. 131).

University of Michigan. (2011, September 16). *U-M library statement on the orphan works project*. Retrieved October 23, 2011, from http://www.lib.umich.edu/news/u-m-library-statement-orphan-works-project

University of NSW v. Moorhouse (1975) HCA 26; (1975) 133 CLR 1 (Austl.)

Vaidhayanathan, S. (2001). *Copyrights & copywrongs: The rise of intellectual property and how it threatens creativity.* New York: NYU Press.

Viala, A. (1985). *Naissance de l'écrivain.* Paris: Éditions de Minuit.

Victoria Writers' Centre. (now Writers Victoria). (2011). Contracts. *Writers Victoria.* Retrieved January 10, 2011, from http://vwc.org.au/publishing/contracts

Villa, D. R. (1992). Postmodernism and the public sphere. *The American Political Science Review, 86*(3), 712–721. doi:10.2307/1964133

Villa, D. R. (Ed.). (2000). *The Cambridge companion to Arendt.* Cambridge, UK: Cambridge University Press. doi:10.1017/CCOL0521641985

Ward, S. (2006, May 6). Educating global journalists. *The Toronto Star.* Retrieved December 29, 2008, from http://www.global.factiva.com.libraryproxy.griffith.edu.au

Wark, M. (2010, July 28). Copyright, copyleft, copygift. *Meanjin, 69*(1). Retrieved September 21, 2010, from http://meanland.com.au/articles/post/copyright-copyleft-copygift

Westbury, M. (2010, July 26). Has the Australia council had its day? *The Age.* Retrieved September 12, 2010, from http://www.theage.com.au/entertainment/art-and-design/has-the-australia-council-had-its-day-20100725-10qgt.html

Westbury, M., & Eltham, B. (2010). Cultural policy in Australia. In M. Davis & M. Lyons (Eds.), *More than luck: Ideas Australia needs now* (pp. 103-110). Retrieved on September 12, 2010, from http://morethanluck.cpd.org.au/wp-content/uploads/2010/06/MTL_InHousePrint_webcopy2.pdf

Wilson, P. (2011). The girl who saved the publisher. *The Deal, 4*(5), 30–32.

Woodmansee, M. (1984). The genius and the copyright: Economic and legal conditions of the emergence of the 'author'. *Eighteenth-Century Studies, 17,* 425–448. doi:10.2307/2738129

Young, S. (2010, November 26). Bond sidesteps Penguin. In *The book is dead.* Retrieved January 9, 2011, from http://shermanfyoung.wordpress.com/2010/11/26/bond-sidesteps-penguin/

Young, S. (2007). *The book is dead: Long live the book.* Sydney: University of New South Wales Press.

About the Author

Francina Cantatore holds the following qualifications: BA, LLB (Hons), MA, Grad Dip Legal Prac (Hons), PhD. After practising in South Africa as a barrister for many years, she relocated to Australia, where she continued her law practice and academic studies. She currently lectures at the Faculty of Law, Bond University, Australia, and is also in practice as a consulting solicitor. She serves on the Board of the Queensland Writers Centre, Australia, and takes a specific interest in copyright in the creative industries, especially in relation to authors' rights. Her PhD research was conducted in this area to provide insight into authors' relationships with copyright and challenges faced by authors in the digital era. Her broader research interests lie in the areas of intellectual property law and consumer and competition law. She has published internationally in these areas and has presented papers at international conferences on consumer law issues and copyright.

Index

A

anti-copyright 35, 81, 106, 161
Australian Government 3-4, 33, 69, 71-73, 76-79, 145, 147, 164, 166
Australian law 9, 13, 19, 30, 41, 144, 146, 171, 201, 206, 213, 221, 229-230
Australian Society of Authors (ASA) 52, 81, 84, 101, 115, 130, 153, 194, 221
author-publisher relationship 6, 82, 84, 216
authorship 1, 3, 7, 14, 26, 29, 34, 42, 45, 48-50, 52-66, 68, 93, 97, 114, 124, 126, 140-142, 166, 193, 212, 217-219, 224, 232
author sphere 2, 31, 81, 193, 201, 219, 221-222

B

Berne Convention 12-13, 15-16, 26, 29, 48, 50, 57, 70, 101
book industry 3, 5, 8, 73, 79, 117, 150, 181, 195, 198-199, 210, 214, 228, 232
business models 5-6, 64, 66, 81-82, 103, 168, 176, 186, 190, 193, 207, 211-213, 216, 227, 231

C

case law 1, 9, 17, 37, 49, 57, 93
collective viewpoints 115, 126
Committee Report 18, 29, 36
contract consultant 118-120, 129, 149, 172
copyright 1-31, 33, 35-48, 50-55, 57-59, 64-66, 68-69, 71-79, 81-83, 85-86, 91, 93, 97-118, 120-122, 124, 126, 128-131, 133-141, 143-158, 161-168, 170, 172-173, 175-176, 178, 180-187, 189-191, 193-194, 196-198, 200-214, 216-232
Copyright Agency Limited (CAL) 15, 38, 69, 71, 74, 128, 131, 144, 220, 229
copyright law 2, 4-7, 9-10, 13-17, 19-20, 22, 24-26, 28-29, 31, 35-38, 40, 46-47, 53, 55, 69, 73, 75, 79, 98, 102, 106, 117, 129, 165, 184, 208, 214, 218, 223-224, 226-227, 229-232
copyright legislation 1-2, 5, 9, 12-14, 16, 24, 36, 38, 45, 53-55, 58, 114, 117, 128, 141, 143-145, 147, 152, 165, 190-191, 197, 217, 227
Creative Commons 3, 45, 81, 105-107, 133, 182, 187, 190, 205, 207, 225

creative environment 39, 69
critical theory 1, 33, 50, 55, 58-59, 64, 67-68

D

digital publishing 4, 81, 89, 107, 116, 153, 167-168, 177-178, 188, 190, 193, 198, 202, 217, 220, 224-225, 229
digital rights 4, 20, 82, 92, 94, 104, 162, 174, 176, 178-179, 199, 203, 205-207, 223

E

ebooks 4, 52, 63-64, 81, 87, 89-93, 95-96, 102, 104, 106-109, 111-113, 127-128, 167, 176-177, 180, 188-189, 198-199, 201, 203, 214, 225, 227-228, 230, 232
Educational Lending Rights (ELR) 69, 76, 131, 220
electronic publishing 1, 6, 16, 24, 83, 121, 177, 193, 204, 211, 216, 220, 224, 230
Ergas Committee 18, 28, 36

G

global considerations 1
Google 1, 5-6, 22, 30, 35, 58, 73, 81, 95, 97-102, 105, 110-113, 128, 145, 151, 161-163, 167-168, 176, 182-186, 188, 190-191, 193, 199, 205, 207-209, 215, 217, 220, 225-227, 230, 232

H

Habermas 7, 9, 28, 31-35, 46-47, 196, 201, 214, 221, 230-231
heavenly library 193, 202-204, 207
honesty box 81, 106-107, 211, 224
Humanities-based approach 114

I

in-depth interviews 36, 114, 116, 118-119, 123, 125-126, 129, 137, 144, 147, 168, 170
intellectual property 2, 7, 12-13, 15-16, 18, 21, 25-26, 29, 35-37, 39, 41-42, 46-48, 65, 67, 70, 74, 79, 97, 113, 138, 145, 154, 161, 168, 189, 213, 215, 231
inter-disciplinary study 114

L

legislative framework 6, 143, 146, 216
literary sphere 6, 31-32, 62, 64, 83, 115, 122, 196-197, 206, 212, 216-217, 219, 221-222, 225, 227, 230

M

mainstream publisher 85, 92, 137, 144-145, 148, 150, 162, 172, 180, 184, 197, 199, 201, 206, 223
moral rights 9, 12, 14, 16, 19-20, 25, 28-30, 34-35, 38, 40-42, 45-46, 49-50, 52, 57, 86-87, 91-92, 103, 116, 128, 133, 140-143, 161, 165-166, 176, 205, 212-213, 218-219, 230
multi-method methodology 114

N

natural rights 11, 28-30, 35, 37-40, 44, 49-51, 103, 107, 136, 146, 217-218, 226

P

parallel importation 2, 4, 8, 16, 19-21, 24, 26, 73, 144, 147, 152-153, 162, 166, 197, 210
philosophical theories 6, 28, 30, 45, 50, 193, 216-217

power balance 81, 201

Productivity Commission 2, 4, 8, 20-22, 25-26, 73, 147, 151, 153, 166, 197-198, 214, 221

public benefit 18-20, 28, 30, 35-37, 39, 43-44, 52-53, 104, 106-107, 201, 209, 212-213

public domain 20, 28, 30, 35-38, 43, 46-48, 98-99, 150, 154, 184

public interest 2, 10, 19, 33, 35, 39, 43-45, 52, 100, 103, 193, 197-198, 209, 218, 223, 227

Public Lending Rights (PLR) 69, 76, 131, 220

public sphere 1-2, 7-9, 28, 30-35, 45-48, 50, 55, 61, 65-66, 69, 73, 81, 83, 103, 129, 143, 152, 193-194, 196, 198, 201-202, 212, 214, 216-217, 219, 221-224, 230-231

publishing contracts 6-7, 83-84, 90, 103, 114, 116, 128, 157, 167, 173, 175, 177-178, 193, 199, 202, 216-217, 224-225, 230

publishing industry 2, 6-7, 21-22, 31, 33, 62, 81-83, 94, 111, 114-115, 121-122, 128-129, 147-148, 165, 167-168, 178, 193, 198, 202, 214, 216-217, 223-224, 230

purposive sampling 114, 116-117, 205

Q

qualitative data 115, 118-121

quantitative research model 114

R

Resale Royalty Right for Visual Artists Act 2009 160, 166, 193, 209

research design 114-115

S

second hand 160, 209-211

survey data 114, 126

T

traditional print 1, 93, 97, 103, 109, 177, 201

traditional publishing 4, 63, 83-84, 133, 168, 173, 177, 189-191, 203, 211, 220, 225

U

utilitarian approach 17, 19, 28, 30, 36-37, 106, 146, 226

utilitarian principles 4, 45, 207, 209